THE BIBLE AS
ENGLISH LITERATURE

THE BIBLE AS
ENGLISH LITERATURE

BY

J. H. GARDINER

ASSISTANT PROFESSOR OF ENGLISH IN
HARVARD UNIVERSITY

CHARLES SCRIBNER'S SONS
NEW YORK 1927

PREFACE

This book springs from a course of study which
I have offered for several years at Harvard University in the Department of English. In this course
my object has been to make students as familiar as
possible with the English Bible, and to throw light
on its literary forms by bringing together facts from
the history of its sources and from the history of the
translation into English. For the latter purpose I
have drawn freely on the larger results of the great
school of learning which is commonly known as the
Higher Criticism. This is in itself, as has often
been pointed out, merely a critical study of the various books of both Old and New Testaments from
the historical point of view; it arrives at its results
by a faithful comparison of the various parts with
each other, and by bringing to bear on them all per-
tinent facts from the monuments and other external
sources of history. I have confined myself almost
wholly to the larger results of the school, on which
there is substantial agreement among scholars · and

v

I have nowhere, I believe, made statements of fact
which cannot be tested by a knowledge of the English
Bible.   I have not cited authorities, partly for the
reason just stated, but more because this book does
not pretend to deal with doubtful questions at first
hand: it is rather an essay in which conclusions already established are used to illuminate purely literary characteristics.   In an appendix I have named a
few words which will serve as a guide for any reader
who may care to go farther with the analytical study
of the Bible; in those books will be found copious
citation of the authorities.

Since this is a study in English literature I have
confined myself wholly to the Authorised Version.
If another generation should return to the general
reading of the Bible the Revised Version may become English literature; but that is a matter for the
future to determine.   For this reason all my quotations come from the Authorised Version, even where
the translation is imperfect or incorrect.   It is well
understood that the Revised Version is a better basis
for the study of Hebrew literature or of New Testament literature.

In all my discussion I have assumed the fact of
inspiration, but without attempting to define it or to
distinguish between religious and literary inspiration.   The two come together in a broad region where

every one who cares for a delimitation must run his line for himself. It is obvious, however, that no literary criticism of the Bible could hope for success which was not reverent in tone. A critic who should approach it superciliously or arrogantly would miss all that has given the book its power as literature and its lasting and universal appeal.

A large part of the book was delivered in the form of a course of lectures at the Lowell Institute during the past winter. The chapter on the poetry, and portions of some other chapters, have appeared as essays in the *Atlantic Monthly*; and I am under obligations to the editor of that magazine for his kind permission to use them.

To several of my colleagues I owe special thanks for their generosity in opening to me their own stores of learning and for advising me in my reading. Chief among them are Professor Toy, who has shown me unwearying kindness in many difficulties, Professor G. F. Moore, Professor Lyon, and Professor Ropes, who, besides giving me much valuable advice, has been good enough to read some of the manuscript.

J. H. GARDINER

18 GRAYS HALL, HARVARD UNIVERSITY,
    June 16, 1906.

CONTENTS

CHAPTER I

CHAPTER II

CHAPTER III

CHAPTER IV

CHAPTER V

CHAPTER VI

CHAPTER VII

CHAPTER VIII

CHAPTER IX

THE BIBLE AS ENGLISH
LITERATURE

CHAPTER I

INTRODUCTION

I

WHEN one begins to study the Bible from the
point of view of English literature, one sees at once
that though it has grown into the substance of that
literature nevertheless it has still its own character
and its own place apart. At first sight sufficient
explanation for this separateness seems to be found
in the fact that it always has been and is still venerated as the word of God. A little further
consideration, however, shows that though this is
one cause it is far from being the only cause or even
the chief cause for this peculiar position of the Bible
in our literature; for all its literary characteristics
and the mode of thought and the purpose of its
writers are demonstrably different from those which
lie behind any other work in the language. This
uniqueness of character and of position of the
Bible in English literature springs from the essen-

1

tial character of the book itself, and not merely
from the attitude of its readers toward it.

Before we go on, however, to study this unique
character of this great work of literature we must
first clearly recognize the closely related fact that in
English literature the Bible is a single book. Before long we shall have to enter into some analysis
of the parts of the book into their component sources,
and this analysis may tend to obscure the essential
unity of the whole. Yet the popular usage which
speaks of the Bible as a single book in spite of the
diversity of its parts, and in an equally natural way
of Biblical style as established fact in literature, is
a sound usage. In English literature the Bible is
a single book, and not a " library of books."

This distinctness and unity of character runs not
only to the style but to the substance. In substance
a minute's consideration will show any one how
naturally he thinks of this book as the sum of the
actions and sayings of men of another region and
another age of the world; and whether these men
of Palestine come from the time of David or from
the time of St. Paul, they lie together in one's mind
as belonging to a single land and a single marvellous
period of the world's history. Moreover, the whole
substance is imbued with a directness and a freshness of inspiration which are unique. It is a right

instinct, for all that Emerson has said, which puts
the sayings of Isaiah and of Amos, of St. Paul and
of St. John on a higher level than the sayings of
Socrates or of Marcus Aurelius, and puts the words
of Jesus in a place apart and above them all. The
older and normal classification is merely a recogni-
tion of established facts in history and literature.
Even as between the Old Testament and the New
Testament the differences seem slight and negligible
when we compare either with anything else in
English literature. Moreover, the two run together
through many common characteristics: Christianity
is deeply rooted in the religion of Israel; and all
through the book, whether in the Old Testament
or the New, there is the same earnestness and underlying warmth of feeling, even in the stories of
Samson and his rude jests on the Philistines, or in
the quite unreligious book of Esther. Everywhere
one feels the consciousness of the original writers
that they were telling the story of the chosen people
of God and setting forth the fulfilment of his
promises to them. And throughout the whole book
there is the unswerving and developing sense that
there is a God in the world whose sway is justice
and righteousness and love, and whose service is the
highest duty of mankind. In all these ways the
substance of the Bible is marked by an essential,

underlying unity of character, which makes it in a
very real way a single book.

This same essential unity of quality is even more
palpable in the style, which in its directness and its
simple nobility is the one standard which we have
in English to control the development of our language. The phrases from the Bible which have
grown into our everyday speech spring impartially
from the Old and New Testaments: we use " the
son of his old age," or " the valley of the shadow
of death," or " the pure in spirit," or " lilies of the
field," without thinking whether they come from
one part of the book or the other. This unity of style
is, as we shall see, largely due to the fact that the
whole book was translated at the same period into
a language of unsurpassed and unfaded vigor,
which now has enough tinge of the archaic to give
it a color of its own. It was Tindale's great achievement that once for all he fixed the language of the
whole Bible: and under the anxious and inspired
care of the revisers who followed in his steps the
style has been brought to a point of simplicity and
dignity, of strong feeling expressed by the rich
music of the prose, of stateliness and directness,
which sets it apart from the style of any other book
in the language.

Thus whether we consider the substance or the

style of the Bible, we only reinforce our original impression that in English literature it is a single book. If we were studying Hebrew literature or New Testament literature we should of necessity break it up and should find the force of the common saying that the Bible is a "library of books"; but for our present purpose it is a single book in as real a sense, though in a different one, as that in which the works of Shakspere constitute a single book. In a volume of his works it is a far cry from the euphuistic ingenuities of *Love's Labour's Lost* or the rant and bombast of some parts of the early chronicle histories or the passionate romance of *Romeo and Juliet* to the intense complication of thought in *Hamlet* or the great-hearted power of *Antony and Cleopatra,* and from them to the placid and autumnal charm of *The Tempest.* But for all these differences they have a common underlying character; and elusive though it may be, we recognize that Shakspere's personality hides behind them all. So in quite another way with the English Bible: though there can be no question here of personality, yet the unity of character is indisputable; for the religion of which it is the written revelation is as distinctly individual as is the character which gives consistency to the words and deeds of a man. At the end of our study I shall recur

to this point, and after the analysis and discussion
of distinctions, try to bring my readers back to this
natural attitude towards the Bible as a whole and
single book.

In the meantime, in the hope of enriching that
impression by pointing out the immense variety of
the different parts which blend into the impression of the whole, I shall dwell on the diversity of the
sources from which they spring, both in substance and
in time. Those of the Old Testament cover in time
certainly more than a thousand years. The earliest
materials go back to a period when the people of
Israel were barely emerging from the wanderings
of a nomadic life. These stories and songs and laws
gradually coalesced in the hands of a long series of
compilers and writers into something like connected
histories; then in the hands of successive schools of
prophets and priests, each with a clearer and higher
perception of the true nature of Jehovah and his
relations to his chosen people, these histories were in
some cases changed in purpose and contents, and expanded by additions, in part of prophetic exhortation, in part of legal and liturgical prescriptions,
until in the narrow and bitter times of the Persian
sovereignty they came into their present form. The
books of poetry, though each incorporates material
from earlier times, came to be the expression of the

thought and aspirations of the Jews of this same late period, a period when they were struggling for their existence both as a nation and as a church with a noble and inextinguishable faith. The prophecy, the key to the whole literature, first taking written form with Amos and Hosea and Isaiah, came to its height with them; and then gradually losing its power, after the times of the Captivity it dried up or ran off into the inspired dreams of the apocalyptic literature, which continued on far beyond the apostolic age of the New Testament. Then in the New Testament, we come to books which were written in a modern and Western language, when the Roman empire held undisputed sway over the world. Thus in point of time the work that we shall be studying ranges in origin from some time before 1200 B.C. to at least as late as the end of the first century A.D.

In material there is a corresponding variety. There are scraps of folk-songs of war and victory, early legends and myths, histories based on contemporary records and full of the vigor of a most vigorous time, great bodies of laws which reflect important changes in civilization, highly developed schemes of liturgy and ecclesiastical law, collections of proverbs so pithy and closely wrought that they still hold their truth, psalms of pious and connected medita-

tion or of jubilant ejaculations of faith, the soaring
messages of the prophecy, the mystical visions of the
apocalypse, the simple, everlasting stories and teachings of the gospels, the fiery and soaring arguments
of St. Paul.

In the Old Testament all this material is Oriental:
it springs from the same civilization as the *Arabian
Nights*. But it has preserved for us the history,
the poetry, the wisdom, the religious ideals and
national hopes of a people whose individuality and
tenacity of thought are perhaps the strongest known
in history. The poetry is marked by a singular concreteness and objectivity both of idea and of idiom,
and by a freedom of form otherwise unknown in
English. The books of wisdom are shrewd or at
times soaring, but they never reason in the modern
sense of the word. The religious ideas develop
without any break which could make the pious Jew
of the fourth century B.C. feel himself cut loose from
ancestors of the tenth or fifteenth century B.C. whose
religion and worship had close kinship to those of
other desert tribes.

In the New Testament side by side with the Oriental simplicity of the first three gospels and of some
of the later books there is a new element, and an approach to modern ways of thought in the fourth gospel, in the epistles of St. Paul, and in *Hebrews*. In

these works we find the first effort to make a theology,
—to philosophize religion. As a whole, the New Testament has its unity in the substance of its doctrines,
in the fact that in all its books it sets forth the
same facts, the same doctrines, the same hopes, and
the same ideals: but the two ways in which it sets
them forth are as different as the East and the West.

Yet all this diversity has grown together into the
unity of our English Bible. The seeds of this unity
were already sown in Old Testament times in the
gradual advance of the people of Israel to higher
and purer ideas of the nature and majesty of
Jehovah. In each age their books of history were
subject to a constant revision which selected and
moulded the material with a strongly governing purpose. In the times of Ezra and Nehemiah the Law
in the form of our Pentateuch became a definite
book, venerated above all other books in existence.
Then the prophetical books, which for the Jew included the historical books after the Pentateuch,
followed the Law to a separate and kindred place
in their esteem; and finally the Old Testament was
completed by the addition of the other books. All
this collecting and editing was done by men with
no sense of literary ownership or of historical development. Thus there was a constant tendency to
confuse and obliterate the special characteristics of

different portions of the literature. Moreover, the
text was still so fluid down to the very beginning
of our era that the Greek of the Septuagint, which
was made after 300 B.C., differs in important re-
spects from the established text of the Hebrew.

At the same time the books of the Apocrypha
show that there was no gulf between the Old Testament and the New. Even the forms are continuous
and overlapping: the apocalyptic, which came to its
full growth in *Daniel,* is carried on in *Revelation*
and in *2 Esdras*; some of the psalms almost surely
come from Maccabean times, less than two hundred
years before the Christian age, and the *Magnificat*
and *Nunc Dimittis* in *St. Luke* are a product of the
same mode of literature. Moreover, in literary form
the first three gospels are indistinguishable from
analogous portions of the Old Testament. Thus the
books of the Old Testament merge insensibly into
those of the New.

The processes of translation still further obliter-
ated differences and created similarities. The Vulgate, which was the Bible of all Europe down to
the first half of the sixteenth century, by its strong
coloring and its beauty and splendor of phrasing to
some extent stamped its character on our version;
and long before the fifteenth century men had lost all
idea of any large differences between the parts of

the Bible. The versions of the sixteenth century still further reinforced the unity of character of the whole Bible. When the devoted labors of William Tindale, his scholarship and his genius, had set the style of the English, the later revisions merely corrected the detail without altering the strong characteristics which he had stamped on it. Moreover, the language of England in the sixteenth century had the vigor which belongs to a vernacular freshly turned to purposes of literature; and its comparative poverty in abstract and learned words separate it from our language of to-day, and even without what is for us a slightly archaic coloring help again to set the Bible a little apart from other books.

Thus the work which we are to consider here came to its full growth in the English in a form which, in spite of its foreign origins and the diversity of its sources, makes it a single book, and the book which of all books in English is the most native and the most deeply ingrained in our literature and our language. The object of this essay will be to throw light on this enduring power, and especially on some of the causes which enabled its appeal to survive so many centuries of time and the translation into a language of wholly different genius. In discussing the book I shall look at it as the one book which in the last three centuries has reached the hearts and expressed the deepest feelings of all classes of English-speaking people, as the book which since the time of the great Puritan uprising of the seventeenth century has so worked itself into the bone and sinew of English literature and of the English language that to-day our common speech is full of its phrases. And looking at the book from this special and narrow point of view I shall confine myself wholly to its characteristics as a work of English literature.

II

Since the Bible is essentially a national literature, however, and the Old Testament especially so, to understand how it came to be what it is one must have a clearer notion of the actual history of the people than can be gained from an uncritical reading of its historical books; and especially one must realize the great change which was wrought in the religious life of the people of Israel, and by necessary consequence in their literature, by the revelations through the prophets. The messages of Amos, Hosea, and Isaiah which preceded and accompanied the national disasters of the eighth century B.C., and those of their successors in later ages, changed not

only the substance but the outward form and structure of the literature.

To begin with, one must realize how much the
course of the history of the tribes of Israel was determined by the situation and character of the country they inhabited. Palestine, constituting as it
does the narrow strip of habitable land between the
desert and the Mediterranean, was the bridge over
which ran the trade routes between the valley of the
Nile and the valley of the Euphrates. Accordingly
the states formed by its changing inhabitants were at
best little more than buffers between the great empires
of Egypt and of Assyria and Chaldea: and they
were constantly subject to the domination of one
or the other or to the almost incessant wars between them. The country itself in the south is
rough, hilly and mountainous, but in the north
opens out into the great plain of Esdraelon or
Megiddo. Thus, though the north was open to invasion, the line of mountains to the west of Jordan,
especially in the south, created almost impregnable
strongholds, such as Samaria and Jerusalem, which
made possible in the dawn of Israelite history the
persistence of the Canaanite clans, later the ex-
ploits of Jonathan and David, and still later, at the
threshold of the Christian era, the marvellous victories of the Maccabees. The greater ruggedness

and sterility of the south largely account for the
survival of the kingdom of Judah for more than a
century after the destruction of the kingdom of
Samaria by the Assyrians.

The people of Israel who were to rule this region
with many vicissitudes for less than a thousand
years, sprang from the nomadic tribes of the Arabian
desert, which produced also the Ammonites, the
Moabites and the Edomites, and probably also the
Assyrians and Chaldeans. Some time, probably in
the second half of the second millennium before
Christ, these clans from the desert seem to have
settled on the northeast border of Egypt. Their origin and early history are very obscure, for the
stories of the patriarchs are probably largely or
wholly legendary; and it is not until the Exodus that
even the outlines of the history become at all distinct. At this period, when the Egyptians afflicted
them with burdens and forced them to build " for
Pharaoh treasure cities, Pithom and Raamses," they
broke loose from their masters under the leadership
of Moses and moved off into the wilderness of Sinai.
Here the tribes renewed their covenant with Jehovah
and became thenceforth definitively Jehovah's people.
This solemn renewal of allegiance to their own God
stamped Israel with an individual character, which
in future ages was to separate them from all other na-

tions. After the death of Moses, under the leadership of Joshua, they made their entry into
Canaan, crossing the Jordan at Jericho just above
the Dead Sea. Their establishment here, as can be
seen from a careful reading of *Joshua* and *Judges*,
was slow and their advance irregular. Some of the
natives of the country maintained themselves in
their strongholds for a long period: Jerusalem, for
example, was not taken until the reign of David.
Then gradually, as they fought their way to supremacy in Palestine, they became transformed
from a more or less incoherent league into a people
settled in cities and engaged in agriculture.

The completion of this slow process came just
before 1000 B.C., when Saul, after beating back the
Philistines, the neighbors of Israel on the sea-coast
of the Mediterranean, established a kingdom which
included all the tribes of Israel. When he died
fighting the Philistines at Gilboa, David, succeeding at first to the leadership of Judah, presently by
shrewd and conciliatory statesmanship, by prowess
as a warrior, and with the aid of such relentless
leaders as Amasa and Joab, established his rule over
all the tribes. He not only consolidated the kingdom, but he widened its borders to Damascus on
the northeast and to Elath on the Red Sea. Under
Solomon the kingdom must have taken on the

features of an Oriental despotism. His wisdom was a wisdom of peace: and he made leagues with his neighbors and enriched himself through trade. He hired mercenaries, he built fortresses by forced labor, and he introduced into his capital at Jerusalem all those luxuries which we are told filled the Queen of Sheba with such wonder that " there was no more speech left in her." The luxury and the oppressiveness of his reign, however, broke up the kingdom. On his death Jeroboam led all the tribes of the north in a rebellion against the dynasty of David, and established the kingdom of North Israel, which until the disaster of 722 B.C. was to be the leader of the two kingdoms.

Then for a couple of centuries these two little kingdoms stood side by side, sometimes in warfare against each other, sometimes in coalition against their neighbors, always overshadowed by the great power of Assyria. In Judah the dynasty of David maintained itself: in North Israel the ruling family changed four times before the final anarchy which preceded the annihilation of the kingdom. When the power of Assyria again strengthened itself after the middle of the eighth century the beginning of the end was at hand. Pekah, the king of Israel, and Rezon, the king of Damascus, " those two tails of smoking firebrands," as Isaiah calls them, formed a coalition which attempted to stem the tide. When they made war on Ahaz of Judah to force him into the coalition, he bribed Tiglath-Pilezer to help him. The latter put an end to the kingdom of Damascus and devastated the northern and eastern frontiers of North Israel. Then after a long siege Sargon took the city of Samaria in 722 B.C., and deported much of the population of the northern kingdom to the far East, putting in their place foreigners from the Euphrates. So ends the first chapter in the history of Israel. Henceforth Judah is left standing as a vassal of the great power of Assyria for another century, but its extinction was merely a question of time.

Down to this period it is probable that the people of Israel differed not very much from the kindred nations across the Jordan, Moab and Ammon, who were of the same Semitic stem. The Moabites served Chemosh, and the Ammonites Milcom in much the same manner that Israel served Jehovah; and there is every reason to believe that down to the middle of the eighth century B.C., a century after the time of Elijah, Israel thought of Jehovah as a god of the same general nature as the gods of their neighbors. He was to them their special tribal god, their champion against Chemosh or Milcom or the special god of any other nation with which they might clash. Probably the religion of Israel was in essence purer and simpler than those of their neighbors; but *Judges* and *Kings* show how continually the religion of Jehovah was in danger of contamination by these other religions. The merciless extermination of the worshippers of Baal under the leadership of Elijah and Elisha in the ninth century B.C. was a successful reaction against the inroads of foreign gods on the allegiance of Israel to Jehovah; but we must suppose that down to this time the religion of Israel differed only in degree of purity from the worship of the surrounding nations, and that often the service of the heathen gods went on side by side with the worship of Jehovah.

With the eighth century, however, a new light breaks for the religion of Israel. If the doctrine which had hitherto been accepted by all the Semitic peoples were true, that the god of each nation would protect it against other gods and their nations, then obviously the power of Jehovah had become weak and limited, for Assyria had overrun and destroyed the kingdom of North Israel. In this crisis we see the saving power of the religion of Israel. As the cloud was approaching, and before it broke, Amos and Hosea had proclaimed a new doctrine. They announced to the people that Jehovah would punish Israel for its unrighteousness, and that he would use the hosts of the heathen for his own purposes:

> But, behold, I will raise up against you a nation, O house of Israel, saith the Lord the God of hosts: and they shall afflict you from the entering in of Hemath unto the river of the wilderness.[1]

> And the Lord said unto me, Amos, what seest thou? And I said, A plumbline. Then said the Lord, Behold, I will set a plumbline in the midst of my people Israel: I will not again pass them by any more:
> And the high places of Isaac shall be desolate, and the sanctuaries of Israel shall be laid waste; and I will rise against the house of Jeroboam with the sword.[2]

And in the next generation Isaiah reinforced this doctrine to Judah:

> Now therefore, behold, the Lord bringeth up upon them the waters of the river, strong and many, even the king of Assyria, and all his glory: and he shall come up over all his channels, and go over all his banks:
> And he shall pass through Judah; he shall overflow and go over, he shall reach even to the neck; and the stretching out of his wings shall fill the breadth of thy land, O Immanuel.[3]

[1] Amos vi. 14.   [2] Ib., vii. 8, 9.   [3] Isa. viii. 7–8.

This was a new and unwelcome doctrine to the
people of Israel and of Judah. Heretofore their religion had meant largely a cheerful round of festivals and the observance of the ritual purity by which
Jehovah was to be propitiated.[1] This new message
declared that Jehovah no longer shielded them from
disaster; but that it was he, their own God, who
was bringing the disaster on them, to punish them
for their unrighteousness and their evil-doing. It
was probably a long time before the people as a
whole rose to the acceptance of this high doctrine;
but its proclamation at just this time is a striking
example of the way in which the religion of Israel
was to be again and again lifted above what seemed
a nullification by events through the revelation of a
wider and more spiritual conception of the nature
of Jehovah and of his relation to his chosen people.
It is this new idea which gives to the earlier editing
of the books of history the touch of awe and wonder for the continuous and loving care of Jehovah
for his chosen people, and which makes these books
as wholes so different from the materials out of which
they were built. Henceforward the religion of Israel
differs not merely in degree but in kind from the
religion of its neighbors.

The outward history of Judah, left alone on its

[1] Cf. Isa. i. 10-20.

hills from the beginning of the seventh century, is obscure. Almost all we know is that it remained a vassal of the Assyrians until the destruction of Nineveh and the overthrow of the Assyrian power in 607 B.C., and that then it passed helplessly into the hands of the Chaldeans, who had succeeded to the empire of Assyria. The weak and foolish kings of the time of Jeremiah intrigued with Egypt against Nebuchadnezzar, and in 597 B.C. the latter occupied Jerusalem and carried away the flower of the people, with most of the priests, to Chaldea, where he settled them in the neighborhood of Babylon. When the intrigues were renewed he returned, and in 586 sacked the city, destroyed the temple and carried away all of the population of Judah except a handful of peasants, whom he left to keep the land from reverting entirely into wilderness. So passed away the kingdom of Judah.

In the meantime, about a generation before this final catastrophe, the discovery of *Deuteronomy* in the temple and its acceptance by Josiah and the people of Judah as the basis on which to renew their covenant with Jehovah worked a revolution in the religious observances, and ultimately in the whole constitution, of the Jewish people. The great unknown prophet who wrote the work, recognizing that so long as each village and town had its own

priest and its own high place just so long would
the unclean rites of the heathen gods creep in to
contaminate the pure worship of Jehovah, ordained
that henceforward all sacrifices should be offered at
Jerusalem:

> But unto the place which the Lord your God
> shall choose out of all your tribes to put his name
> there, even unto his habitation shall ye seek, and
> thither thou shalt come:
>
> And thither ye shall bring your burnt offerings,
> and your sacrifices, and your tithes, and heave
> offerings of your hand, and your vows, and your
> freewill offerings, and the firstlings of your herds
> and of your flocks:
>
> And there ye shall eat before the Lord your God,
> and ye shall rejoice in all that ye put your hand
> unto, ye and your households, wherein the Lord
> thy God hath blessed thee.
>
> Ye shall not do after all the things that we do
> here this day, every man whatsoever is right in
> his own eyes.[1]

Though *Deuteronomy* provided that the Levites
from the rest of the country should minister in the
temple at Jerusalem, in practice the priests of Jerusalem maintained their exclusive rights, and the other
Levites became doorkeepers and servants. Thus came
about the distinction between priests and Levites

[1] Deut. xii. 5-8.

which was to continue till the final destruction of
the temple. At the same time this concentration of
the worship at one place enormously increased the
influence and the professional feeling of the priests
and so paved the way for the establishment of the
hierarchy; and out of this hierarchy grew the ecclesiastical organization which kept the Jews from
slowly sifting away into the nations among which
they were scattered.

On the literature the influence of *Deuteronomy*
and of the priestly ideas which grew out of it was
no less dominant than on the organization of the
nation. From now on the records of the race were
rewritten from " history with a moral " into " history for the moral." This reconstruction at first in
the hands of writers full of the Deuteronomic idea
of the covenant between Jehovah and his people
brought *Judges, Samuel,* and *Kings* into their present form. Then as it passed into the hands of men
of narrower professional interests it led to the working out of the great body of laws and liturgical and
ritual prescriptions found in the middle books of the
Pentateuch. At the same time, as we shall see, the
problems produced by a literal application of *Deuteronomy* to the later condition of the Jews brought
forth the great book of *Job* and many of the psalms.

Outwardly the history of the Jews who lived in

Palestine for the six centuries or less from the time
of the exile to the final destruction of Jerusalem
is chiefly a history of oppression and distress. From
this period dates also the Dispersal, which had its beginning in conquest and deportation, but soon became
dependent on the instinct for commerce. The Jews
who spread in all directions through the known world
became in point of numbers and prosperity of more
consequence than the Jews who still lived in Palestine. But wherever they lived, whether in Persia or
in Egypt, or on the borders of the Mediterranean,
they held together as a nation through their passionate devotion to their religion and their unquenchable
faith in Jehovah. The history of the Jews in Palestine during this period is extremely obscure: in the
fourth century b.c., we have hardly a single fact of
their history. It is known that the struggle of the
Egyptians for freedom from Persian rule was in part
fought over the territory of Palestine, and it is almost certain that the Jews must have suffered bitterly from the armies of the Persians. In the next
century, after the conquest of Alexander the Great,
the Jews probably had for eighty years a period of
some peace and quiet under the rule of the first
three Ptolemies. We know that they were in high
favor at the Egyptian court, and prosperous in Alex-
andria. All through this period they must have

been gaining the larger experience of the world which appears in the later literature of the Old Testament and even more in the Apocrypha. With the renewed war between Egypt and the Seleucidan kings of Syria, the Jews found themselves in their old unhappy position of inhabiting the bridge over which the hostile forces must fight. The balance swung to the Syrians under Antiochus III., who in the first years of the second century B.C. wrested Palestine from the Ptolemy of the time. His son, Antiochus IV. Epiphanes, who came to the throne in 175 B.C., made a determined and deliberate attempt to stamp out the religion of the troublesome nation which inhabited the highlands in the south of his kingdom. He desecrated the temple by setting up an image of Zeus in the Holy of Holies,—the abomination of desolations, as *Daniel* calls it,— he gave orders for the destruction of all copies of the law, he forbade circumcision and the observance of the sabbath, and started an active and bloody persecution against all Jews who resisted his commands. At first it seemed as if the end were come. Then at last an aged priest, Mattathias, in the little mountain village of Modin, in desperation struck down a Jew who was offering the unclean sacrifice and the Syrian officer who was enforcing it. With his five sons he fled to the mountains, and there with a little band as desperate as himself he beat back the party sent by the Syrians against him. Then in successive marvellous victories his son, Judas Maccabeus, beat back one expedition after another until finally in 165 he defeated the viceroy Lysias himself. After the death of Antiochus in 164 Judas and the two brothers who successively followed him in the leadership were able in 143 by military valor and by shrewd intrigues with the claimants for the throne of the Seleucidæ to establish the Jews once more as an independent kingdom, a kingdom which was to last eighty years. During this time the sons and descendants of Mattathias became more and more merely civil rulers, and the high priesthood, which they held hereditarily, became almost a civil office.

With the coming of the Romans came the beginning of the end. Pompey in 63 B.C. took Jerusalem and plundered the temple, though he did not disturb the daily sacrifice. Syria, including Palestine, was now a Roman province. In 37 B.C. Herod, the ruler of the little Idumean kingdom, succeeded in having himself made by the Romans king over the Jews. His reign was marked by magnificent building of cities with fortresses, temples and theatres; the rebuilding of the temple at Jerusalem lasted till 4 B.C. With his death his kingdom was divided, and Judea was henceforth shifted by the

Romans from one political division and one ruler to another. All through this time the Jews had been turbulent. They were bitterly divided against each other and continually intriguing. Finally in 66 A.D. the country blazed out into a war which forced the Romans to bring large reinforcements to Palestine. Vespasian came to the gates of Jerusalem, where the parties of the Jews had been fighting against each other, but the final capture of the city, whose garrison was divided against itself, was delayed until the coming of Titus in September, 70 A.D. This time the Romans did the work thoroughly. The city was sacked, and the inhabitants sold as slaves or used in the combats in the public games; and the plunder of the temple was exhibited in the triumph of Vespasian and Titus in Rome. So came the final end of the Jews as a nation with a local and settled home.

Meantime their religion, starting from the impetus given by the great prophets of the eighth century, Amos, Hosea and Isaiah, soared to constantly higher planes. The great writer who wrote the original *Deuteronomy*, besides concentrating the worship at Jerusalem, formulated in the 7th century B.C. the doctrine of the dependence of the outward fortunes of Israel on its faithfulness to the covenant with Jehovah.

The Lord did not set his love upon you, nor choose you, because ye were more in number than any people: for ye were the fewest of all people:

But because the Lord loved you, and because he would keep the oath which he had sworn unto your fathers, hath the Lord brought you out with a mighty hand, and redeemed you out of the house of bondmen, from the hand of Pharaoh king of Egypt.

Know therefore that the Lord thy God, he is God, the faithful God, which keepeth covenant and mercy with them that love him and keep his commandments to a thousand generations;

And repayeth them that hate him to their face, to destroy them: he will not be slack to him that hateth him, he will repay him to his face.

Thou shalt therefore keep the commandments, and the statutes, and the judgments, which I command thee this day, to do them.[1]

In the next century, during the Exile, another great unknown prophet, whom we may call the Isaiah of the Exile, advanced to a new and higher doctrine. Through his mouth Jehovah proclaimed:

I am the Lord, and there is none else, there is no God beside me: I girded thee, though thou hast not known me:

That they may know from the rising of the sun,

[1] Deut. vii. 7–11.

and from the west, that there is none beside me. I am the Lord, and there is none else.

I form the light, and create darkness: I make peace, and create evil: I the Lord do all these things.[1]

And he sets forth as the corollary of this doctrine the futility of idol-worship. The notable passage of grim humor in *Isaiah* describes how a man, after hewing down an ash,

burneth part thereof in the fire; with part thereof he eateth flesh; he roasteth roast, and is satisfied: yea, he warmeth himself, and saith, Aha, I am warm, I have seen the fire:

And the residue thereof he maketh a god, even his graven image: he falleth down unto it, and worshippeth it, and prayeth unto it, and saith, Deliver me; for thou art my God.[2]

When one remembers that these mighty doctrines were uttered by the prophet of a people whom the Chaldeans must have looked on as one of the least important of their captive nations, one sees how far the religion of Israel had risen. In the succeeding centuries the Jews rose to still further heights. Clinging as they did with a passionate earnestness to the promises of the prophets and at the same time driven by the coercive weight of circumstances to

[1] Isa. xlv. 5–7. [2] Ib. xliv. 16–17.

see that these promises could not be fulfilled in their own day, gradually they came to realize that their faith would be rewarded in a future life; and in *Daniel* and the other apocalyptic writings, the doctrine of immortality is set forth clearly and specifically.

> And many of them that sleep in the dust of the earth shall awake, some to everlasting life, and some to shame and everlasting contempt.
>
> And they that be wise shall shine as the brightness of the firmament; and they that turn many to righteousness as the stars for ever and ever.[1]

From this period between the Captivity and the period of the Maccabees come probably many of the psalms, and the great poem of *Job*. Meditation on the meaning of the world had come, but it was guided by men whose faith in their God was unquenchable.

Thus in the thousand years or less in which the history of the people of Israel can be traced, we find them changed from a small and loosely bound league of nomadic tribes to a congregation widely scattered through the world, and bound together only by their allegiance to a law understood and followed in the most scrupulously literal way. In their religion they have passed from the simple, unthinking

---

[1] Dan. xii. 2–3.

devotion of a desert tribe to its tribal god to a realization that Jehovah is the God of all the earth, and that though his chosen people may for a time seem to be oppressed and helpless, yet it is in his power to set them above all the heathen who surround them. It is the history of a people who in spite of disasters which often brought it to the verge of annihilation, yet by its inextinguishable faith rose superior to the events of this life and attained to an elevation of religious thought which has made it for all its small numbers and its helplessness one of the great powers in the shaping of the modern world.

The books of the New Testament are hardly affected by external history, for the Christian Church accepted the empire of Rome as a matter of course. The spread of Christianity to the Jews of the Dispersal and then to the Gentiles led to the translation of the gospel into terms of Western thought under the leadership of St. Paul, and *Revelation* was written under the stress of the early persecutions against the Christians; but otherwise the books written to aid the spread of the gospel were little influenced by external history. The Christian Church in the apostolic days was in no way a political organization, and was only indirectly influenced by the political events of the time. Most of the epistles of the New Testament and the Fourth Gospel reflect the background of modern thought from the Greek-speaking world to which they were addressed: but it is only in this indirect way that the books of the New Testament are affected by the permanent shift in the mastership of the world from the long succession of Oriental powers to the Greeks and Romans.

Such then is the background of country and of history from which the various materials of our English Bible sprang. For the most part the region was even more Oriental than Cairo or Damascus and the rest of the great Mohammedan world of to-day; but it was the home of a people of extraordinary individuality, and endowed moreover with a religious and moral sense which rose constantly to higher levels of spiritual elevation. Without this vitality of their religion there is no reason to suppose that the people of Israel would have survived the incessant warfares and conquests which they underwent any more than did their kindred, the people of Moab or of Ammon; but through it their great men brought forth books which have turned the history of the world. Incidentally, translated into English, and grown into a single book, these books have become the greatest single monument of our own literature.

For convenience of study I will first discuss the several literary types into which the books may be classified, roughly following the order in which they come in our English Bible; then I will set forth the processes of translation and revision which led up to the Authorised Version of 1611; and finally I will discuss the qualities and characteristics of that version as we read it to-day.

CHAPTER II

THE NARRATIVE

I

In any adequate study of the narrative of the Bible there must be a considerable amount of analysis and discrimination; for the narrative of the New Testament differs from that of the Old Testament, and within the Old Testament itself there is great variety of type. Nevertheless, one can say that all the narrative of the Bible shows a combination of two sets of qualities: on the one hand it has a simplicity and a limpid and vivid clearness which make it appeal to all sorts and conditions of men; on the other hand through its whole range it has an undercurrent of earnestness and strong feeling. Thus the style clothes and transfigures even homely events with beauty and spiritual power; and the concreteness and clearness crystallize the deep feeling expressed by the strong rhythm and the varied music of the style. These two sets of characteristics, then, the simplicity and vivid clearness on the one hand,

and the earnestness and rich depth of feeling on the
other, we may take as the most characteristic attributes of these narratives.

By a discussion of these attributes in the light
thrown on the various books by modern scholarship
we shall be able partly to trace some of the causes
from which they proceed. We shall find that from
the substance and ideas of the Hebrew books of
history and from the nature of their language spring
the causes of the directness and the concreteness of
the Old Testament narratives: and we shall see that
the history of the Jews helps to explain the in-
creasingly deeper and more spiritual insight into the
meaning of their history which produced the solemnity and elevation of these works. At the same
time, the way in which the various types of narrative have been put together has produced a literary
effect different from anything else that we have in
English literature. A final consideration which I
shall put off to the chapter on the translation is the
fact that in the English this narrative, though a
translation, has a freshness and vigor of motion
above all other narratives in the language. Here
again, we shall find some explanation in the history
of the period when the translation was made, and
in the character and circumstances of the men
who made it.

In our ordinary speech the phrase " Biblical narrative " seems to express a definite enough fact for our present purpose; yet when one thinks over the various books of the Bible, their differences begin to stand out and give us pause. The contrast between the two opening chapters of *Genesis*, or between the simple, primitive stories of *Judges* and *Samuel* and the intensity and earnestness of *Deuteronomy*, or between the pastoral and limpid simplicity of *Ruth* and the repetitious and ponderous narrative of *Daniel*, stare one in the face, and seem to make it impossible to generalize. In the end, as I have said, we shall find that all these narratives agree in combining concrete simplicity and deep earnestness of feeling to a degree which sets them apart from anything else in English literature; in the meantime we shall gain a deeper understanding of all the Biblical narrative by briefly examining these contrasts as they appear in three important types of it in the Old Testament. The New Testament narrative I will touch on later. We shall find that these three types of Old Testament narrative spring from three different ages of the history and the religious thought of the Jews, and that the contrasting qualities of the different types are to a large extent explicable by the different circumstances under which they were produced. I will discuss first that which is earliest in time, then for the sake of contrast that which is latest, and finally that which is intermediate.

The type of narrative that springs most readily to one's mind when one speaks of the Biblical narrative is the vivid kind of story which for the most part fills *Genesis, Samuel,* and *Kings.* For swiftness, for the unerring sense of effective detail, these stories are our standard in English. The story of the Garden of Eden, and the fall of man, and the stories of Abraham, Isaac, and Jacob show us this vivid narrative at its clearest and simplest. Even in this vivid and simple narrative, however, there is considerable variety. The stories of this type in *Genesis* are pastoral, almost idyllic, in contrast to the histories of the bloody Joab and his slaughter of Amasa and Absalom, or of the primitive feuds of Gideon and Jephthah in *Judges,* or of Elisha and Jehu and their merciless extermination of the worshippers of Baal. These later stories produce an effect of a stern reality, beside which the stories of the patriarchs have, as has been said, " the freshness of the elder world." Nevertheless all of them are separated from the other types of which I shall speak, by their vividness, by their intense interest in human life, by their being told primarily for the interest in the events and in the people. One thinks first of all of their simplicity, clearness, and vividness.

These characteristics can be made more palpable by putting an example from the earliest type beside one from the latest type. If one begins to read *Genesis* with one's critical sense alert, the transition from the first to the second chapter shows a surprising change of style and of atmosphere. The first chapter is a solemn epitome of the whole process of the creation which tends to fall into a series of formulas, and which has many repetitions.

> And God said, Let there be lights in the firmament of the heaven to divide the day from the night; and let them be for signs, and for seasons, and for days, and years:
>
> And let them be for lights in the firmament of the heaven to give light upon the earth: and it was so.
>
> And God made two great lights; the greater light to rule the day, and the lesser light to rule the night: he made the stars also.
>
> And God set them in the firmament of the heaven to give light upon the earth,
>
> And to rule over the day and over the night, and to divide the light from the darkness: and God saw that it was good.
>
> And the evening and the morning were the fourth day.[1]

What is more significant even than the formal precision of this chapter is the fact that the belief un-

[1] Gen. i. 14–19.

derlying it is an austere monotheism: the God who performs these great wonders of creation is a remote and omnipotent being.

In the second chapter, after the fourth verse, all this is changed. The creation of man fills the centre of interest: the creation of plants and animals is incidental; the creation of the heavens and the earth is assumed. The style throughout is that of the first type of which I have spoken, simple, direct, vivid to the point of homeliness in its details.

> And the Lord God said, It is not good that the man should be alone; I will make him an help meet for him.
>
> And out of the ground the Lord God formed every beast of the field, and every fowl of the air; and brought them unto Adam to see what he would call them: and whatsoever Adam called every living creature, that was the name thereof.
>
> And Adam gave names to all cattle, and to the fowl of the air, and to every beast of the field; but for Adam there was not found an help meet for him.
>
> And the Lord God caused a deep sleep to fall upon Adam, and he slept: and he took one of his ribs, and closed up the flesh instead thereof;
>
> And the rib, which the Lord God had taken from man, made he a woman, and brought her unto the man.
>
> And Adam said, This is now bone of my bones, and flesh of my flesh: she shall be called Woman, because she was taken out of Man.

> Therefore shall a man leave his father and his mother, and shall cleave unto his wife: and they shall be one flesh.
>
> And they were both naked, the man and his wife, and were not ashamed.[1]

Here, in contrast to the first chapter, God is on familiar terms with the man whom he has created: he brings the beasts of the fields and the fowls of the air to Adam " to see what he would call them "; and in the third chapter he walks in the garden " in the cool of the day." One does not need much scrutiny to see the great difference not only in the manner of writing but in the mode of conceiving the act of creation: where the first chapter is stately, abstract, and reverent, the second is vivid, simple, and naïve.

Two more examples will make clearer the difference in thought and substance between these different types of narrative. Of the two accounts of the promise to Abraham the first one begins as follows:

> And when Abram was ninety years old and nine, the Lord appeared to Abram, and said unto him, I am the Almighty God; walk before me, and be thou perfect.
>
> And I will make my covenant between me and thee, and will multiply thee exceedingly.
>
> And Abram fell on his face: and God talked with him saying,

[1] Gen. ii. 18–25.

As for me, behold, my covenant is with thee, and thou shalt be a father of many nations.

Neither shall thy name any more be called Abram, but thy name shall be Abraham; for a father of many nations have I made thee.[1]

The second account begins with the story of how Abraham entertained the angels unawares:

And the Lord appeared unto him in the plains of Mamre; and he sat in the tent door in the heat of the day;

And he lift up his eyes and looked, and lo, three men stood by him: and when he saw them, he ran to meet them from the tent door, and bowed himself towards the ground,

And said, My Lord, if now I have found favor in thy sight pass not away, I pray thee, from thy servant:

Let a little water, I pray you, be fetched, and wash your feet and rest yourselves under the tree:

And I will fetch a morsel of bread, and comfort ye your hearts; after that ye shall pass on: for therefore are ye come to your servant. And they said, So do, as thou hast said.

And Abraham hastened into the tent unto Sarah, and said, Make ready quickly three measures of fine meal, knead it, and make cakes upon the hearth.

And Abraham ran unto the herd, and fetcht a

[1] Gen. xvii. 1–5.

calf tender and good, and gave it unto a young man; and he hasted to dress it.[1]

And it even tells how the Lord disputes with Sarah:

> Then Sarah denied, saying, I laughed not; for she was afraid. And he said, Nay; but thou didst laugh.

In the simplicity of this story, even the actions of God are conceived with the same homely concreteness as are the dealings of the patriarchs with each other. Again, as in the case of the first two chapters of the book, we find in contiguous passages strongly contrasted types of narrative, the one naïve, concrete, and vivid, the other in comparison abstract, stately, and reverent.

Let us consider more carefully the simple and vivid narrative. It is characterized by a lively and naïve interest in the affairs of human life, and by natural and unpremeditated story-telling. Such are the simpler of the stories of the patriarchs, the story of Rebecca at the well, of Jacob and his tortuous dealings with his brother Esau and his father-in-law Laban, and the stories of Joseph, with that most touching scene of all where he could no longer refrain from disclosing himself to his brethren. In other books of the Bible we come to examples of this style with its full human interest in the stories of

[1] Gen. xviii. 1–7.

Jephthah and of Samson, in the story of Saul seeking his father's asses, in the various stories of David and Saul, in the story of David and Bathsheba, and of the rebellion of the arrogant Absalom and his wretched death at the hands of Joab, in the stories of Elijah and Ahab, and in that of Elisha, Naaman, and Gehazi. In all these stories the interest lies almost wholly in the actions and in the people. They show no evidence of any pondering on the meaning of history; the events and the actors in them are sufficient for the narrators. The narrative moves directly and rapidly, yet with extraordinary vividness of characterization. The contrast between Jacob and Esau is perhaps the best example of this compact portrayal of character: Jacob farsighted and wily in a peculiarly Oriental way, yet withal sobered and deepened by his foresight of the great future which the promises of Jehovah had laid out for his race; Esau bluff and honest, but reckless of any good beyond that of the present moment. So in the stories of David and his troubles with his sons: the few chapters give us a most vivid glimpse of this Oriental court of David, the great warrior and the farsighted statesman, yet soft as a woman in dealing with the fractious and unruly Absalom. And consider the little glimpse of the bloody and treacherous Joab and his assassination of Amasa:

And Joab said to Amasa, Art thou in health, my brother? And Joab took Amasa by the beard with the right hand to kiss him.

But Amasa took no heed to the sword that was in Joab's hand: so he smote him therewith in the fifth rib, and shed out his bowels to the ground, and struck him not again; and he died. So Joab and Abishai his brother pursued after Sheba the son of Bichri.[1]

It is difficult to see how narrative style can have more of the essential virtues than we find in such stories as these.

Yet if we knew only these stories in the Old Testament, we should miss a notable element of what makes up our impression of the Biblical narrative. For after all, that narrative is not merely a standard for vividness; it is also a standard for depth of meaning and a solemn stateliness of style. For these qualities one must turn to the other two of these three types of narrative. The latest of these, which is found chiefly in the Pentateuch, and which we may call the priestly, is bare of vivifying detail. The first chapter of *Genesis* in comparison with the second is austere and abstract: by itself and beside the warm human interest of the other stories it seems lacking in life. It does not scintillate with the words

[1] 2 Sam. xx. 9–10.

and the movement of living beings; it sets forth the
newly created universe and the world of the patriarchs as an empty expanse in which the Lord God
of Israel stands at a remote and awful distance.
And if one follows out the passages in which this
type of narrative occurs through the Pentateuch one
gets only an outline of the history, and an outline
in which religious institutions and ceremonies overshadow the individuals of the race. Examples of
this bare but solemn narrative are the story of the
creation in *Genesis i*, of God's covenant with Noah
after the Flood, of the covenant and promise to
Abraham in *Genesis xvii*, of Abraham's purchase of
the field of Ephron the Hittite at Machpelah for a
buryingplace in *Genesis xxiii*, and of the Lord's
commission to Moses to lead the children of Israel
out of Egypt in *Exodus vi*. Besides these and many
other passages of narrative, the great mass of laws
and liturgical prescriptions and the exhaustive gene-
alogies and chronology scattered through these books
of the Pentateuch belong to the same priestly source,
and add their solemn precision and formality to
the general effect. Yet throughout this bare and
unimaginative type of narrative is marked by a
dignity and elevation which go a long way to color
one's impression of the Biblical narrative as a whole.
The very austerity of its conception of creation and

of history lifts one above the petty concerns of daily life.

At the same time the repetitiousness of style, which is one of its characteristics, establishes a strength of rhythm which deepens and emphasizes the meaning of the history.

> And Moses spake unto the children of Israel, and every one of the princes gave him a rod apiece, for each prince one, according to their fathers' houses, even twelve rods: and the rod of Aaron was among their rods.
>
> And Moses laid up the rods before the Lord in the tabernacle of witness.
>
> And it came to pass, that on the morrow Moses went into the tabernacle of witness; and, behold, the rod of Aaron for the house of Levi was budded, and brought forth buds, and bloomed blossoms, and yielded almonds.
>
> And Moses brought out all the rods from before the Lord unto all the children of Israel: and they looked, and took every man his rod.[1]

If this solemn rhythm colors and deepens even such a simple narrative as this, when it appears in a statement of the promises to the chosen people of God, it adds indefinitely to the impressiveness and weight of the narrative. Here is part of the passage in *Exodus* where the Lord gives to Moses the formal

[1] Num. xvii. 6–9.

commission to lead the people out of the house of bondage:

> And I have also heard the groaning of the children of Israel, whom the Egyptians keep in bondage; and I have remembered my covenant.
>
> Wherefore say unto the children of Israel, I am the Lord, and I will bring you out from under the burdens of the Egyptians, and I will rid you out of their bondage, and I will redeem you with a stretched out arm, and with great judgments:
>
> And I will take you to me for a people, and I will be to you a God: and ye shall know that I am the Lord your God, which bringeth you out from under the burdens of the Egyptians.
>
> And I will bring you in unto the land concerning the which I did swear to give it to Abraham, to Isaac, and to Jacob; and I will give it to you for an heritage: I am the Lord.[1]

In the English the portions of the histories which come from this source have always this sonorousness and fullness of sound. It is a curious fact that in the lists of words and phrases which are given in the manuals as being characteristic of this source there is a larger proportion of Latinate words than elsewhere in the Bible. Here are a few of them from the list in Driver's *Introduction to the Literature of the Old Testament*, which, it may be noted, is based on a study of the Hebrew: *to be fruitful, to multiply,*

[1] Ex. vi. 5–8.

according to their generations, everlasting covenant, princes of the congregation, according to the command of the Lord. Where there are many such words the large proportion of open vowels and liquid consonants makes the language almost intone itself. This rich coloring of this priestly type of narrative is an important part of one's total impression of the style of the Bible: for a necessary element in that impression is dignity and solemnity. The great stretches of ecclesiastical law in *Exodus, Leviticus,* and *Numbers* are arid so far as any literary interest is concerned; yet even in the dry details of the sacrifices and of the clothing of the priests the style has often a richness of coloring and a consequent glow of feeling which are curiously out of keeping with the character of the substance.

The third type of narrative which must be taken into account in forming an estimate of the Biblical narrative as a whole is that of *Deuteronomy* and the analogous passages in the other histories; in time of origin this is intermediate between the other two. The amount of narrative in *Deuteronomy* itself is comparatively small, but the influence of its very individual style has spread through other books. This influence is analogous to that of the priestly type of narrative in deepening and strengthening the feeling. Here, however, the style has a power of

sustaining periods and a sonorous and flowing eloquence, unlike that of any other writing of the Old
Testament:

> But the Lord hath taken you, and brought you
> forth out of the iron furnace, even out of Egypt,
> to be unto him a people of inheritance, as ye are
> this day.
>
> Furthermore the Lord was angry with me for
> your sakes, and sware that I should not go over
> Jordan, and that I should not go in unto that good
> land, which the Lord thy God giveth thee for an
> inheritance:
>
> But I must die in this land, I must not go over
> Jordan: but ye shall go over, and possess that good
> land.
>
> Take heed unto yourselves, lest ye forget the
> covenant of the Lord your God, which he made
> with you, and make you a graven image, or the
> likeness of any thing, which the Lord thy God
> hath forbidden thee.
>
> For the Lord thy God is a consuming fire, even a
> jealous God.[1]

Such a style as this clearly adds an important element to the great work in which it is contained.
Here are freedom and a vivid instinct for fact, joined
with a sonorous and elevated diction to give expression to a high and austere conception of religion.
There is no writer in the Bible whose style is more

[1] Deut. iv. 20–24.

individual and distinct than the great unknown prophet who wrote the original *Deuteronomy*; and both his lofty conceptions of the obligations of Israel to Jehovah and his rolling and eloquent style made a deep impression on the Jews of the generations immediately before the Exile and during the next two or three centuries. Writers eager to impress his teachings on their contemporaries recomposed the history for the period covered by our books of *Judges, Samuel,* and *Kings* in order to illustrate and burn in this theory of history, that the prosperity or distress of the children of Israel sprang immediately from their obedience or disobedience to the commandments of the just and merciful God who had brought them out of the land of Egypt into a land flowing with milk and honey: and in recomposing the history they added many short passages to make the lesson unmistakable. After the manner of all writers of antiquity such passages are apt to take the form of speeches put into the mouths of the chief actors in the history, as, for example, the first farewell of Joshua, in *Joshua xxiii,* the farewell of Samuel in *1 Samuel xii,* and the prayer of Solomon at the dedication of the temple. All such passages, and there are many of them besides such speeches, by their sonorous phrasing and their rolling periods add to the earnestness and elevation of

the books in which they are imbedded. Like the
narrative of the priestly type with its austere dignity and abstract and stately elevation, *Deuteronomy*
and the analogous passages in the other books help
to deepen and enrich the impression made by the
narrative books as a whole.

I hope that this very brief review of so huge a
field will have sufficed to make clear the fact that
these stories of the Bible, in spite of their general
effect of simple and vivid clearness suffused and enriched by a singular depth and earnestness of feeling, are made up of distinct elements which can be
discovered and isolated by analysis. This analysis
has been one of the chief results of the great school
of modern scholarship which is commonly known as
the Higher Criticism: and it has shown in the most
interesting way that not only deep and essential
differences in religious thought but purely literary
differences in style in the English Bible can be explained by the diverse historical circumstances which
produced the original books. The clear and unpremeditated directness of the simpler stories of the
Old Testament, the eager and rolling eloquence of
Deuteronomy, and the formal and stately austerity
of the priestly narrative all are explicable, in part
at any rate, by the conditions from which they
sprang. For in their origins these three types of

narrative represent three different stages of the history and of the religious thought of the people of Israel. Almost all of the simple and vivid narrative has come down from the early times, before the great prophets Amos, Hosea, and Isaiah had set forth the deeper meaning of the religion of Jehovah. In these stories, God seems to be thought of almost as an elder brother walking on the earth and guarding his chosen people. The idea which these early generations held of Jehovah and of their relation to him is illustrated by the speech of Rab-shakeh to the men of Hezekiah when the former was besieging Jerusalem:

> . . . Hearken not unto Hezekiah, when he persuadeth you, saying, The Lord will deliver us.
> Hath any of the gods of the nations delivered at all his land out of the hand of the king of Assyria?
> Where are the gods of Hamath, and of Arpad? where are the gods of Sepharvaim, Hena, and Ivah? have they delivered Samaria out of mine hand?
> Who are they among all the gods of the countries, that have delivered their country out of mine hand, that the Lord should deliver Jerusalem out of mine hand?[1]

This whole region, as we have seen, held that the god of each nation was charged with the protection of

[1] 2 Kings xviii. 32–35.

that nation against other nations and their gods: and there is every reason to suppose that this was still the controlling idea of the religion of Israel down to the eighth century B.C. Thus the religion from which most of this simplest type of narrative sprang was that of a people in its childhood, and of a people who in spiritual insight had not yet risen above their neighbors. Then in the eighth century B.C., when the shadow of the great empire of Assyria began to darken the horizon of Israel, the new light came; and it brought as one of its consequences a change in the character of the literature of Israel. Now it was revealed to the prophets that their people were the servants of a God who controlled the nations of the earth, and who used the heathen to chastise Israel for its unrighteousness and its backsliding; and in the next century *Deuteronomy* brought this new and inspiring ideal to an almost legal formulation. Each of these stages of revelation had its effects on the form and even on the style of the narrative.

An even greater change followed the revelation made in the sixth century B.C. that the God of the Jews was the one God, who had made the heavens and the earth, and all that therein is. This high thought stimulated Ezekiel to propound an ideal scheme for the rebuilding of the temple and the reconstitution of its services in a manner befitting the

God of the whole earth. He was also a priest, probably a chief founder of that school of priestly writing which produced the latest of the three types of narrative we have been considering; and his prophecies and visions witness to the immense stimulus given to the priests as a class by this consciousness that they were the special servants of the one God. The vision which occupies the last nine chapters of his book is proof of the enthusiasm with which they entered into the work and the spiritual elevation with which they undertook it:

> Afterward he brought me to the gate, even the gate that looketh toward the east:
>
> And, behold, the glory of the God of Israel came from the way of the east: and his voice was like a noise of many waters: and the earth shined with his glory.
>
> And it was according to the appearance of the vision which I saw, even according to the vision that I saw when I came to destroy the city: and the visions were like the vision that I saw by the river Chebar; and I fell upon my face.
>
> And the glory of the Lord came into the house by the way of the gate whose prospect is toward the east.
>
> So the spirit took me up, and brought me into the inner court; and, behold, the glory of the Lord filled the house.

And I heard him speaking to me out of the house;
and the man stood by me.

And he said unto me, Son of man, the place of
my throne, and the place of the soles of my feet,
where I will dwell in the midst of the children of
Israel forever, and my holy name, shall the house
of Israel no more defile, neither they, nor their
kings, by their whoredom, nor by the carcases
of their kings in their high places.[1]

In estimating the legal and historical writing of the
school of the priests during the Exile and the
century succeeding, one must not leave out of account this fact that they were filled with this new
and uplifting conception of their religion and of the
unique place which their nation in consequence occupied among the peoples of the earth. It is this
great idea which fills the set formulas of the first
chapter of *Genesis* with such nobility and which imparts depth and richness of feeling to what is otherwise bare and formal throughout this priestly type
of the narrative. Thus it came about that a style
of writing which seems so remote from the warmth
and living vividness of the stories of the patriarchs
or the history of David had a peculiar rich depth
of expressiveness; for the later generations of the
Jews were able to feel the power of their God in a
way impossible to their forefathers, who had not

[1] Ezek. xliii. 1-7.

passed through the fiery furnace of affliction to so
noble a conception of his nature.

Speaking very broadly, then, we may say that the
limpid simplicity and the instinct for living and
vivifying detail in the first of our three types of
narrative reflect the habits of thought of a people
whose interests lay in the present, whose religious
life was simple and primitive; that the broader view
of *Deuteronomy* and its intensity of feeling reflect
a time when Judah in times of bitter and seemingly
hopeless distress rose to a view of history and a conception of religion that were both more spiritual and
intellectually far in advance of the writers of the
simpler stories; and that finally, in the latest type
of narrative we have the still nobler and more spiritual thought of a generation which has soared above
the mythology of the great nations that held them
captive and the unthinking anthropomorphism of
their own ancestors to the austere and uplifting conception of Jehovah as the one and only God who
had made the heavens and the earth. The spirit and
ideas of each of these periods are preserved in the
rich mosaic of the historical books of our Old Testament.

Yet in the end we must remember that analysis
is not literature: and that although this analysis is
worth making since it helps one to see perspective

instead of a flat surface, yet in the end the natural way of reading is the true way for literature. I may compare one's original way of reading these stories to the effect of a Chinese picture, where there are rich colors and strongly outlined figures, but no distinction of foreground and background, since there is no perspective. But after following out the analysis, one's reading is like a picture which, keeping the rich color and the sharp outline, now has depth and distance, so that one sees the thought of age before age of the people of Israel, reaching back into the mists of antiquity, as blue mountains peer over one another's shoulders off to the dim horizon. Thus the clear and vivid simplicity of the earlier narratives is deepened and ennobled by the searching earnestness of the later ones; and the austere bareness of the latter is vivified by the warm human interest of the former.

II

Beside any other narrative in English literature, however, the differences between these three types of narrative become insignificant. In the first place they are separated from us by a great gulf in the manner of thought. That difference I shall discuss more fully in the chapter on the wisdom books of the Old Testament: but one can feel it if one realizes that the first two chapters of *Genesis* are, each in its own way, statements of what we should call theories of the universe. It seems a far cry from the story of the Garden of Eden and the serpent tempting Eve to the nebular hypothesis and the theory of evolution; yet in purpose they are alike: each is an effort which men have made to explain to themselves how the universe in which they live came into being. Yet though these theories of *Genesis* are separated by a gulf from modern science, nevertheless the writer of the first chapter of *Genesis* reached an intellectual height far above that of the contemporary writers of Babylonia, for whom the creation of the world sprang from the tangle of an elaborate pantheon. There is no more striking proof of the spiritual power of the religion of Israel than the way in which the priests of this small and oppressed people rose above the fogs of mythology and reduced its confusion to the terms of a pure and simple monotheism. They still had to phrase their understanding of the creation in the form of a narrative, for as we shall see they had no other way either of thinking or of expressing it; but even intellectually this simplification is a large advance on the mythological confusion of other Semitic nations of the period.

In the same way these Hebrew writers had also to phrase what we should call theories of history in the narrative form. When they wished to set forth their understanding of the meaning of history they inserted a compact retrospect, generally putting it into the mouth of one of the actors. The character of these additions depends on the age from which they come, and reflects the successive advances which, as we have just seen, the Jews made in their understanding of the nature of Jehovah and of their relation to him. The earliest of them go back to the century after the great prophets Amos, Hosea, and Isaiah had declared that the God of Israel ruled all the nations of the earth, and that he demanded righteousness from his people. The destruction of Samaria by the Assyrians in 722 B.C. came as an overwhelming proof of this doctrine; and the more enlightened among the Jews, beginning to meditate on the history of their race, saw the events of their own times bound up with the purposes of Jehovah in past and in future ages. In consequence their history took on for them a fresh and inspiring meaning. Examples of this new conception may be found in the promises added to the story of Abraham and his sacrifice of Isaac in *Genesis xxii*, and in the commission given to Moses at the burning bush in *Exodus iii*; it is set forth most distinctly in the second farewell of Joshua to the people of Israel.

> And Joshua said unto all the people, Thus saith the Lord God of Israel, Your fathers dwelt on the other side of the flood in old times, even Terah, the father of Abraham, and the father of Nachor: and they served other gods.
>
> And I took your father Abraham from the other side of the flood, and led him throughout all the land of Canaan, and multiplied his seed, and gave him Isaac.
>
> And I gave unto Isaac Jacob and Esau: and I gave unto Esau Mount Seir, to possess it; but Jacob and his children went down into Egypt.
>
> I sent Moses also and Aaron, and I plagued Egypt, according to that which I did among them: and afterward I brought you out.
>
> And I brought your fathers out of Egypt: and ye came unto the sea; and the Egyptians pursued after your fathers with chariots and horsemen unto the Red sea.
>
> And when they cried unto the Lord, he put darkness between you and the Egyptians, and brought the sea upon them, and covered them; and your eyes have seen what I have done in Egypt: and ye dwelt in the wilderness a long season.
>
> And I brought you into the land of the Amorites, which dwelt on the other side Jordan; and they fought with you: and I gave them into your hand, that ye might possess their land; and I destroyed them from before you.

Then Balak the son of Zippor, king of Moab, arose and warred against Israel, and sent and called Balaam the son of Beor to curse you:

But I would not hearken unto Balaam; therefore he blessed you still: so I delivered you out of his hand.

And ye went over Jordan, and came unto Jericho: and the men of Jericho fought against you, the Amorites, and the Perizzites, and the Canaanites, and the Hittites, and the Girgashites, the Hivites, and the Jebusites; and I delivered them into your hand.

And I sent the hornet before you, which drave them out from before you, even the two kings of the Amorites; but not with thy sword, nor with thy bow.

And I have given you a land for which ye did not labour, and cities which ye built not, and ye dwell in them; of the vineyards and oliveyards which ye planted not do ye eat.

Now therefore fear the Lord, and serve him in sincerity and in truth: and put away the gods which your fathers served on the other side of the flood, and in Egypt; and serve ye the Lord.

And if it seem evil unto you to serve the Lord, choose you this day whom ye will serve; whether the gods which your fathers served that were on the other side of the flood, or the gods of the Amorites, in whose land ye dwell: but as for me and my house, we will serve the Lord.

And the people answered and said, God forbid

that we should forsake the Lord, to serve other
gods.

. . . . . .

And Joshua said unto the people, Ye cannot
serve the Lord: for he is an holy God; he is a jealous
God; he will not forgive your transgressions nor
your sins.

. . . . . .

And the people said unto Joshua, Nay; but
we will serve the Lord.[1]

In all the passages of this type and period there is
a peculiar freshness of thought and feeling: it is as
if the writers were standing awestruck in the light
of a new dawn which had made for them a new
heaven and a new earth; or as if they had struggled
to a Pisgah height from which they saw history
stretched out before them and behind with a new
inspiring significance.

A century later these explanatory additions to the
history come almost wholly from Deuteronomist
writers. The conception is in general the same as
that of the passage which I have just quoted; but
the statement of it shows a certain definiteness and
crystallizing, and the phrasing generally has a tendency towards fixed and regular formulas. This
developed and established theory of history is set
forth compactly in *2 Kings xvii*, where the Deuter-

[1] Josh. xxiv. 2–16, 19, 21.

onomist editors of the book pass judgment on North
Israel after the fall of Samaria:

> In the ninth year of Hoshea the king of Assyria
> took Samaria, and carried Israel away into Assyria,
> and placed them in Halah and in Habor by the
> river of Gozan, and in the cities of the Medes.
>
> For so it was, that the children of Israel had
> sinned against the Lord their God, which had
> brought them up out of the land of Egypt, from
> under the hand of Pharaoh king of Egypt, and had
> feared other gods,
>
> And walked in the statutes of the heathen, whom
> the Lord cast out from before the children of Israel,
> and of the kings of Israel, which they had made.
>
> And the children of Israel did secretly those
> things that were not right against the Lord their
> God, and they built them high places in all their
> cities, from the tower of the watchmen to the
> fenced city.
>
> And they set them up images and groves in every
> high hill, and under every green tree:
>
> And there they burnt incense in all the high
> places, as did the heathen whom the Lord carried
> away before them; and wrought wicked things to
> provoke the Lord to anger:
>
> For they served idols, whereof the Lord had said
> unto them, Ye shall not do this thing.
>
> Yet the Lord testified against Israel, and against
> Judah, by all the prophets, and by all the seers,
> saying, Turn ye from your evil ways, and keep my
> commandments and my statutes, according to all

the law which I commanded your fathers, and which I sent to you by my servants the prophets.

Notwithstanding they would not hear, but hardened their necks, like to the neck of their fathers, that did not believe in the Lord their God.

And they rejected his statutes, and his covenant that he made with their fathers, and his testimonies which he testified against them; and they followed vanity, and became vain, and went after the heathen that were round about them, concerning whom the Lord had charged them, that they should not do like them.

And they left all the commandments of the Lord their God, and made them molten images, even two calves, and made a grove, and worshipped all the host of heaven, and served Baal.

And they caused their sons and their daughters to pass through the fire, and used divination and enchantments, and sold themselves to do evil in the sight of the Lord, to provoke him to anger.

Therefore the Lord was very angry with Israel, and removed them out of his sight: there was none left but the tribe of Judah only.[1]

The book of *Judges*, in its original form, was composed to illustrate and prove this conception of history, which is set forth compactly at the beginning of the book in chapter iii; and it is also the substance of many of the speeches put into the mouths

[1] 2 Kings xvii. 6–18.

of the great men of Israel. The first farewell of Joshua, the farewell of Samuel, the prayer of Solomon at the dedication of the temple, all, as we have seen, sum up the way in which this school of writers understood their history. All of these passages, it will be noticed, are put in narrative form.

The additions made by the priestly writers after the Exile, though still narrative in form, reduce the narrative to its simplest terms. The covenant of God with Abraham in *Genesis xvii*, which I have already quoted, as in a case in point:

> And when Abram was ninety years old and nine, the Lord appeared to Abram, and said unto him, I am the Almighty God; walk before me, and be thou perfect.
>
> And I will make my covenant between me and thee, and will multiply thee exceedingly.
>
> And Abram fell on his face: and God talked with him.

Here the ascription to God of actual talk with men is reduced to the simplest form; it is not amplified with vivifying detail as in the case of the earlier stories; and the writer seems to use it almost as a formula. Even nearer to an actual abstraction is the solemn commission to Moses:

> And God spake unto Moses, and said unto him, I am the Lord:
>
> And I appeared unto Abraham, unto Isaac,

and unto Jacob, by the name of God Almighty, but by my name Jehovah was I not known to them.

And I have also established my covenant with them, to give them the land of Canaan, the land of their pilgrimage, wherein they were strangers.

And I have also heard the groaning of the children of Israel, whom the Egyptians keep in bondage; and I have remembered my covenant.

Wherefore say unto the children of Israel, I am the Lord, and I will bring you out from under the burdens of the Egyptians, and I will rid you out of their bondage, and I will redeem you with a stretched out arm, and with great judgments.[1]

In the earlier sources the angel of the Lord appears to Moses out of the burning bush; and in another chapter of the same origin the Lord turns Moses' rod into a serpent, and then makes his hand leprous and turns it again as his other flesh. In comparison with such passages, this which I have quoted is as abstract as it can be and still remain narrative. Like *Genesis i* this passage approaches the very edge of complete abstraction, but it does not pass over it. In such a place the writer of a modern history would abandon narrative and take to exposition or argument or some kindred mode of philosophizing. These ancient writers had no such resource: and in this lack

[1] Ex. vi. 2-6.

is to be seen a profound and essential difference in the literature of the Old Testament from our literature of to-day. The Hebrew language had, as we shall see directly, no forms to express analysis and generalization; and when these ancient writers tried to set forth the way in which the universe came into being and history developed, of necessity they told of it in a story. Some of these stories are primitive to the extent of anthropomorphism; and looking at them as explanations of the universe, one feels what a long way back we must go to reach the frame of mind of the people who made them; yet such stories are only extreme examples of the primitive simplicity of thought which shows even in the priestly writings after the Exile, and which helps to explain both the difference of this literature from our modern writing and its perennial power.

III

I shall recur to this subject in each of the next two chapters: in the meantime we can get light on the distinctive simplicity of these narratives and of all the Old Testament literature by a brief consideration of the nature of the Hebrew language. In this chapter I shall speak of the general structure of the language; the character of the vocabulary I shall discuss in the chapter on the poetry.

Renan summed up the essential difference in the structure of the Hebrew from our modern languages when he pointed out that Hebrew " lacked one of the degrees of combination which we hold necessary for the complete expression of the thought. To join the words in a proposition is as far as they go; they made no effort to apply the same operation to the propositions." [1] In other words, the old Hebrew language never reached the point at which it was able to construct sustained periods or closely linked chains of thought. Their only means of joining facts and ideas together was the conjunction *vav*, which was in itself hardly more definite than a gesture to indicate that things somehow belonged together. In the King James Version it is translated indifferently *and*, *but*, or *so*; and sometimes incorrectly *when*. Thus we get the constant succession of *ands* which are so familiar a characteristic of the Biblical style. In consequence of this poverty in connectives the Hebrew language could not express swiftly and compactly the relations of facts and ideas to each other; and it was wholly incapable of expressing most of the subtle

[1] E. Renan: *Histoire Générale des Langues Sémitiques*, 1858. Chap. I.

modulations which give variety and flexibility to
modern writings. It was a language in which solid
fact followed solid fact in hardly changing sequence.
Indeed in the Hebrew, sentences could be complete
without a verb. There is one verse in our translation of the book of *Proverbs* which has maintained
the form: to the Hebrew mind, " A whip for the
horse, a bridle for the ass, and a rod for the fool's
back," [1] was a complete sentence; the mere juxta-
position of the ideas sufficiently expressed its sense
of the relation between them. Furthermore the
language had very few inflections. The verb had
only two tenses, and these did not express time; the
one set forth the act as still going on, whether in
the past, the present, or the future, and the other
as completed at some time in the past, the present,
or the future. Nor were there any moods to express absoluteness or dependence of the action. To
quote Renan again: " Perspective is almost entirely
lacking in the Semitic style. One seeks in vain for
the half lights which give to the Aryan tongues, as
it were, the double power of expression. One must
even allow that the idea of style as we understand
it was wholly lacking among the Semitic people.
Their period is very short; the extent of discourse
which they embrace at a time never passes one or

[1] Prov. xxvi. 3.

two lines. Wholly preoccupied with the present thought they do not construct in advance the mechanism of the phrase and take no thought of what has gone before or of what is coming. One would say that their style was like the freest conversation caught in its flight and fixed directly by writing."

We shall see later how this character of the language blocked the way to anything like reasoning in our modern sense. Obviously it goes a long way to fix the character of the narrative. Stories in which the writer could indicate no shades of meaning, and none of the subtler, underlying relations which would set forth his individual inference and judgments about the facts, would seem irrationally primitive to readers of Pater and Conrad and Henry James; and even beside such old-fashioned directness as that of Thackeray or Jane Austen a style so limited would seem helpless. But without coming down to our own times we can find within the covers of the Bible a contrast which will bring out this essential simplicity of what we look on as the typical Biblical narrative. Down to the end of the third gospel there is no narrative in the Bible which departs from the types we have been considering: in the latter part of the *Acts of the Apostles* the style becomes radically different. Let me quote short passages first from the Old Testament, then from *Acts*:

> And Saul armed David with his armour, and he put an helmet of brass upon his head; also he armed him with a coat of mail.
>
> And David girded his sword upon his armour, and he assayed to go; for he had not proved it. And David said unto Saul, I cannot go with these; for I have not proved them. And David put them off him.
>
> And he took his staff in his hand, and chose him five smooth stones out of the brook, and put them in a shepherd's bag which he had, even in a scrip; and his sling was in his hand: and he drew near to the Philistine.
>
> And the Philistine came on and drew near unto David; and the man that bare the shield went before him.
>
> And when the Philistine looked about, and saw David, he disdained him: for he was but a youth, and ruddy, and of a fair countenance.
>
> And the Philistine said unto David, Am I a dog, that thou comest to me with staves? And the Philistine cursed David by his gods.[1]

In this passage, in which there are both narrative and speeches, there are no connectives but *and* between the separate clauses and sentences, except *for* twice, and no clause which goes beyond two lines in length.

---

[1] 1 Sam. xvii. 38–43.

With it compare this passage from the latter part of the *Acts of the Apostles*, where the influence of the Greek shows plainly in the style:

> And when they were escaped, then they knew that the island was called Melita.
>
> And the barbarous people shewed us no little kindness: for they kindled a fire, and received us every one, because of the present rain, and because of the cold.
>
> And when Paul had gathered a bundle of sticks, and laid them on the fire, there came a viper out of the heat, and fastened on his hand.
>
> And when the barbarians saw the venomous beast hang on his hand, they said among themselves, No doubt this man is a murderer, whom, though he hath escaped the sea, yet vengeance suffereth not to live.
>
> And he shook off the beast into the fire, and felt no harm.
>
> Howbeit they looked when he should have swollen, or fallen down dead suddenly; but after they had looked a great while, and saw no harm come to him, they changed their minds, and said that he was a god.[1]

Here there are hardly two sentences alike: the clauses show great variety in length; and for connectives we find *when, but, though, howbeit, after*;

[1] Acts xxviii. 1–6.

the *ands* are comparatively insignificant. One feels immediately the difference between the two styles. In contrast with the *Acts of the Apostles* the passage from *Samuel* sounds, as Renan has suggested, almost like the writing of a child. On the other hand, in contrast to the vivid and unpremeditated simplicity of the Old Testament, the passage from *Acts* has a touch of art: one feels that it was written by a man who knew rhetoric, who had some acquaintance with the value of style as style, and who was intent not merely on setting forth the facts but who also took pleasure in the finished beauty of the writing. Another even more accentuated example of this full-fledged rhetorical narrative of the latter chapters of *Acts* may be found in the speeches which are given to St. Paul. Here is a portion of his answer before Felix:

> Then Paul, after that the governor had beckoned unto him to speak, answered, Forasmuch as I know that thou hast been of many years a judge unto this nation, I do the more cheerfully answer for myself:
>
> Because that thou mayest understand, that there are yet but twelve days since I went up to Jerusalem for to worship.
>
> And they neither found me in the temple disputing with any man, neither raising up the people, neither in the synagogues, nor in the city:

Neither can they prove the things whereof they now accuse me.

But this I confess unto thee, that after the way which they call heresy, so worship I the God of my fathers, believing all things which are written in the law and in the prophets:

And have hoped toward God, which they themselves also allow, that there shall be a resurrection of the dead, both of the just and unjust.

And herein do I exercise myself, to have always a conscience void of offence toward God, and toward men.

Now after many years I came to bring alms to my nation, and offerings.

Whereupon certain Jews from Asia found me purified in the temple, neither with multitude, nor with tumult.

Who ought to have been here before thee, and object, if they had ought against me.

Or else let these same here say, if they have found any evil doing in me, while I stood before the council.

Except it be for this one voice, that I cried standing among them, Touching the resurrection of the dead I am called in question by you this day.[1]

In this little speech are to be found most of the devices by which a highly developed oratory reaches its effects. Less important facts are so subordinated

[1] Acts xxiv. 10–21.

as to modify the more important in a variety of ways, the order is inverted so as to bring striking ideas into relief, and the thought is elaborately bound together by connectives. Clearly this was written by a writer who belongs to the same world as Xenophon and Herodotus, as Cæsar and Cicero, writers whose faces are westward and towards our modern world.

Let me cite one more example, this time from modern English, to bring into higher relief this objectivity and simplicity of the Bible narrative. One thinks of Bunyan's *Pilgrim's Progress* as an example of an extremely simple style. Here is a short passage from the First Part:

> I looked then after Christian to see him go up the hill, where I perceived he fell from running to going, and from going to clambering upon his hands and his knees, because of the steepness of the place. Now about midway to the top of the hill was a pleasant arbor, made by the Lord of the hill for the refreshing of weary travellers; thither therefore Christian got, where also he sat down to rest him. Then he pulled his roll out of his bosom, and read therein to his comfort; he also now began afresh to take a review of the coat or garment that was given him as he stood by the cross. Thus pleasing himself awhile, he at last fell into a slumber, and thence into a fast sleep, which detained him in that place until it was almost night;

and in his sleep the roll fell out of his hand.   Now
as he was sleeping, there came one to him, and
awaked him, saying, *Go to the Ant, thou sluggard;
consider her ways, and be wise.*   And with that Christian suddenly started up, and sped him on his way,
and went apace till he came to the top of the hill.

In this passage the clauses run to three and four and
even five lines; and instead of all the clauses being
co-ordinate and of equal value, every sentence shows
subordination of one idea to another by *where*, by
relatives, by participles and other devices of a modern language.   Such writing as this is of another
kind than that of the Bible narrative.   The simplicity of *Pilgrim's Progress* expresses far more
ratiocination and consciousness of the finer relations
between ideas than does even the most advanced
style in the Biblical narrative.   Like the speeches
ascribed to St. Paul in *Acts* Bunyan's writing belongs to a mode of thought and of style which are
unknown in the Old Testament.

IV

In the New Testament, the most common type
of narrative stands between the unbroken co-ordina-
tion and simplicity of the Old Testament and the
fully developed Greek style of the latter chapters of

Acts. It is almost certain that the first three Gospels consist of material which was originally composed in Aramaic, the Semitic dialect which gradually took the place of Hebrew in Palestine after the exile. The general character of this Aramaic language, being the same as that of Hebrew, tended to fix on the narrative portions of these gospels the same general style that we find in the Old Testament: and though the influence of the Greek in which they were finally written shows in the frequency of participles and *when* clauses, yet there are almost no sustained periods. In consequence these gospels and the early part of *Acts* seem almost as foreign beside the later part of *Acts* as does the Old Testament itself. Beside the Gospels, on the other hand, *Judges* and *Samuel* and *Kings* seem to belong to a world of the past: and this effect may in part be ascribed to the fact that their style is actually archaic in a way that the style of the gospels is not. In the last-named we have simplicity, but it is not a primitive simplicity.

A good example of the average style of the New Testament narrative may be taken from the account of the death of John the Baptist in the *Gospel According to St. Mark.* This gospel is the simplest of the four, and at the same time is especially full of little touches of vivifying and convincing detail.

For Herod himself had sent forth and laid hold upon John, and bound him in prison for Herodias' sake, his brother Philip's wife: for he had married her.

For John had said unto Herod, It is not lawful for thee to have thy brother's wife.

Therefore Herodias had a quarrel against him, and would have killed him; but she could not:

For Herod feared John, knowing that he was a just man and an holy, and observed him; and when he heard him, he did many things, and heard him gladly.

And when a convenient day was come, that Herod on his birthday made a supper to his lords, high captains, and chief estates of Galilee;

And when the daughter of the said Herodias came in, and danced, and pleased Herod and them that sat with him, the king said unto the damsel, Ask of me whatsoever thou wilt, and I will give it thee.

And he sware unto her, Whatsoever thou shalt ask of me, I will give it thee unto the half of my kingdom.

And she went forth, and said unto her mother, What shall I ask? And she said, The head of John the Baptist.

And she came in straightway with haste unto the king, and asked, saying, I will that thou give me by and by in a charger the head of John the Baptist.

And the king was exceeding sorry; yet for his

oath's sake, and for their sakes which sat with him, he would not reject her.

And immediately the king sent an executioner, and commanded his head to be brought: and he went and beheaded him in the prison,

And brought his head in a charger, and gave it to the damsel: and the damsel gave it to her mother.

And when his disciples heard of it, they came and took up his corpse, and laid it in a tomb.[1]

Here the subordination of subsidiary to principal facts helps to add swiftness to the narrative; and at the same time the absence of all subtleties keeps the story real and solid. In such passages the art of story-telling, without losing any of its substantial power, is brought to a still higher degree of perfection than in the Old Testament. This variety and modulation of the style makes possible the ethereal power of the description in *St. Luke* of the shepherds watching in the field by night, perhaps the most beautiful short piece of narrative in the whole Bible:

And there were in the same country shepherds abiding in the field, keeping watch over their flock by night.

And, lo, the angel of the Lord came upon them, and the glory of the Lord shone round about them: and they were sore afraid.

[1] Mark vi. 17-29

And the angel said unto them, Fear not: for, behold, I bring you good tidings of great joy, which shall be to all people.

For unto you is born this day in the city of David a Saviour, which is Christ the Lord.

And this shall be a sign unto you; Ye shall find the babe wapped in swaddling clothes, lying in a manger.

And suddenly there was with the angel a multitude of the heavenly host praising God, and saying,

Glory to God in the highest, and on earth peace, good will toward men.

And it came to pass, as the angels were gone away from them into heaven, the shepherds said one to another, Let us now go even unto Bethlehem, and see this thing which is come to pass, which the Lord hath made known unto us.

And they came with haste, and found Mary, and Joseph, and the babe lying in a manger.

And when they had seen it, they made known abroad the saying which was told them concerning this child.

And all they that heard it wondered at those things which were told them by the shepherds.

But Mary kept all these things, and pondered them in her heart.

And the shepherds returned, glorifying and praising God for all the things that they had heard and seen, as it was told unto them.[1]

[1] Luke ii. 8–20.

Here St. Luke's trained sense for style reaches its highest point; in recording the tradition which had come to him, he keeps its absolute simplicity; and at the same time his knowledge of the art of writing makes it possible for him to touch it with a sheer beauty of style which expresses feelings hardly known to the Old Testament. Thus without any suggestion of the somewhat palpable art which we feel in the latter part of *Acts*, the gospels seem the work of writers who lived in our half of the world and on the hither side of antiquity.

V

Yet when one turns from the style to the substance one feels again that all these narratives belong to another world. For these ancient writers, whether in the Old Testament or the New, there were no subtleties: they took note only of the solid facts of life; they had no interest in inferences and modifications and other complications of thought which might be built upon them. I can bring out this difference more concretely by an example from Browning's *Saul*. Here the compact narrative of *Samuel* is expanded to a poem of seven pages of close print. Let me quote first a few verses of the original:

But the spirit of the Lord departed from Saul, and an evil spirit from the Lord troubled him.

And Saul's servants said unto him, Behold now, an evil spirit from God troubleth thee.

Let our lord now command thy servants, which are before thee, to seek out a man, who is a cunning player on an harp: and it shall come to pass, when the evil spirit from God is upon thee, that he shall play with his hand, and thou shalt be well.

And Saul said unto his servants, Provide me now a man that can play well, and bring him to me.

.   .   .   .   .   .

And David came to Saul, and stood before him: and he loved him greatly; and he became his armour bearer.

And Saul sent to Jesse, saying, Let David, I pray thee, stand before me; for he hath found favour in my sight.

And it came to pass, when the evil spirit from God was upon Saul, that David took an harp, and played with his hand: so Saul was refreshed, and was well, and the evil spirit departed from him.[1]

This is almost the whole of the passage on which Browning builds. Compare a small part of Browning's development of part of the last verse; the mere expansion, however, is the least of the differences between the two stories.

[1] 1 Sam. xvi. 14–17; 21–23.

                    Then I, as was meet,
Knelt down to the God of my fathers, and rose
    on my feet,
And ran o'er the sand burnt to powder. The
    tent was unlooped;
I pulled up the spear that obstructed, and under
    I stooped;
Hands and knees on the slippery grass-patch,
    all withered and gone,
That extends to the second enclosure, I groped
    my way on
Till I felt where the foldskirts fly open. Then
    once more I prayed,
And opened the foldskirts and entered, and was
    not afraid,
But spoke, Here is David, thy servant! And
    no voice replied.
At first I saw naught but the blackness: but
    soon I descried
A something more black than the blackness—
    the vast, the upright
Main prop which sustains the pavilion: and
    slow into sight
Grew a figure against it, gigantic and blackest
    of all.
Then a sunbeam, that burst thro' the tent-roof,
    showed Saul.

            .   .   .   .   .   .

Then I tuned my harp,—took off the lilies we
    twine round its chords

Lest they snap 'neath the stress of the noontide
—those sunbeams like swords!
And I first played the tune all our sheep know,
as one after one,
So docile they came to the pen-door till folding
be done.
They are white and untorn by the bushes, for
lo, they have fed
Where the long grasses stifle the water within
the stream's bed;
And now one after one seeks its lodging as star
follows star
Into eve and the blue far above us,—so blue
and so far.

Browning chose, we may assume, wholly to neglect
the spirit of the Biblical narrative. Leaving out of
account the ambling measure, itself so incongruous
beside the stately march of the Bible story, one sees
that in place of the grave restraint, and the absorption in the solid realities of life, he lets his thought
spin itself out into a network of subtleties; and the
imaginations which he puts into the mouth of David
are those of the modern day, not of the East, and
of the ancient past.

Oh, our manhood's prime vigor! No
spirit feels waste
Not a muscle is stopped in its playing, nor sinew
unbraced.

Oh, the wild joys of living! the leaping from
    rock up to rock,
The strong rending of boughs from the fir-tree,
    the cool silver shock
Of the plunge in a pool's living water, the hunt
    of the bear
And the sultriness showing the lion is crouched
    in his lair.
And the meal, the rich dates yellowed over with
    with gold dust divine,
And the locust-flesh steeped in the pitcher,
    the full draught of wine,
And the sleep in the dried river-channel where
    bulrushes tell
That the water is wont to go warbling so softly
    and well.
How good is man's life, the mere living! how
    fit to employ
All the heart and the soul and the senses forever
    in joy!

This David of Browning's imagination could not
have lived before the Italian renaissance. The pleasures of these men of the East from whom the Old
Testament sprang were grave; and though they en-
joyed their sensations, they did not know that they
had them. There is a phrase in one of Mr. Kipling's stories which describes the difference. In
Her Majesty's Servants, the animals get to talk-
ing about the things each is afraid of, and the bul-

locks cannot understand why at the flight of the bullets the elephant stampedes, while they graze in peace. Then the elephant explains to them the difference: " You can only see out of your heads, I can see into mine." That phrase sums up the difference between the Oriental and ancient world from which come these stories of the Bible, and the modern world from which springs Browning's poem. The thought of the East was essentially simple. It knew only the objective and solid facts of which man has direct sensation, and the simple and primitive emotions which are his reaction to them. It has no perception of the subtler shades and shadows of feeling in which modern writers delight, nor of the complicated webs of thought which grow from men's efforts to reason out the universe. Nothing will more accentuate the chasm which stands between us and that ancient world than an attempt to imagine Browning's *Saul* written in the style of these Biblical narratives. The writers of the book of *Samuel* could not have conceived the subtleties and arabesques of this poem; and if they had been able to do so, their language would have provided no means of expressing them.

Yet to this very limitation we must ascribe much of the permanent expressive power of the Bible narratives. They are an unbroken stream of objective realities. Their whole texture is composed of the things which men can feel and see and hear. The very lack of the means for subordinating ideas took away from the writers the power of coloring the facts with their own personality. In Browning's poem the simple realities of the original story of David are overlaid and obscured by his own imaginings. These imaginations, though in themselves interesting to many people, are individual and personal and therefore of limited appeal, where the Old Testament story is impersonal and universal and therefore permanent. Our more elaborate art may build more complicated structures, and carry its chiselling of detail to a higher degree of subtlety; but in so far as it loses its hold on the qualities which belong to the Biblical narrative it loses power. For, after all, swiftness of movement, sparing but vivifying use of background, unflagging earnestness of purpose, and depth of feeling are the qualities which give to narrative the surest hold on the human imagination.

CHAPTER III

I

In the preceding chapter on the narratives of the Bible, we have found that their most essential and distinctive characteristic is the transfiguring of a limpid and simple vividness by deep earnestness and elevation of feeling; so that stories of the rough and homely life of the early days of Israel are made worthy to stand by the narratives of the gospel. In this chapter I am to discuss the poetry of the Bible; and here again we shall find the same combination of a primitive simplicity and concreteness of expression with the profound and ennobling emotion that transfigures the experience of man into an expression of permanent verities. The distinguishing characteristic of the poetry of the Bible is its absolute objectivity: it knew only facts which are concrete and which mean always the same to all men. This complete objectivity and concreteness joined to the strong rhythm and the rich coloring of the style give palpable form to feelings which are too large and too deep-seated to be explained by articulate language.

Let us begin with a brief survey of the poetry in something like chronological order. Here, even more than with the rest of the literature, we must remember that we have only a portion of all the poetry of Israel, and that perhaps a small portion. Whole classes of it must have disappeared. The literature was collected during and after the Exile by men who were passionately and wholly devoted to preserving the religion of Jehovah from the attacks of the heathen and to making it a living force for righteousness among the remnant of their own nation. They were thinking of higher matters than beauty of expression: they were concerned with the revelations of God to man, not with the imaginations of men's hearts. For them no writing was of value which did not bear on the history of God's chosen people and on the revelation to them of his will. The Pentateuch, as containing the Law, set the standard of admission to the Old Testament: to that were added first the other books of history and the books of the prophets, as supplementing and illustrating the Law, then these books of poetry and the rest of the Old Testament as in one way or another sacred through their relations to the religion of Israel as set forth in the Law. That there must have been other poetry than that which we have admits of no doubt: there must have been other songs of victory than those of Deborah, other dirges than those of David on Saul and Jonathan and on Abner, other poems of manners than those in *Proverbs* on the drunkard and the sluggard, other love and wedding songs than those in the *Song of Solomon*. What we have left merely shows how large and rich was the art of poetry among the people of Israel from the earliest times. Moreover, the dominance of the psalms and the wisdom poems in our Old Testament can hardly represent the original range of the old Hebrew poetry. During the troubled times of the Exile and the succeeding centuries, when the Jews were tossed from one conquerer to another, and harried and spoiled in the unceasing wars for the control of Palestine, all but their most essential writings must have disappeared. In the desperate struggle to keep themselves and the religion of Jehovah from being crushed and annihilated by the heathen they had no time to think of songs of love and feasting and the making and copying of poetry which served no more substantial purpose than beauty. We must remember, then, that in the poetry of the Old Testament we have only a portion of Hebrew literature, and that rigidly selected for a direct and practical religious purpose.

Now when we look at these remnants of the poetry, and especially when we arrange it in what is probably chronological order, we find great changes in form from the early poetry to the later. The early poetry we may take in a large sense as that which comes from before the eighth century B.C., when the revelations of the great prophets Amos, Hosea, and Isaiah made the turning point both in the history and in the literature of Israel. Of this early poetry we have few examples. The Song of Deborah in *Judges* is held to be the earliest of all: it is undoubtedly the song of triumph which was composed and uttered by Deborah herself to celebrate the great victory won by her people. A couple of centuries later than this perhaps would be the dirge which David sang at the death of Saul and Jonathan, the " Song of the Bow," as it is called in our version, in *2 Samuel i*. Probably from about the same period comes the Blessing of Jacob in *Genesis xlix*; and from a somewhat later time the Blessing of Moses in *Deuteronomy xxxiii*, the oracles of Balaam in *Numbers xxiii–xxiv*, and a few smaller fragments. These poems, except the Song of Deborah and David's lamentation, in the course of transmission became separated from the occasions which gave them birth; and the composers of our books inserted them in places which seemed to them appropriate. All these poems we may accept as having been written before the middle of the eighth century B.C.

Reading these early poems together one finds that they have in common a stirring rush and vigor of expression and an abrupt and swiftly changing diction. Here is a portion of the Song of Deborah:

> The kings came and fought; then fought the kings of Canaan in Taanach by the waters of Megiddo; they took no gain of money.
>
> They fought from heaven; the stars in their courses fought against Sisera.
>
> The river of Kishon swept them away, that ancient river, the river Kishon. O my soul, thou hast trodden down strength.
>
> Then were the horsehoofs broken by the means of the pransings, the pransings of their mighty ones.
>
> Curse ye Meroz, said the angel of the Lord; curse ye bitterly the inhabitants thereof; because they came not to the help of the Lord against the mighty.[1]

Here every verse has a new figure; and one feels the freshness and opulence of resource of the singer. For comparison let me cite the last psalm of the *Psalter*:

> Praise ye the Lord. Praise God in his sanctuary: praise him in the firmament of his power.
>
> Praise him for his mighty acts: praise him according to his excellent greatness.

[1] Judges v. 19-23.

Praise him with the sound of the trumpet: praise him with the psaltery and harp.

Praise him with the timbrel and dance: praise him with stringed instruments and organs.

Praise him upon the loud cymbals: praise him upon the high sounding cymbals.

Let everything that hath breath praise the Lord. Praise ye the Lord.[1]

The contrast is exaggerated, for in these liturgical psalms, as in many of our modern hymns, the words are of importance chiefly as affording a continuous medium for music; but the poverty and convention-ality of the thought and the formal regularity of the verse throw into relief the spontaneity and variety of the earlier poem. The change is from a poetry in which the words and imagery spring freshly from the immediate occasion to a poetry which is the handmaid of music.

Let me cite another pair of examples in which the contrast is less extreme, a few verses from one of the oracles of Balaam and about as many from *Psalm xxxiv.* Here is the third oracle which Balaam uttered at the behest of Balak:

And he took up his parable, and said, Balaam the son of Beor hath said, and the man whose eyes are open hath said:

He hath said, which heard the words of God,

[1] Ps. cl.

which saw the vision of the Almighty, falling into a trance, but having his eyes open:

How goodly are thy tents, O Jacob, and thy tabernacles, O Israel!

As the valleys are they spread forth, as gardens by the river's side, as the trees of lign aloes which the Lord hath planted, and as cedar trees beside the waters.

He shall pour the water out of his buckets, and his seed shall be in many waters, and his king shall be higher than Agag, and his kingdom shall be exalted.

God brought him forth out of Egypt; he hath as it were the strength of an unicorn: he shall eat up the nations his enemies, and shall break their bones, and pierce them through with his arrows.

He couched, he lay down as a lion, and as a great lion: who shall stir him up?   Blessed is he that blesseth thee, and cursed is he that curseth thee.[1]

With this consider the familiar passage from *Psalm xxxiv*:

This poor man cried, and the Lord heard him, and saved him out of all his troubles.

The angel of the Lord encampeth round about them that fear him, and delivereth them.

O taste and see that the Lord is good: blessed is the man that trusteth in him.

O fear the Lord, ye his saints: for there is no want to them that fear him.

Num. xxiv. 3–9.

The young lions do lack and suffer hunger: but they that seek the Lord shall not want any good thing.[1]

Between these two passages there are the same differences as between the other two, though in less exaggerated form. The oracle of Balaam is probably an early poem inserted here by some editor who saw its appropriateness to the place. The profusion and the constant change of figure are the instinctive and spontaneous response to the vivid intensity of the feeling: one feels that the imagery is struck out fresh from the mint of the imagination for the special occasion. In the psalm, on the other hand, for all the beauty and the expressiveness of its phrasing, one feels a background of familiar literature: it is as if this poet found his imagery in the great storehouse of earnest and pious expression which had come down to him as a heritage from earlier generations, and as if this literature were a more living fact to him than the life behind it from which its imagery was drawn. I can put the distinction more concretely and not too whimsically perhaps by suggesting that the lions who " lack and suffer hunger " in the psalm were probably known to this later poet chiefly through literature: but that the earlier poet in his figure, " He couched, he lay

[1] Ps. xxxiv. 6–10.

down as a lion, and as a great lion," may have been writing of a danger which he had himself known. Certainly the difference in vividness seems to carry us nearer the realities of life: in the psalm the lion seems not much more than a fine figure of speech. Very few early poems have survived in their original form; but these examples will serve to bring out the difference between the spontaneity and freshness of the early poetry and the finished and deliberate art of the later. The early poetry gives the impression of being born in the very heat of joy or grief or triumph: the later poems seem in comparison the work of an art which has been brought by long growth and study to a high degree of finish.

The Psalms, however, we must remember, were poems which were used as hymns in the musical services of the temple; and we may suppose that their adaptation to this purpose to some extent smoothed their freedom of structure to a somewhat more formal regularity. It is dangerous to put too much argument on a single example, especially when we know so little about the principles that governed Hebrew poetry: but the poem which stands as the third chapter of *Habakkuk*, which by its superscription "upon Shigionoth" seems to have been written for music, is somewhat less fixed and regular in its form than the psalms. Here is a part of it:

God came from Teman, and the Holy One
from mount Paran. Selah. His glory covered
the heavens, and the earth was full of his
praise.

And his brightness was as the light; he had
horns coming out of his hand: and there was the
hiding of his power.

Before him went the pestilence, and burning
coals went forth at his feet.

He stood, and measured the earth: he beheld,
and drove asunder the nations; and the everlasting
mountains were scattered, the perpetual hills did
bow: his ways are everlasting.

I saw the tent of Cushan in affliction: and the
curtains of the land of Midian did tremble.

Was the Lord displeased against the rivers?
was thine anger against the rivers? was thy wrath
against the sea, that thou didst ride upon thine
horses and thy chariots of salvation?

Thy bow was made quite naked, according to
the oaths of the tribes, even thy word. Selah.
Thou didst cleave the earth with rivers.

The mountains saw thee, and they trembled:
the overflowing of the water passed by: the deep
uttered his voice, and lifted up his hands on
high.

The sun and moon stood still in their habitation:
at the light of thine arrows they went, and at the
shining of thy glittering spear.

Thou didst march through the land in indignation, thou didst thresh the heathen in anger.[1]

[1] Hab. iii. 3–12.

As compared with the regular stanzas of *Psalm xviii*
this poem seems what the musicians would call a
free composition. Here is one stanza of the psalm:

> Then the earth shook and trembled; the founda-
> tions also of the hills moved and were shaken,
> because he was wroth.
>
> There went up a smoke out of his nostrils, and
> fire out of his mouth devoured: coals were kindled
> by it.
>
> He bowed the heavens also, and came down:
> and darkness was under his feet.
>
> And he rode upon a cherub, and did fly: yea, he
> did fly upon the wings of the wind.
>
> He made darkness his secret place; his pavilion
> round about him were dark waters and thick
> clouds of the skies.
>
> At the brightness that was before him his thick
> clouds passed, hail stones and coals of fire.
>
> The Lord also thundered in the heavens, and the
> Highest gave his voice; hail stones and coals of
> fire.[1]

Beside the poem the psalm seems evenly, and as it
were deliberately, wrought out, with due and artistic
regard for the regular forms of a recognized poetic
literature: it seems to owe more to the polishing and
the orderly arrangement which are the heritage of
poets who come late in the history of their art. The
change, however, is merely from one form of beauty

[1] Ps. xviii. 7–13.

to another. The early poems have a certain freedom and wildness which carry back one's imagination to the youth of the kingdom of Israel; the later poems are the product of a developed civilization: both are the outpouring of earnest and deep feeling.

How highly developed in form this poetry of the Old Testament came to be in the later days may be seen from the number of alphabetic or acrostic poems which we have left. In the four chapters of *Lamentations* and in certain of the psalms the verses or groups of verses in the Hebrew begin with the successive letters of the alphabet. Of these alphabetic poems *Psalm cxix* is the most familiar example, for in the Authorised Version the names of the Hebrew letters are set at the head of each of the sections. This psalm as one reads it section by section seems a somewhat deliberate exercise; and noting its artificial form one is inclined to let it go with a passing comparison to the poems in the form of altars or wings which make George Herbert's *Temple* seem so far from our simpler taste of to-day. But let me cite a few verses from the first chapter of *Lamentations*:

Is it nothing to you, all ye that pass by? behold, and see if there be any sorrow like unto my sorrow, which is done unto me, wherewith the Lord hath afflicted me in the day of his fierce anger.

From above hath he sent fire into my bones, and it prevaileth against them: he hath spread a net for my feet, he hath turned me back: he hath made me desolate and faint all the day.

The yoke of my transgressions is bound by his hand: they are wreathed, and come up upon my neck: he hath made my strength to fall, the Lord hath delivered me into their hands, from whom I am not able to rise up.[1]

Any one who reads this passage for the first time will agree, I think, that it has no suggestion that the poet was tied to any artificial form. Not only has this Hebrew poetry advanced to the invention of elaborate forms of art, but it has gone to the further point of complete mastery of them; so that the intense thought and feeling of the poet flows freely and naturally into moulds which one would expect to be intolerable bonds. One thinks of Milton's great sonnets as examples in English of this masterful acceptance of seemingly impossible bondage. Here is that on *The Late Massacre in Piemont*:

Avenge, O Lord, thy slaughter'd saints, whose bones,
Lie scatter'd on the Alpine mountains cold;
Even them who kept thy truth so pure of old,
When all our fathers worshipp'd stocks and stones.
Forget not: in thy book record their groans

[1] Lam. i. 12–15.

Who were thy sheep, and in their ancient fold
Slain by the bloody Piemontese, that roll'd
Mother with infant down the rocks. Their moans
The vales redoubled to the hills, and they
To Heaven.   Their martyr'd blood and ashes
   sow
O'er all the Italian fields, where still doth sway
The triple Tyrant, that from these may grow
A hundred-fold, who, having learnt thy way,
Early may fly the Babylonian woe.

Here as in *Lamentations,* and in most of the
alphabetic psalms, the feeling of the poet is wrought
to such heat that it fuses the barriers of form and
pours itself forth with its freedom endowed with new
force and weight.   When men can utter their feelings with so little let and hindrance from forms as
artificial as the sonnet or the alphabetic poem, we
may assume that the art of poetry has reached a
high degree of perfection.   But in such poetry we
have come a long way from the undeliberate and
spontaneous outburst of triumph which we find in
the Song of Deborah, though that in itself speaks
of long ages of practice and development.

So far I have spoken chiefly of the early poetry,
and of *Psalms* and *Lamentations.*   Besides these, and
coming like them from the later period, is the great
series of poems which make up the book of *Job*: all
the early chapters of this great book deal with the

problem which of all others in these days of bitter
despair brought even blacker depths of distress to
the soul of the pious Jew: how could he reconcile
it with the promises of Jehovah that the heathen and
the wicked were obviously prosperous, while he who
served him so faithfully suffered such bitter misery?
In chapter xxviii comes the poem in praise of wisdom, and after the somewhat unnecessary piety of
Elihu, the splendid poems of the later chapters with
the answer of Jehovah from the whirlwind and the
stirring descriptions of the horse, of behemoth, and
of leviathan.

In *Proverbs*, besides the great mass of shrewd and
penetrating apothegms there are several series of
short poems in praise of wisdom, and mingled in
with these certain little poems of manners, of which
the following is an example:

> Who hath woe? who hath sorrow? who hath
> contentions? who hath babbling? who hath wounds
> without cause? who hath redness of eyes?
> They that tarry long at the wine; they that go
> to seek mixed wine.
> Look not thou upon the wine when it is red,
> when it giveth his colour in the cup, when it moveth
> itself aright.
> At the last it biteth like a serpent, and stingeth
> like an adder.[1]

[1] Prov. xxiii. 29–32.

And at the end of the book there is the alphabetic poem in praise of the virtuous woman.

Besides all these poems there is the book which we know as the *Song of Solomon*. For many ages it has been the custom of the Church to interpret this book symbolically; and the headings of the chapters in our Authorised Version follow this custom. Of more recent years, however, scholars have recognized that these warm and vigorous lyrics are the expression of a more earthly love, and that the book is probably a collection of folk songs sung at wedding festivals. At first under this view the book was supposed to be a drama, in which Solomon makes love to the Shulamite maiden. There are many difficulties with this theory of the book, however, not the least among which is the fact that the scholars who hold it cannot agree whether there are two or three actors, nor on the limits of the acts. When to this difficulty is added the fact that if the book be a drama it stands unique not only in Hebrew literature, but also, I believe, in Semitic literature, we may fairly turn to some less exacting theory. That may be found in the idea which is constantly gaining ground that the book preserves a collection of fragments of wedding songs sung at a ceremony which still persists in Syria to-day, in which the bride and groom are feasted for a week under the guise of queen and king, with many songs in praise of their beauty and prowess. Thus this book would save for us a fragment from a whole field of poetry otherwise lost. The theory certainly explains the unrestrained fervor of these poems.

Finally, no consideration of the nature of Hebrew poetry can leave out of account the fact that, at any rate in the earlier times, the prophets delivered their messages, whether of reproof or of comfort, of new and uplifting conceptions of religion, or of guidance for political action, in a form which was as much poetical as is that of *Job*, though it is not so regular. It may be closely compared to the Song of Deborah or to David's Lament over Saul and Jonathan. Here is an example from the prophet Amos, and one from Isaiah:

> Can two walk together, except they be agreed?
> Will a lion roar in the forest, when he hath no prey? will a young lion cry out of his den, if he have taken nothing?
> Can a bird fall in a snare upon the earth, where no gin is for him? shall one take up a snare from the earth, and have taken nothing at all?
> Shall a trumpet be blown in the city, and the people not be afraid? shall there be evil in a city, and the Lord hath not done it?
>
>   .   .   .   .   .
>
> The lion hath roared, who will not fear? the Lord God hath spoken, who can but prophesy?[1]

[1] Amos iii. 3–6, 8.

Hear, O heavens; and give ear, O earth: for the Lord hath spoken, I have nourished and brought up children, and they have rebelled against me.

The ox knoweth his owner, and the ass his master's crib: but Israel doth not know, my people doth not consider.

Ah sinful nation, a people laden with iniquity, a seed of evil doers, children that are corrupters: they have forsaken the Lord, they have provoked the Holy One of Israel unto anger, they are gone away backward.

Why should ye be stricken any more? ye will revolt more and more: the whole head is sick, and the whole heart faint.

From the sole of the foot even unto the head there is no soundness in it; but wounds, and bruises, and putrifying sores: they have not been closed, neither bound up, neither mollified with ointment.

Your country is desolate, your cities are burned with fire: your land, strangers devour it in your presence, and it is desolate, as overthrown by strangers.

And the daughter of Zion is left as a cottage in a vineyard, as a lodge in a garden of cucumbers, as a besieged city.

Except the Lord of hosts had left unto us a very small remnant, we should have been as Sodom, and we should have been like unto Gomorrah.[1]

In some cases the prophet adopted not only the verses of poetry but also more extended forms. In

[1] Isaiah i. 2–9.

Isaiah ix–x there are four strophes or stanzas, each ending with the refrain: "For all this his anger is not turned away, but his hand is stretched out still." Both *Jeremiah* and *Ezekiel* have several examples of the Qinah or Lamentation measure, one of the recognized modes of Hebrew poetry, in which the second member being shorter than the first produces a falling cadence. It is the measure of all the chapters of *Lamentations.* The origin of the poetical form of the prophecies is, in part at any rate, due to the fact that the prophets uttered their oracles in a state of high emotional tension, when the ordinary beat of prose would have been inadequate to give expression to the prophet's superheated imagination. The poetical form was thus a necessity of expression for them.

The art of poetry does not come to an end, however, with the Old Testament times. In the New Testament the canticles in the early chapters of *St. Luke* show what beautiful poems could be written at the very beginning of our era. The *Magnificat* and the *Nunc Dimittis* and the *Benedictus*, as they are called in the *Book of Common Prayer*, are of the nature of the psalms, but not restricted by being adapted to the temple service. Their golden and mature beauty brings the psalm-writing to a close for us at almost its highest point. In language these poems are saturated with the idioms and figures of the Old Testament poetry, but adapted with a new vividness of imagination to the occasions which give them birth; in them the passionate distress and jubilation of *Job* and of the *Psalms* give way to a confident and settled hope. In place of the fierce workings of the soul of a nation in anguish these poems declare the serenity and peace which herald the dawn of the new era.

II

Let us now turn to a more specific consideration of this poetry as we read it in our English Bible: we must begin, however, by looking at the principles which governed Hebrew verse. These principles can be recovered only in part, but fortunately the one principle which really affects the form of the English has been clearly made out, the principle of parallel structure: in the Hebrew poetry the line was the unit, and the second line balanced the first, completing or supplementing its meaning. The first verse of *Psalm cl* is a good example: " Praise God in his sanctuary; praise him in the firmament of his power." This principle could be applied to produce considerable variety. The second member of the verse might be synonymous with the first, as in the example I have just quoted. It might be in antithesis, as "A soft answer turneth away wrath: but grievous words stir up anger." It might add something to complete the thought: "By the rivers of Babylon, there we sat down, yea, we wept, when we remembered Zion." Or it might be the application of a figure: "A word fitly spoken is like apples of gold in pictures of silver," or "As the door turneth upon its hinges, so doth the slothful upon his bed." Sometimes the first member of one line took its thought from a word in the last member of the line before.

> I will lift up mine eyes unto the hills, from whence cometh my help.
> My help cometh from the Lord, which made heaven and earth.[1]

There might be more than two lines to complete the verse: the normal form of the colloquies in *Job* consists in a balance of couplets:

> My brethren have dealt deceitfully as a brook, and as the stream of brooks they pass away;
> Which are blackish by reason of the ice, and wherein the snow is hid:
>
> What time they wax warm, they vanish: when it is hot they are consumed out of their place.
> The paths of their way are turned aside; they go to nothing, and perish.[2]

[1] Ps. cxxi. 1–2.   [2] Job vi. 15–18.

In the Qinah or Lamentation measure, as I have said, the second member of the line was shorter than the first. Even in the translation the effect can be felt, as in *Lamentations*, of a falling cadence which makes the poem almost seem as if it were written in a minor key. But whatever the variety of form, the unvarying element in the Hebrew poetry is the constant balance of lines of about equal length.

This principle, however, was not rediscovered until a century after our translation was made. Therefore the men who made our translation did not attempt to arrange the lines in a different form from the prose of the rest of the book. The result has been in the English to produce a kind of writing which is unique in our literature, since it is neither regular prose nor regular poetry, but shares the power of both. It has the strong balance and regularity which result from this underlying parallel structure of the Hebrew, and at the same time all the freedom and naturalness of prose. When in reading the historical books one comes across a poem the difference in effect is striking: without one's realizing why the style suddenly seems as it were to take on energy and movement. I cite an example from *Joshua*:

> Then spake Joshua to the Lord in the day when the Lord delivered up the Amorites before the

children of Israel, and he said in the sight of Israel.
Sun, stand thou still upon Gibeon; and thou, Moon,
in the valley of Ajalon.

And the sun stood still, and the moon stayed,
until the people had avenged themselves upon
their enemies.   Is not this written in the book of
Jasher?   So the sun stood still in the midst of the
heaven, and hasted not to go down about a whole
day.[1]

Here the strong balance of the lines of the poem
strengthens the rhythm, so that as the poem stands
imbedded in the prose it seems almost excited in
utterance.

On the other hand, since in the English this balance and strong rhythm are always united to entire
freedom this Biblical poetry is quite clear of any suggestion of artificiality or sophistication.   For us to-
day verse and poetry are a mode of utterance apart
from the speech of every-day life.   They are art, and
art carries always for us the implication of an attention to form which makes impossible an entirely
unstudied spontaneity.   Even blank verse, the freest
of all our forms of poetry, is lacking in the naturalness of prose.   Consider this passage from the fourth
act of *Richard II*:

Many a time hath banish'd Norfolk fought
For Jesu Christ in glorious Christian field,

[1] Josh. x. 12–13.

Streaming the ensign of the Christian cross
Against black pagans, Turks, and Saracens;
And toil'd with works of war, retired himself
To Italy; and there at Venice gave
His body to that pleasant country's earth,
And his pure soul unto his captain Christ,
Under whose colors he had fought so long.

This is as simple as it can be; there are only two adjectives which are not a necessary part of the meaning, and no other attempt to adorn or beautify the facts than comes from the verse itself. Yet as compared with the earnest solemnity of the *Psalms* or of *Job* it is the writing of a man who is playing at life: it is the efflorescence of feeling rather than an irrepressible and inevitable expression of it. Even the great soliloquies in Hamlet produce something of the same effect: for all their searching into the foundations of the human soul they are still play-acting, a noble blossoming out of the imagination in a noble time, if you like, but still flowers from a " garden of pleasant delights," to modify the title of one of the Elizabethan poetry books. The noble sonnet in which Milton poured out his prophetic indignation which I have quoted seems to be an exception, and there are a few great poems of our own day, such as Tennyson's *Crossing the Bar* and Mr. Kipling's *Recessional* and *White Man's*

Burden, which sum up in burning phrase the feeling of a race. But even these, beside the poetry of the Old Testament, only emphasize the fact that the poet is for us a man apart, a seer looking on at life and penetrating its mysteries by the flash of genius: whereas these psalms are part of the bone and sinew of the Jewish life. In them there are no rules of art between us and the soul of the nation. In this Old Testament poetry as we read it in the Authorised Version we find the heightened beat of the rhythm, which expresses strength of emotion, and which is the peculiar virtue of poetry; and we have it combined with an entire freedom and naturalness which forestall any straying of our attention from the message to the form in which it is couched. It is in large part because of this unique form that the poetry of the Old Testament seems so much a universal and unstudied expression of the deepest feeling. Thus the very fact that our translators made no attempt to reproduce the exact form of the verse in English has added to its power; and I am inclined to suspect that the modern fashion of printing the poetry of the Old Testament in broken lines is quite as much of a hindrance as a help to the reader who wishes to get the full feeling which it contains. One hears grumbling to-day at the difficulty imposed on our

reading of the Bible by the division into verses. We
may well remember that when the Bible was known
thoroughly and universally, it was always so read.
We may assume, then, that the Hebrew poetry when
translated into an English which knew nothing of
its technical rules created for us a new kind of
writing, which, standing between our verse and our
prose, shared in the especial virtues and expressiveness of each.

III

Let us now go a step further and see how the
language itself affected this poetry which we are
studying. We have seen in the last chapter how
little apparatus the Hebrew language had for expressing any complication of thought through variety and modification of sentences and their structure:
it is a closely related fact that its vocabulary had no
words except for the concrete objects of the external
world. All the words of the old Hebrew went back
immediately to things of sense, and in consequence
even their every-day language was figurative in a
way which we can hardly imagine. The verb *to be
jealous* was a regular form of the verb *to glow*; the
noun *truth* was derived from the verb meaning *to
prop, to build,* or *to make firm.* The word for *self*

was also the word for *bone*. To quote Renan again:
"*Anger* is expressed in Hebrew in a throng of ways,
each picturesque, and each borrowed from physio-
logical facts. Now the metaphor is taken from the
rapid and animated breathing which accompanies the
passion, now from heat or from boiling, now from
the act of a noisy breaking, now from shivering.
Discouragement and *despair* are expressed by the
melting of the heart, *fear* by the loosening of the
reins. *Pride* is portrayed by the holding high of
the head, with the figure straight and stiff. *Pa-
tience* is a long breathing, *impatience* short breathing,
desire is thirst or paleness. *Pardon* is expressed by
a throng of metaphors borrowed from the idea of
covering, of hiding, of coating over the fault. In
Job God sews up sins in a sack, seals it, then
throws it behind him: all to signify that he forgets
them. . . . Other more or less abstract ideas have
found their symbol in the Semitic languages in a
like manner. The idea of truth is drawn from
solidity, or stability; that of beauty from splendor,
that of good from straightness, that of evil from
swerving or the curved line, or from stench. *To
create* is primitively to mould, *to decide* is to cut,
to think is to speak. *Bone* signifies the substance, the
essence of a thing, and serves in Hebrew for our
pronoun *self*. What distinguishes the Semitic lan-

guages from the Aryan is that this primitive union of sensation and idea persists,—so that in each word one still hears the echo of the primitive sensations which determined the choice of the first makers of the language."

This characteristic of the Hebrew language and one of the accepted doctrines of modern psychology, —the theory commonly known as the James-Lange theory of the emotions,—fit together like the two parts of a puzzle. According to this theory emotion is inseparable from sensation, or rather, emotion consists of a mass or complex of bodily sensations. Professor James sums it up in the following questions: " What kind of an emotion of fear would be left if the feeling neither of quickened heart-beats nor of shallow breathing, neither of trembling lips nor of weakened limbs, neither of goose-flesh nor of visceral stirrings, were present, it is quite impossible for me to think. Can one fancy the state of rage and picture no ebullition in the chest, no flushing of the face, no dilatation of the nostrils, no clenching of the teeth, no impulse to vigorous action, but in their stead limp muscles, calm breathing, and a placid face? The present writer for one, certainly cannot.—In like manner of grief: what would it be without its tears, its sobs, its suffocation of the heart, its pangs in the breastbone? A feelingless cognition that certain circumstances are deplorable, and nothing more. Every passion in turn tells the same story. A purely disembodied human emotion is a nonentity." [1]

The Hebrew language is an unfailing illustration of this theory: it expressed emotion always by naming the sensations of which the emotion consists. Here is an expression from the *Psalms* of helpless despair:

> Save me, O God; for the waters are come in unto my soul.
>
> I sink in deep mire, where there is no standing: I am come into deep waters, where the floods overflow me.
>
> I am weary of my crying: my throat is dried: mine eyes fail while I wait for my God.[2]

Notice the number of sensations which are named; " my throat is dried," " mine eyes fail," and the sensation of sinking in deep mire, with all its implication of spasmodic and desperate struggling. Another example may be found in the following passage in *Job*; and here again notice how many actual sensations are named:

> Now a thing was secretly brought to me, and mine ear received a little thereof.
>
> In thoughts from the visions of the night, when deep sleep falleth on men,

[1] W. James, *Psychology*, vol. ii., p. 452.   [2] Ps. lxix. 1–3.

Fear came upon me, and trembling, which made all my bones to shake.

Then a spirit passed before my face; the hair of my flesh stood up:

It stood still, but I could not discern the form thereof: an image was before mine eyes, there was silence and I heard a voice, saying,

Shall mortal man be more just than God? shall a man be more pure than his Maker? [1]

The shaking of the bones, the hair of the flesh standing up, the sense of an object indistinctly present, the silence, all go together to make a most vivid description of the terror that flies by night; and here again the emotion is set forth by means of the concrete sensations of which it consists. For a somewhat different example, let me cite another passage from the *Psalms*, the first few verses of what is known as the *Venite* in the *Book of Common Prayer*; here the emotion of joyful worship is expressed by the acts in which it is expressed:

O come, let us sing unto the Lord: let us make a joyful noise to the rock of our salvation.

Let us come before his presence with thanksgiving, and make a joyful noise unto him with psalms.

For the Lord is a great God, and a great King above all gods.

In his hand are the deep places of the earth: the strength of the hills is his also.

[1] Job iv. 12–17.

The sea is his, and he made it: and his hands formed the dry land.

O come, let us worship and bow down: let us kneel before the Lord our Maker.[1]

Here though the emotion is more spiritual than in the other cases, yet it is still phrased in terms of bodily sensation, the singing, the joyful noise, the bowing down and kneeling. Often the emotion, instead of being set forth by the bodily sensation that constitutes it, is indirectly portrayed by naming the concrete objects which inevitably produce these sensations.

Thou visitest the earth, and waterest it: thou greatly enrichest it with the river of God, which is full of water: thou preparest them corn, when thou hast so provided for it.

Thou waterest the ridges thereof abundantly: thou settlest the furrows thereof: thou makest it soft with showers: thou blessest the springing thereof.

Thou crownest the year with thy goodness; and thy paths drop fatness.

They drop upon the pastures of the wilderness: and the little hills rejoice on every side.

The pastures are clothed with flocks; the valleys also are covered over with corn; they shout for joy, they also sing.[2]

[1] Ps. xcv. 1–6.
[2] Ps. lxv. 9–13.

Such a passage arouses all the sensations of a warm day in spring when a man walks with head erect, his lungs filled with the warm, rich air, and his nostrils opened to the manifold sweet smells of the earth and of the growing things about him. The deep emotion of content and happiness is thus expressed not by naming the sensations but by naming the objects which inevitably produce them, a mode of expression which is just as powerful as the other.

Comparatively simple cases like these will show, I think, how the principle works out: that the naming of two or three specific sensations or of a few concrete objects carries with it a large and complex mental state which taken all together is the emotion of fear, of reverence, or of joy. And seeing this truth clearly for the simpler cases one can understand how it explains the less palpable and more complex cases, and how the concrete imagery of such a passage as the following has the power to express feelings and thoughts which lie still deeper within the soul:

> Bless the Lord, O my soul. O Lord my God, thou art very great; thou art clothed with honour and majesty.
> Who coverest thyself with light as with a garment: who stretchest out the heavens like a curtain:

Who layeth the beams of his chambers in the
waters: who maketh the clouds his chariot: who
walketh upon the wings of the wind:

Who maketh his angels spirits; his ministers a
flaming fire:

Who laid the foundations of the earth, that it
should not be removed for ever.

Thou coveredst it with the deep as with a garment: the waters stood above the mountains.[1]

The means employed are the same, but the emotions
to be expressed being larger and more diffused one
cannot follow out the mechanism of the expression
so definitely.   Nevertheless the unsurpassed vividness of the Hebrew poetry and its unfailing hold on
our imagination may be ascribed to this fact, that
it always expressed emotions directly and concretely
through sensations instead of describing them by
words which are abstract and therefore pale.

We can go even further, and find in this special
characteristic of the Hebrew language the cause for
the permanent appeal of these ancient poems.   The
great body of our sensations and feelings does not
change from generation to generation.   The horror
of despair at sinking in deep mire, the dread at the
creeping mysteries of the night, or the delight in
uttering forth our joy in song, all are the same thing
for us to-day that they were for these ancient

[1] Ps. civ. 1–6.

Hebrews two thousand years ago and for their ancestors a thousand years before them; and the sight of the stars in the great field of heaven lifts us out of ourselves in the same way that it has moved our ancestors for innumerable generations. We moderns have built up a superstructure of abstract reasoning which they did not have; but all the great mass of our consciousness is the same that it has been for ages and, so far as we can see, as it will be for ages to come. Thus a literature which is able to express itself through these inalterable sensations has a permanence of power impossible to any literature which is phrased largely in abstractions and in inferences from these sensations. In this primitive simplicity of thought, therefore, we can find one reason at any rate for the permanent power of the Hebrew poetry.

Emotion and feeling, however, have other modes of expression than through the connotation of words of sensation: their most typical and highest expression is through music. Every one knows that music can give bodily form to moods far too impalpable and evanescent for articulate language. Even the man who has no ear for music knows what it is to have his flesh stirred and his feet set moving by the playing of a military band; and to music-lovers the full rhythms and harmonies of a great orchestra reach feelings which lie so deep in the soul that no words can find them. Herein lies the other side of the power of literature: since it stands for the spoken word it can borrow some of this power of music to express disembodied emotion. In this power our Authorised Version sets the standard for the English language: it is throbbing with the earnestness of the great men who in the stress of the Reformation, when England was struggling free from the power of the Pope, wrought out their translation of the Scriptures. It was a time when all writing was musical: I have yet to meet a work of the sixteenth century written in the bare and jolting style of so many of our books to-day. To the original translators and to the revisers who followed them we owe the strong and moving rhythm and the rich but subdued music which gives our Bible its capacity of uttering forth the deep things of the soul.

One source of this rich music we must not neglect: that is the Latin of the Vulgate. Later on I must discuss its influence more fully; here I will merely point out that all the men who made our version were intimately acquainted with it: and that its most notable qualities to us are its strong rhythm and its rich sonorousness of tone, qualities which more than all others express earnestness and rever-

ence of feeling. A short psalm, " Behold, how good
and how pleasant it is for brethren to dwell together
in unity!" will show for the present the marvellous power of this language to enrich its words
with ringing music. Notice how full it is of open
vowels and liquid consonants, sounds on which the
voice insensibly dwells.

> Ecce, quam bonum et quam jucundum habitare
> fratres in unum:
> Sicut unguentum in capite, quod descendit in
> barbam, barbam Aaron.
> Quod descendit in oram vestimenti ejus:
> Sicut ros Hermon, qui descendit in montem
> Sion,
> Quoniam illic mandavit Dominus benedictionem
> et vitam usque in sæculum.

The deepest and strongest feelings which are expressed in the psalms are the feelings of awe in
the presence of the omnipotent God, feelings which
are naturally expressed in worship. Now music is
an inseparable part of worship; and we may well
hold that this music of the Biblical poetry was derived in part by reflection from the Vulgate. Thus
we may feel that we have in our English some share
of the passionate earnestness of St. Jerome, ringing
down through the centuries to deepen and enrich the
meaning of the English.

IV

Now let us turn from the essential questions of style which concern the translation, and search behind them into the intensity and elevation of feeling which made this marvellous style a necessity of expression. Here explanation can make but a short step; for we are in a realm where the only ultimate explanation is the fact of inspiration; and that is only another way of saying that we are in the presence of forces above and beyond our present human understanding. We can see a little further into the power of these poems, however, if we take into account the times in which they were probably written and consider the experiences which called them forth. I will speak here only of the *Psalter* and *Job*.

It is now generally held by scholars of the modern school that the *Psalter* is the hymn book of the second temple; and most scholars who accept the new views of the Bible at all agree that some of the psalms at any rate were composed as late as the time of the Maccabean revolution, 165 B.C. The dates of the separate psalms may be very divergent. Some of them may have been originally composed before the Exile, some of them perhaps by King David himself;

but as the *Psalter* is a hymn book the date of the original composition of any given psalm is a matter of
small importance. For since a hymn book is a collection of poems made for a very practical purpose, it
has no reason for existence if it does not express
the feelings and aspirations of the generation which
uses it. Therefore if the *Psalter* as we have it comes
from the latest period of Jewish history it must
embody the sufferings and aspirations, the faith and
the passionate zeal of the Jews of the third and
the second centuries before Christ. It would come,
therefore, from nearly the most critical period of
their history, a time full of bitter suffering and distress, when they were harassed by enemies from
without, and torn by dissensions from within. In
Psalms lxxiv and *lxxix* Jerusalem is described as
sacked and the temple profaned; and the outburst of
bitter indignation in *Psalm lv*,

> But it was thou, a man mine equal, my guide
> and mine acquaintance.
> We took sweet counsel together, and walked
> unto the house of God in company.
> Let death seize upon them, and let them go down
> quick into hell: for wickedness is in their dwellings,
> and among them,

is probably aimed at the party among the Jews in
these centuries which was ready to compromise with

the heathen, perhaps even to contaminate the worship of Jehovah by the assimilation of heathen rites.
The depths of this misery is sounded by many of the
psalms, as the faith by force of which they won their
way through the furnace of affliction is measured by
such glowing words as those of *Psalm lxviii*:

> Let God arise, let his enemies be scattered: let
> them also that hate him flee before him.
> As smoke is driven away, so drive them away:
> as wax melteth before the fire, so let the wicked
> perish at the presence of God.
> But let the righteous be glad; let them rejoice
> before God: yea, let them exceedingly rejoice.
> Sing unto God, sing praises to his name: extol
> him that rideth upon the heavens by his name
> JAH, and rejoice before him.
> A father of the fatherless, and a judge of the
> widows, is God in his holy habitation.
> God setteth the solitary in families: he bringeth
> out those which are bound with chains: but the
> rebellious dwell in a dry land.
> O God, when thou wentest forth before thy
> people, when thou didst march through the wilder-
> ness; Selah:
> The earth shook, the heavens also dropped at
> the presence of God: even Sinai itself was moved
> at the presence of God, the God of Israel.

The jubilant triumph of some of the psalms, too,
seems to reflect such an unexpected and miraculous

escape as came to the Jews through the victories of
Judas Maccabæus:

> It is better to trust in the Lord, than to put con-
> fidence in man:
> It is better to trust in the Lord, than to put con-
> fidence in princes.
> All nations compassed me about: but in the
> name of the Lord will I destroy them.
> They compassed me about; yea, they compassed
> me about: but in the name of the Lord will I
> destroy them.
> They compassed me about like bees; they are
> quenched as the fire of thorns: for in the name of
> the Lord I will destroy them.
> Thou has thrust sore at me, that I might fall:
> but the Lord helped me.
> The Lord is my strength and song, and is become
> my salvation.[1]

Certainly there is no time before the Exile which
will furnish the background of hopeless misery and
depression, suddenly interrupted by unbounded joy
and thanksgiving, which lies behind the *Psalter* as
a whole. The very intensity and desperateness of
the suffering and the suddenness of the reaction help
us to understand the intensity of feeling uttered
forth in these marvellous poems.

Job also comes probably from the Exile or the
succeeding century, the time when, as we have seen,

[1] Ps. cxviii. 8–14.

the problem of the origin of evil came home to the
Jews with such bitter poignancy. *Deuteronomy*
taught them that Jehovah would reward their faithfulness to the statutes and ordinances which he had
commanded them, and that he would punish whoever
disobeyed; and in the manner of their age and country they looked for an immediate reward or an immediate punishment. Yet they who were striving
with the most anxious care to fulfil every jot and
tittle of the law were crushed by poverty and oppression, while their heathen conquerors, living in open
defiance of the laws of Jehovah, grew old in wealth
and happiness. For them, and especially for those
whose faith was strongest, the dilemma must have
been critical. This noble poem witnesses to the earnestness with which they attacked the problem and the
triumphant faith with which they came back to the
solution that the ways of God are too great for man
to understand, that the fear of the Lord is the beginning and the end of wisdom. *Job* utters not only
the whole bitterness of their despair, but also the
faith in the omnipotence of their God which rose
untouched by difficulties and sufferings.

Then the Lord answered Job out of the whirlwind, and said,

Who is this that darkeneth counsel by words
without knowledge?

Gird up now thy loins like a man; for I will demand of thee, and answer thou me.

Where wast thou when I laid the foundations of
the earth? declare, if thou hast understanding.

Who hath laid the measures thereof, if thou
knowest? or who hath stretched the line upon it?

Whereupon are the foundations thereof fastened?
or who laid the corner stone thereof;

When the morning stars sang together, and all
the sons of God shouted for joy?[1]

This truth, that the *Psalter* and *Job* are the em-
bodiment of intensely real emotions, must not be left
out of account in reading them. The way in which
Job solves the problems it discusses I must consider
at greater length in the next chapter; here we can
recognize that the intensity and elevation of spirit
which give it its nobility spring from the triumph
of an inextinguishable faith in a desperate crisis.

V

Finally, the distinctive character of Hebrew
poetry appears in a significant limitation, which is
especially illustrated by *Job*. To use a technical
term, Hebrew poetry never reached the point of rep-
resentation: in other words, it never passed beyond
the point of expressing the writer's own emotions to

[1] Job xxxviii. 1–7.

the point where he could imagine himself into the feelings of other persons, whether real or invented. The same limitation appears in the historical books in the speeches which the writers, after the manner of all historians of antiquity, whether Oriental or classical, put into the mouths of the chief persons of the history. The Deuteronomist writers of *Kings*, for example, composing a prayer which would be fitting for Solomon at the dedication of the temple, put into his mouth words and ideas of which the people of Israel had no knowledge until three hundred years after his death. They made him speak in the language and thought of *Deuteronomy,* a book which was called forth by the great change in the fortunes of Israel after the destruction of Samaria. They could not imagine to themselves how Solomon would really have felt; all they could do was to put their own hopes and yearnings into his mouth. This lack of the faculty of constructive imagination is a chief note of the Hebrew literature.

In the poetry this limitation resulted in the absence from our Old Testament of all poetry which cannot be roughly classified as lyrical. The Hebrew mind had no apparatus for inventing characters, or for understanding the thoughts and feelings of other men. Ostensibly *Job* is either a drama or a debate; yet though Satan is a protagonist in the prose introduction, he is not mentioned at all in the poem; in the colloquies the speeches of the three friends can be interchanged without injury to the book, and in Chapter xxvii, as it stands, Job shifts over and occupies the ground which has been held by his friends against him. Clearly the authors of this great book came into no clear imagination or understanding of Job as an individual and consistent character. They made no effort to get into the point of view and temperament of the ostensible hero of the poem: as we say nowadays they made no attempt to create a character. He is best understood as a generalized figure of suffering Israel, a conception which was apparently dear to the hearts of the Jews at this period; it was set forth by the Isaiah of the Exile in several passages of which the following is one:

He was oppressed, and he was afflicted, yet he opened not his mouth: he is brought as a lamb to the slaughter, and as a sheep before her shearers is dumb, so he openeth not his mouth.

He was taken from prison and from judgment: and who shall declare his generation? for he was cut off out of the land of the living: for the transgression of my people was he stricken.

And he made his grave with the wicked, and with the rich in his death; because he had done no violence, neither was any deceit in his mouth.

Yet it pleased the Lord to bruise him; he hath

put him to grief: when thou shalt make his soul an offering for sin, he shall see his seed, he shall prolong his days, and the pleasure of the Lord shall prosper in his hand.[1]

The same idea appears in certain of the psalms:

For my loins are filled with a loathsome disease: and there is no soundness in my flesh.

I am feeble and sore broken: I have roared by reason of the disquietness of my heart.

Lord, all my desire is before thee; and my groaning is not hid from thee.

My heart panteth, my strength faileth me: as for the light of mine eyes, it also is gone from me.

My lovers and my friends stand aloof from my sore; and my kinsmen stand afar off.

They also that seek after my life lay snares for me: and they that seek my hurt speak mischievous things, and imagine deceits all the day long.

But I, as a deaf man, heard not; and I was as a dumb man that openeth not his mouth.

Thus I was as a man that heareth not, and in whose mouth are no reproofs.[2]

During the bitter times of the Exile, and the century or two succeeding, the Jews seem to have found comfort in thus figuring themselves as a nation which was suffering because of its very faithfulness to Jehovah, and to have had a melancholy pleasure

[1] Isa. liii. 7–10.   [2] Ps. xxxviii. 7–15.

in describing these sufferings at length, always with
the expression of the hope in the mercy and power
of their God. It is probable that *Job* can thus be
best understood. In a sense he is individualized,
but no more so than is the suffering servant of
Jehovah by the Isaiah of the Exile, or than the
suffering Israel described in the *Psalms*. If one
reads the poem carefully, one will see that it could
be applied to many men of a considerable variety
of temperaments; indeed, the further fact that the
piety of the Job of the prologue, which consists so
much in offering sacrifices, is different from the
larger-minded piety of the Job of the colloquies,
seems a pretty strong proof that the authors had
little idea of what we mean by consistent characterization. They made no effort to make Job individual in the sense that Hamlet and Henry Esmond
are individuals; furthermore, there is no evidence
that the men of their race were ever conscious of the
possibility of such an effort.

This unconsciousness of the possibilities of the
creative imagination marks the abyss which lies between the Old Testament literature and our modern
literature. From the time of the Greeks down representative art is the largest and most important part
of pure literature. All the drama, all story-writing,
and all poetry except lyrical are representative, in that

their effort is to set forth the actions and feelings of persons whom their writers know only indirectly and by force of the creative imagination. In the Bible there is no such literature. If one remembers that the only other work with which English-speaking people are familiar, which comes from the same Oriental background as the Bible, is the *Arabian Nights*, one will realize better the distance from us of this Old Testament literature. R. L. Stevenson pointed out in his essay *A Gossip on Romance* that the people of the *Arabian Nights* are mere puppets; that their stories are a pure succession of incident and event, unbroken and undiluted by any understanding of character on the part of the authors, or attempt to make the people real. These Israelite writers are on a somewhat higher plane, for they could tell a simple story in terms of the most vivid detail; and, as we have seen, they could in a simple, unconscious sort of way make the different actors in their stories seem like distinct people; but their creative imagination did not go so far as to enable them to invent a character, or even so far to detach themselves from their own experiences as to imagine consistently and convincingly the mental workings of anyone whose circumstances or temperament differed much from their own. We shall see in the next chapter that Hebrew thought never attained to ab-

stract reasoning. Here I wish only to make clear
that the thought of Hebrew authors was primitively
simple; it was never able to push beyond its own
experience in order to create that of other men.

In this limitation, on the other hand, we may find
part of the power of this literature. The Hebrew
poetry has power over our feelings because it is always in dead earnest. There is no play-acting here.
When we see or read *Hamlet*, or *Macbeth*, or *King
Lear*, we are absorbed in the distress and suffering
pictured before us; but always we have behind our
absorption the sense of detachment from real affairs.
Unconsciously we feel that we can afford to take
part by imagination in the suffering, because after
all it is not real. To understand and appreciate the
poetry of the Old Testament one must remember
that it always is real. The sufferings, or the joy,
or the faith are the personal experience of real men.
Their poetry had always the direct and practical
purpose of unburdening real feeling: there is no
" make-believe " in these poems of the Old Testament.
Even in *Job* the apparent form of a drama is the
thinnest of masks for the deep feelings which lie underneath. The book is not an effort of the author
to imagine how such a man as Job would have felt
under such trials, but rather the expression of actual
distress over the hopeless plight of his people. The

mental tortures under which Job writhes are therefore those of real people in real and harrowing perplexity; and the overwhelming power of the answer of the Almighty is the direct witness of a faith which could not be daunted by the most grievous trials.

Thus we may bring this brief survey of the poetry of the Bible to an end. In form and style it has power which springs from the unblurred concreteness and directness of the old Hebrew language, and from the strong but unconscious rhythm and the richness of music. Behind the manifold variety of the imagery and the deep music of the style, we can see, and not too vaguely, the intensity of faith which soared above all earthly troubles to the highest conception of God yet reached by man, the faith which we shall trace in the constantly wider and more spiritual messages of the prophets, rising during the period which produced the psalms to a clear grasp of immortality and the blessings of paradise.

CHAPTER IV

THE WISDOM BOOKS

I

I HAVE already pointed out that since the Hebrew language had no apparatus for embodying any complication of thought, all the narrative of the Old Testament is extremely simple in form. In like manner we have seen that the poetry embodies only man's immediate experience and the deep emotions which are his reaction to that experience, and that the Jews never reached the point of figuring to themselves the feelings of fictitious persons. As in the narrative, the mental habit behind the poetry is of extreme simplicity.

In this chapter and in the next I shall discuss those parts of the Bible which contain the nearest approach to what we call philosophising: in the Old Testament, the books of wisdom—*Proverbs, Ecclesiastes* and *Job*; and in the New Testament the Fourth Gospel and the Epistles. I shall confine the discussion of them almost entirely to a single point, the habit of mind and the manner of thought which they reveal to us; for we shall gain much light on the literature of the Bible as a whole if we can see wherein the mode of thought of these ancient writers was similar to ours and wherein it was dissimilar; moreover, by understanding this point we shall see better in the end how this literature which is so foreign could weave itself so deeply into the texture of English thought and speech.

Proverbs is a somewhat miscellaneous collection, in part of short poems on various subjects, in still larger part of the shrewd and pithy apothegms in which the Oriental mind delighted to sum up its observations on man and his life. It begins with nine chapters in which are contained a number of short poems generally in praise of wisdom, though some contain particular admonitions and warnings. Then comes the main portion of the book, which is also the most typical: its character is summed up in the heading of the tenth chapter in the Authorised Version, " From this chapter to the five and twentieth are sundry observations of moral virtues, and their contrary vices." This classification, however, is somewhat too sweeping, for at verse 17 of Chapter xxii begins a new section, the so-called Words of the Wise. Here instead of separated and isolated proverbs we have brief poems on various subjects,

sometimes only a couple of verses long, sometimes
six or eight verses, such as the poem on the drunkard
which I have already cited, and the following poem
on the sluggard:

> I went by the field of the slothful, and by the
> vineyard of the man void of understanding;
> And, lo, it was all grown over with thorns, and
> nettles had covered the face thereof, and the stone
> wall thereof was broken down.
> Then I saw, and considered it well: I looked
> upon it, and received instruction.
> Yet a little sleep, a little slumber, a little folding
> of the hands to sleep:
> So shall thy poverty come as one that travelleth;
> and thy want as an armed man.[1]

Then follows another collection of separate proverbs
and axioms, " proverbs of Solomon, which the men
of Hezekiah king of Judah copied out "; these, however, are somewhat classified, as is recognized by such
a heading as that of Chapter xxvi in the Authorised
Version, " Observations about fools, about sluggards,
and about contentious busybodies." The rest of the
'book is thoroughly miscellaneous; Chapter xxx begins with a very obscure passage denominated " the
words of Agur," and runs on into a series of numer-
ical proverbs, such as:

[1] Prov. xxiv. 30–34.

There be four things which are little upon the earth, but they are exceeding wise:

The ants are a people not strong, yet they prepare their meat in the summer;

The conies are but a feeble folk, yet make they their houses in the rocks;

The locusts have no king, yet go they forth all of them by bands;

The spider taketh hold with her hands, and is in kings' palaces.[1]

The last chapter begins with the " words of king Lemuel, the prophecy that his mother taught him," and concludes with an alphabetical poem which describes the virtuous woman. Between these very different parts there are no transitions and no attempt on the part of the authors or compilers to create the possibility of continuous thought. The canons of Hebrew authorship never demanded the welding together of dissimilar parts into a single whole.

The exact date both of the individual proverbs and poems and of the book as a whole is indeterminable; but in its present state the book like the other wisdom books, though incorporating material which in ultimate origin may be early, comes most probably from the later period after the Exile when the experience of the Jews became so much widened. To

[1] Prov. xxx. 24–28.

this conclusion point the tacit assumption of monotheism, the absence of any definite national traits,
the predominant interest in urban life, the somewhat
technical use of the words *wisdom* and the *wise*, and
the general unity of the group of wisdom books. But
after all, the settlement of dates in works of such
character can never be very exact, especially when
one takes into account the unbroken and slow-chang-
ing tradition of ideas among Eastern peoples: if the
customs of Syrian peasants in our own day throw
light on the nature of the *Song of Solomon* one can
hardly look for much difference in ways of thought
between the days of Jeremiah and those of Alexander. In view of such facts, and also of the fact
that much Hebrew authorship consisted in compilation and amplification of existing materials we may
fairly suppose that *Proverbs* gives us materials which
were originally produced by many writers of very
different ages: and that Jews of times as far apart
as the seventh century and the third held in general about the same views of life, and thought in
about the same way.

Thus we may look on the book as offering us the
reflections on life of sages who lived in an indefinite
past and with the restricted experience of the Oriental world. Yet it is indubitably stimulating to us
to-day, and it impresses one at each new reading by

the soundness and shrewdness of its conclusions. As one turns over its pages one's eye catches observation after observation that has established itself in our everyday thought. In Bartlett's *Familiar Quotations* there are sixty-nine quotations from *Proverbs,* far more than from any other book in the Bible except *Psalms,* and we must remember that the latter has become especially familiar through its almost universal use in church services. Such an adhesion to modern thought attests the fact that the single proverbs are terse in the strict sense of the word: all but the very essence of the thought is polished away, and the phrasing reduced to the least possible number of words. As one reads them one cannot help thinking of the gravity and deliberation of the East, where men have time to ruminate on the meaning of life, and where the absence of science and analytical philosophy confines the attention of wise men to the affairs of daily life. Moreover, one feels the scorn for the garrulousness of the fool in a region where rulers are despots who seize every opening for extortion, and punish ruthlessly every insult or offense; in such a world it behooves a man to think out his thoughts and not to utter them rashly.

With the terseness goes the shrewd insight into human nature. Here insight is better than reasoning, since reasoning cannot more than begin to state all the premises. One's judgment of men and affairs is built on a multitude of facts and feelings, of instincts and prejudices good and bad, many of them so subtle or so vague that it is impossible to phrase them; yet they all go into the scale and help to settle our likings and our acts. It is the accuracy and justice with which *Proverbs* sums up these intuitive judgments that gives it its lasting hold on our interest. In a way things intellectual are the superficial parts of humanity: the great mass of mankind has no share in them, since in the long run men are governed by their feelings and their instincts and intuitions. It is this portion of our mental life which is summed up so compactly and with such aptness of expression in this book.

Ecclesiastes, though in subject of much less range than *Proverbs*, is hardly less orderly: quite as much as the latter it reads like a notebook in which the sage set down his meditations and observations on life as they happened to come to him. Though there are some connected poems in the book, as a whole it is brought together with no more method than we should put to the filling of a scrapbook. Indeed one scholar in his effort to compel chaos into order has proposed the theory that in some ancient copy of the book the sheets became transposed, so that the middle part became the end and the two ends the middle part. This is only the wildest of the many efforts to find a continuous structure in the book. All such efforts are based on the mistaken assumption that a book of wisdom would of necessity have order, a necessity which the Hebrew mind never felt. There is no more striking evidence of the difference of the Hebrew thought from our own than this obliviousness to all that we mean by the word " composition."

The teachings of *Ecclesiastes*, its despairing, cynical acceptance of the vanity of all man's endeavor, I will refer to presently. Though it seems to show some acquaintance with the Greek philosophy, in its mode of thought it does not differ from *Proverbs*. In one respect, however, it is in contrast to both *Proverbs* and *Job*, and indeed to all the other books of the Old Testament except *Nehemiah* and the books of the prophets: here we seem to come into touch with the individuality of the author, for he quotes proverbs and then adds his own comment.

> The wise man's eyes are in his head; but the fool walketh in darkness: and I myself perceived also that one event happeneth to them all.
>
> Then said I in my heart, as it happeneth to the fool, so it happeneth even to me; and why was I then more wise?   Then I said in my heart, that this also is vanity.
>
> For there is no remembrance of the wise more

than of the fool for ever; seeing that which now is in the days to come shall all be forgotten. And how dieth the wise man? as the fool.

Therefore I hated life; because the work that is wrought under the sun is grievous unto me: for all is vanity and vexation of spirit.[1]

It is better to hear the rebuke of the wise, than for a man to hear the song of fools.

For as the crackling of thorns under a pot, so is the laughter of the fool· this also is vanity.[2]

Each of these passages begins with a proverb which might have been found in either *Proverbs* or *Ecclesiasticus*; but there it would have been merely recorded. The author of *Ecclesiastes*, on the other hand, seems to use the proverb as the text or starting point of his own thought; and the latter is the more important. It is this habit of pointing the traditional wisdom of the sages in a new direction that makes the work of the Preacher seem so individual and so modern beside the impersonal aphorisms of the shadowy and legendary Solomon to whom *Proverbs* is ascribed.

Job stands by itself in the wisdom literature, since, as we have already seen, it is a great series of poems dealing with a single problem, the origin of suffering and the doctrine of retribution. Its solu-

[1] Eccles. ii. 14–17.   [2] Ibid., vii. 5–6.

tion of this problem I will consider presently: in the mean time let us consider its outward form. The structure of the book is of the loosest. The prose prologue and epilogue with which it begins and ends have only a superficial connection with the poems: the three friends seem to know nothing of the specific nature of the sufferings which have brought Job to the dust, or of the explanation of his sufferings which is offered by the prologue. Moreover, Satan, who is protagonist in the prologue, is ignored in the epilogue. In the colloquies, which occupy Chapters iii–xxvi, the regular cycle of answers to Job's complaints by each of the three friends in turn is disturbed at the end: the last speech of Bildad is only six verses, and that of Zophar is omitted. Furthermore, in Chapter xxvii, as we have seen, Job shifts his ground to the position so far occupied by his friends, and Chapter xxviii consists of a poem in praise of wisdom which is closely like that in *Proverbs viii* and which is in no way connected with the rest of *Job*. Then after Job's bitter description of his sufferings in Chapters xxix–xxxi, we come in Chapters xxxii–xxxvii to the speeches of Elihu which seem to be a pious and less forcible iteration of the doctrine already relentlessly enforced by the three friends. Moreover, the description of behemoth and leviathan in Chapters xl and xli are to our modern ideas too detailed and too remote from the purpose of the book to fall smoothly into place in it. Here, as in the case of *Ecclesiastes,* the effort to reduce such irregularities to order must not tempt us into an uncritical ascription to a past age of the world of an instinct which it did not possess. Even if the book were at one time more orderly and consecutive, which is perhaps doubtful, we must recognize that the present disturbances and dislocations would have offended no one in these simple and uncritical generations.

I have already pointed out that in substance *Job* ultimately owes its origin to a literal interpretation of the doctrines of *Deuteronomy.* The original writer of that book formulated the teachings of the great prophets into a covenant between Jehovah and his people, with promises of reward if they should obey the statutes and ordinances which he set before them and warnings of bitter punishment if they should disobey. As time went on both promises and rewards were applied to the individual, and, being taken literally, were understood as of immediate fulfilment; or else, where they were still applied to the people as a whole, they led the prophecy on, as we shall see, into the apocalypse. Applied to the individual this doctrine produced the idea which is the basis of many of the psalms, as well as of *Job,* that suffering and distress of necessity imply sin on the part of the sufferer, and that righteousness is surely and immediately rewarded by happiness and prosperity.

> Fret not thyself because of evildoers, neither be thou envious against the workers of iniquity.
> For they shall soon be cut down like the grass, and wither as the green herb.
> Trust in the Lord, and do good; so shalt thou dwell in the land, and verily thou shalt be fed.
> Delight thyself also in the Lord; and he shall give thee the desires of thine heart.[1]

It is this doctrine that Jesus controverts in the passage in *St. Luke* concerning " the Galileans, whose blood Pilate had mingled with their sacrifices," and the " eighteen, upon whom the tower in Siloam fell and slew them." [2] It seems to have been a cardinal doctrine in the thought of the Jews in the last centuries of the old era.

The relation of *Job* to this doctrine is illuminating as to its character. The school of wise men or sages from which it is probable that all the wisdom books proceeded seems to have set itself to scrutinize the world in a temper approaching what we should call the scientific. It looked at facts in a cool and dispassionate way which is in strong contrast to the

[1] Ps. xxxvii. 1–4.   [2] Luke xiii. 1–5.

intensity and heated imagination of the prophets; and looking thus at the facts of their time, these sages could not help seeing the contradiction between this traditional doctrine and the facts which faced them. They, who were the chosen people of Jehovah, whose persistence as a people was now determined wholly by their faithfulness to his law, were the prey of heathen conquerors, and subject to such scorn and oppression as is so vividly described by Nehemiah. *Job* shows us one of the ways in which these sages met this crucial dilemma.

It is a significant fact that the author discusses the problem in a series of poems, and that these poems show hardly any progress. Eliphaz and Bildad and Zophar start from the same point in each of the three cycles of speeches, and Job in his replies meets them always in almost the same way: they assume that since he is suffering, therefore he has sinned; he protests that he has not sinned, and sets forth his helplessness in the hands of Jehovah. Only in Chapter xxi does he come to the point of questioning this universal doctrine of his race, and then with horror at his own presumption:

> Mark me, and be astonished, and lay your hand upon your mouth.
> Even when I remember I am afraid, and trembling taketh hold on my flesh.

Wherefore do the wicked live, become old, yea, are mighty in power?

.   .   .   .   .

One dieth in his full strength, being wholly at ease and quiet.

His breasts are full of milk, and his bones are moistened with marrow.

And another dieth in the bitterness of his soul, and never eateth with pleasure.

They shall lie down alike in the dust, and the worms shall cover them.

.   .   .   .   .

How then comfort ye me in vain, seeing in your answers there remaineth falsehood? [1]

The final solution of the problem in the answer of the Lord from the whirlwind in Chapter xxxviii is merely a declaration of the impotence of man:

Who is this that darkeneth counsel by words without knowledge?

Gird up now thy loins like a man; for I will demand of thee, and answer thou me.

Where wast thou when I laid the foundations of the earth? declare, if thou hast understanding.

.   .   .   .   .

Hast thou entered into the springs of the sea? or hast thou walked in the search of the depth?

Have the gates of death been opened unto thee? or hast thou seen the doors of the shadow of death?

Hast thou perceived the breath of the earth? declare if thou knowest it all. [2]

[1] Job xxi. 5–7; 23–26; 34.   [2] Ibid., xxxviii. 2–4; 16–18.

And Job, overwhelmed and in the dust, declares:

> Who is he that hideth counsel without knowledge? therefore have I uttered that I understood not; things too wonderful for me, which I knew not.
>
> Hear, I beseech thee, and I will speak: I will demand of thee, and declare thou unto me.
>
> I have heard of thee by the hearing of the ear: but now mine eye seeth thee.
>
> Wherefore I abhor myself, and repent in dust and ashes.[1]

This is the final word of *Job*: the acknowledgment that the ways of God are past man's understanding; and that the fear of the Lord is the beginning and the end of wisdom.

Judged by the canons of strict logic or of our modern conception of God as supremely just, this treatment of the problem is incoherent and inconsequent. We must not lose sight, however, of the fact that we are dealing with the Oriental world. It has been pointed out that " the doctrine of retribution in the present life which [the author of *Job*] finds inadequate is common to the friends and to the religion which has in all ages been that of the genuine Arab—the so-called *din Ibrahim* (or 'religion of Abraham'). The Eloah and Shaddai of Job are the irresponsible Allah who has all power in heaven and

[1] Job xlii. 3–6.

on earth, and before whom, when mysteries occur in human life which the retribution-doctrine cannot solve, the Arab and every true Moslem bows his head with settled, sad resignation." [1]   This conception of God as an inscrutable, omnipotent Being who justifies His actions to no man, before whom mankind is as the dust of the earth, is chiefly familiar to us today through Fitzgerald's rendering of the *Rubáiyát* of Omar Khayyám:

> We are no other than a moving row
> Of Magic Shadow-shapes that come and go
>   Round with the Sun-illumin'd lantern held
> In Midnight by the Master of the Show;
>
> But helpless Pieces of the Game He plays
> Upon this Chequer-board of Nights and Days;
>   Hither and thither moves, and checks, and slays,
> And one by one back in the Closet lays.
>
> The Ball no question makes of Ayes and Noes,
> But Here or There as strikes the Player goes;
>   And He that toss'd you down into the Field,
> *He* knows about it all—HE knows—HE knows.

This is not far from the doctrine of *Ecclesiastes*; but in *Job* God is assumed to act through love of his people; he is not wholly irresponsible.   The book

[1] Cheyne, *Job and Solomon*, p. 98

breathes the settled conviction that God has chosen his people Israel and that he has a special care over them. Moreover, the author is not, as he has sometimes been held, a sceptic. Though Job cries out against the injustice of his sufferings and breaks through the settled tradition of his people by declaring that the righteous do suffer and the wicked do prosper, yet underneath he has always the faith in God: the cry "though he slay me yet will I trust him" is a necessary element in any just understanding of the book. Its force lies in its capacity to bring home even to us to-day the pressing and crucial nature of the problem, and to make us feel the puny and ephemeral weakness of mankind before the eternal purposes of God. There is no other work in English literature which approaches this power of *Job* to hold us face to face with the overwhelming forces of nature, and to marshal them into a means of setting forth deep and ideal truths. Its appeal is to the highest emotions of which man is capable; and, except perhaps for the Elihu speeches, it maintains itself without flagging at this high pitch of feeling.

Ecclesiastes struggles with the same problem, and comes in a way to the same conclusion, but in so different a spirit that the similarity is only superficial. In spite of the fragmentariness and disarray of the book it strikes a single note, the futility of all man's struggles to understand and justify the universe.

> I said in mine heart concerning the estate of the sons of men, that God might manifest them, and that they might see that they themselves are beasts.

> For that which befalleth the sons of men befalleth beasts; even one thing befalleth them: as the one dieth, so dieth the other; yea, they have all one breath; so that a man hath no preeminence above a beast: for all is vanity.

> All go unto one place; all are of the dust, and all turn to dust again.

> Who knoweth the spirit of man that goeth upward, and the spirit of the beast that goeth downward to the earth?

> Wherefore I perceive that there is nothing better, than that a man should rejoice in his own works; for that is his portion: for who shall bring him to see what shall be after him? [1]

> Truly the light is sweet, and a pleasant thing it is for the eyes to behold the sun:

> But if a man live many years, and rejoice in them all; yet let him remember the days of darkness; for they shall be many. All that cometh is vanity. [2]

This mood is familiar to all men at one time or another, and it is the prevailing mood with the weaker brother; the weariness of the flesh easily

[1] Eccles. iii. 18–22.   [2] Ibid., xi. 7–8.

passes over into weariness of spirit; and at such times the conventions and the apparent universality of *Ecclesiastes* sweep over the field of thought like the face of night over a troubled country. The simplicity and conclusiveness of the solution are soothing; the Preacher is easier to follow than is Job, for even intellectually idealism and optimism are harder doctrines to cling to and need a robuster frame of mind. The shady side of experience is the more obvious, since we take the good of life as our right and without notice, whereas its disappointments come to us as a personal grievance. It is far easier to hold that things are going to the dogs than to extend one's view over a long enough stretch of time to see that they are improving. Moreover, all the delights of the world, even innocent indulgence in the pleasures of the flesh, pull one away from the higher view; the only possible philosophy for the man who chooses the things of this life and turns his back on the things of the spirit is an irresponsible agnosticism; for such men *Ecclesiastes* is the whole of the law and the prophets.

This mood of almost luxurious hopelessness marks the great gap between *Ecclesiastes* and *Job*. Out of the depths of suffering and mental torture the latter still raises a voice of praise and acknowledgment to the Almighty. The author of *Ecclesiastes* lies down before his difficulties, and draws over his eyes the veil of present creature comforts.

II

Now turning to look at all these books of wisdom as a class of literature, the first fact that I wish to emphasize is that they are poetical in form. From that fact it follows as a corollary that they are composed of the simplest kinds of sentences; for we have seen that in Hebrew poetry, since the line is the unit and the lines must be strictly balanced, there can be no sustained periods. In the second place, as I pointed out at some length in the last chapter, the vocabulary of Hebrew is uniformly concrete, and that to a degree which it would be impossible to match in modern books, even in those on the simplest subjects. A page of Bunyan's *Pilgrim's Progress* has more abstract words than the whole of *Job*. Besides this simplicity of structure and this unfailing concreteness of diction, which follow from the nature of Hebrew poetry, there are in these books no connectives or other devices for building the discourses together into sustained and continuous thought. *Proverbs* is a collection of diverse material with no attempt to bind the parts together. In *Job*, Satan, who is the protagonist of the prologue, does not appear in the poems, nor in the epilogue; nor do the poems refer to the specific griefs and trials of the flesh from which Job suffers in the story. Even in the poems, the joining of issue between Job and his comforters is very uncertain: and in Chapter xxvii he shifts over to their side of the argument. The answer of the Lord from the whirlwind loses itself in the descriptions of behemoth and of leviathan; and it is nowhere summed up to a specific conclusion. Thus *Job* is a discussion of a metaphysical question in which there are no abstract words, no logical structure, and not even an attempt at an unbroken chain of reasoning. If one tries to imagine writing today on even the simplest subject in science or philosophy without such necessities of style one will see how far away from us is this poetical wisdom of the Old Testament. Even *Ecclesiastes*, which reflects an acquaintance with Greek philosophy, constantly falls back into the poetical aphorisms of the Hebrew wisdom:

> Again, I considered all travail, and every right work, that for this a man is envied of his neighbour. This is also vanity and vexation of spirit.
>
> The fool foldeth his hands together, and eateth his own flesh.
>
> Better is an handful with quietness, than both the hands full with travail and vexation of spirit.[1]

[1] Eccles. iv. 4–6.

In the strictest sense of the word these Hebrew books of wisdom are literature, for they are always poetical and therefore concerned more with feeling than with thought.

Furthermore, when one compares the contents of these Hebrew books of wisdom with those of our modern philosophy and science one very soon notices that those contents were drawn always and wholly from experience, never from inference and speculation. These books are concerned with such things as the hatred that stirs up strife, pride, the light of the righteous, the fountains of the deep, the doors of the shadow of death. It is such wisdom as might have been gathered by a sage sitting at the gateway of a town, shrewdly observing and ruminating on the affairs of the men who pass him, but never pushing his thought beyond such matters of immediate observation. It is the wisdom of the market place and the highway rather than the wisdom of the study.

So completely is this true that this homely and concrete wisdom of the Jewish sages would not make even a starting point for our science and philosophy. The latter go to sensation and experience only for confirmation of results already reached by abstraction. Astronomy, abstracting from its direct observations of the heavenly bodies their motions in relation to each other, and making great leaps by inference, arrived at the law of universal gravitation. Then by means of pure calculation based on observed deviations of Uranus it pointed its telescopes to the exact place where the faint light of Neptune would strike the eye. So in practical matters. A civil engineer plans a bridge without knowing who will manufacture the steel or who will put it together. He works out in the quiet of his office abstractions which give him mastery over the inert matter and forces of nature; and without the abstraction and inference he would be helpless. Moreover, science uses these abstractions as ultimate and absolute facts, with the same confidence that the Eastern sage had in his shrewd observations in the market place. The force of gravity, electricity, evolution and adaptation to environment, are all figments of inference which we know only by putting together attributes or effects abstracted from a host of concrete inferences of the most diverse kind. Our forms of language differ from those of the Hebrew sages chiefly from the necessary consequences of this difference of thought. We reason by analysis and abstraction, and they did not. Therefore our language has abstract words and a full and increasing apparatus for transitions and for summarizing great reaches of thought: theirs had none.

This difference in mental constitution goes so deep

to the essence of this Biblical literature that I will venture to examine it somewhat more deeply. Let us to turn to psychology and see how the process of reasoning is understood today. Professor James in the chapter on Reasoning in his *Psychology* sums up its essence in these words: " The great difference, in fact, between that simpler kind of rational thinking which consists in the concrete objects of past experience merely suggesting each other, and reasoning distinctively so called, is this, that whilst the empirical thinking is only reproductive, reasoning is productive. An empirical, or ' rule-of-thumb ' thinker can deduce nothing from data with whose behavior and associates in the concrete he is unfamiliar." . . . Reasoning " *contains analysis and abstraction.* Whereas the merely empirical thinker stares at a fact in its entirety, . . . the reasoner breaks it up and notices some one of its separate attributes. This attribute he takes to be the essential part of the whole fact before him. This attribute has properties or consequences which the fact until then was not known to have, but which now it is noticed to contain the attribute it must have." . . . And further on, " The first thing is to have seen that every possible case of reasoning involves the abstraction of a particular partial aspect of the phenomena thought about, and that whilst Empirical Thought simply associates phenomena in their entirety, Reasoned Thought couples them by the conscious use of this extract." [1]

Socrates, who was possibly a contemporary of the author of *Job,* gives in the *Republic* in his search for the nature of justice an admirable example of this process of reasoning by abstraction. "First," he suggested, " let us investigate its character in cities; afterwards let us apply the same inquiry to the individual, looking for a counterpart of the greater as it exists in the form of the less." In other words, he proposed to break up the concrete cases in which justice and injustice appear, in order to separate out or "extract" the single attribute of justice or injustice. The individual and concrete case was of no interest to him once it had yielded up the attribute which he was trying to abstract from it. This analysis which makes possible the extraction of a single attribute is the engine by which our philosophy and science have made all their gains.

In the books of Hebrew wisdom there is no case of reasoning analogous to this discussion between Socrates and his friends. The Hebrew mind proceeded entirely by empirical processes. In such passages as, " A wise man feareth and departeth from evil; but the fool rageth and is confident," or " A soft answer turneth away wrath; but grievous words stir up an-

[1] William James, *Psychology,* II, 329 ss.

ger," or " A wicked man travaileth with pain all the
days of his life,"—in all such assertions, each case
is seen only in its entirety: it is not broken up by
analysis in order that a single attribute,—of folly, of
conciliation, of wickedness,—may be picked out and
followed to its consequences. In these books of wisdom there is no trace of that patient comparison and
analysis of the separate concrete cases which are the
substance of direct experience, none of the sagacious
and deliberate stripping away of the unlike attributes
and qualities in order to reach a clear perception and
definition of the single quality or attribute of folly
or prudence or wisdom. In *Proverbs* the fool is
characterized by a number of Hebrew words: the
most common is that which describes him as dense
and headstrong; another conveys the idea of his de-
generateness and corruptness, another that he is
merely a simpleton. The words seem to be used as
synonyms; but there is never an attempt to compare
them, and by analysing typical cases under each to
define the common attribute which makes us think
and speak of such different varieties of fools all under the same general term. The like cases are
grouped together empirically and with such shrewdness that the empirical conclusions are as true to-day
as when they were written, two thousand years ago;
but neither here nor elsewhere in the Old Testament

is there any case of the further step which would
make reasoning possible.   We pass into a wholly
new realm of intellectual life, I am tempted to say
into a new stage of the evolution of man, when we
pass from the Old Testament wisdom to the debates of
Socrates and his friends and the intellectual life of
the modern world.

An immediate result of this lack of the reasoning
faculty appears in the absence from these books of all
ideas about the universe and of all secondary causes.
To their thought every fact and every action in the
universe proceeded direct from God: In *Job* such
diverse things as these are brought together:

> Canst thou bind the sweet influences of Pleiades,
> or loose the bands of Orion?
> Canst thou bring forth Mazzaroth in his season?
> or canst thou guide Arcturus with his sons?
> Knowest thou the ordinances of heaven? canst
> thou set the dominion thereof in the earth?
>
> .   .   .   .   .   .
>
> Canst thou send lightnings, that they may go,
> and say unto thee, Here we are?
>
> .   .   .   .   .   .
>
> Wilt thou hunt the prey for the lion? or fill the
> appetite of the young lions,
> When they couch in their dens, and abide in the
> covert to lie in wait?
> Who provideth for the raven his food? when his
> young ones cry unto God, they wander for lack of
> meat.[1]

[1] Job xxxviii. 31–33, 35, 39–41.

For the Hebrew thought, all things, small and great, rested immediately on the providence of God. Our modern thought has built up between the power of the Almighty and the phenomena so splendidly described in the later chapters of *Job* a structure of general laws and theories, such as the nebular hypothesis and the law of adaptation to environment, by which, as we say, we explain the phenomena. The Hebrew sage felt no need of such explanation, for he had no faculty for reasoning by which he could construct such secondary causes. We rest our universe on this structure of natural laws, just as the Indian cosmogony made the world rest on an elephant, which stood on a turtle: and just as this turtle was left standing on space, so in the end do our systems and natural laws leave the universe unexplained. The simpler thought of the Hebrew accepted the inscrutability of life in the first instance: for them the universe lay directly in the hand of the omnipotent God who had created it.

Now this absence of abstract reasoning had a determining effect on the character of all the Hebrew literature: and joined to the uniform concreteness of the language it explains the fact that the Hebrew wisdom was never free from emotional elements. In a language in which the words, as we saw in the last chapter, always carried the suggestion of physical sensation, the thought for which they were symbols could never have attained those clear and colorless reaches of mental life where emotion and personal affection give way to impersonal and abstract generalizations. Tied to such a language the Hebrew wisdom could never have disentangled itself from emotion. Our learning makes no real step until it has reached objects of thought which are unperturbed by feeling: for them such objects had no existence. Whether it be in the proverb, " A merry heart doeth good like a medicine, but a broken spirit drieth the bones," or in the passionate outcry of Job, " They shall lie down alike in the dust, and the worms shall cover them "—their wisdom was always a wisdom that touched the personal life and therefore involved the feelings.

This essentially emotional character of the Hebrew wisdom is further heightened by the poetical form of all the wisdom books of the Old Testament. For poetry, rising to a more heightened and figurative diction than prose, utters forth directly the potent feelings and intuitions which are the deepest springs of our thought and action. Still further, by means of its heightened and regular rhythm it can body forth some of those indefinable feelings which lie beyond the power of words in the realm of music. Poetry is thus of necessity more richly clothed with feeling than is prose: indeed, poetry without feeling and emotion is inconceivable. This poetical form of the Hebrew wisdom therefore still further emphasizes its difference from our science and philosophy. In a wisdom which because of its very form must be shot through and through with elements of sense and emotion there is little application for Bacon's favorite apothegm, "Dry light is ever the best"; it could never contemplate the facts of experience solely in the colorless light of the intellect; and having no abstract reasoning its literature could have neither science nor philosophy nor theology.

The best summary that I know of the habit of mind which lies behind these books of wisdom is contained in a letter of a Turkish Cadi to a friend of Layard, the explorer of Nineveh.

My illustrious Friend, and Joy of my Liver!

The thing you ask of me is both difficult and useless! Although I have passed all my days in this place, I have neither counted the houses nor have I inquired into the number of the inhabitants; and as to what one person loads on his mules and the other stows away in the bottom of his ship, that is no business of mine. But, above all, as to the previous history of this city, God only knows the amount of dirt and confusion that the infidels may have eaten before the coming of the sword of Islam. It were unprofitable for us to inquire into it.

O my soul! O my lamb! seek not after things which concern thee not. Thou camest unto us and we welcomed thee: go in peace.

Of a truth thou hast spoken many words; and there is no harm done, for the speaker is one and the listener is another. After the fashion of thy people thou hast wandered from one place to another, until thou art happy and content in none. We (praise be to God) were born here, and never desire to quit it. Is it possible, then, that the idea of a general intercourse between mankind should make any impression on our understandings? God forbid!

Listen, O my son! There is no wisdom equal unto the belief in God! He created the world, and shall we liken ourselves unto him in seeking to penetrate into the mysteries of his creation? Shall we say, behold this star spinneth round that star, and this other star with a tail goeth and cometh in so many years! Let it go! He from whose hand it came will guide and direct it.

But thou wilt say unto me, Stand aside, O man, for I am more learned than thou art, and have seen more things. If thou thinkest that thou art better in this respect than I am, thou art welcome. I praise God, I seek not that which I require not. Thou art learned in the things I care not for: and as for that which thou hast seen I defile it. Will much knowledge create thee a double belly, or wilt thou seek Paradise with thine eyes?

O my friend! if thou wilt be happy, say, There

is no God but God! Do no evil, and thus wilt thou fear neither man nor death; for surely thine hour will come!

The meek in spirit (El Fakir),
IMAUM ALI ZADÈ[1]

This is merely a modern rendering of the conclusion of *Ecclesiastes*:

When I applied mine heart to know wisdom, and to see the business that is done upon the earth: (for also there is that neither day nor night seeth sleep with his eyes:)

Then I beheld all the work of God, that a man cannot find out the work that is done under the sun: because though a man labour to seek it out, yet he shall not find it; yea farther; though a wise man think to know it, yet shall he not be able to find it.[2]

For the modern Oriental as for the ancient the beginning and the end of wisdom is the fear of God.

Yet one must not forget the other aspect of this literature we are studying, that these books have maintained their hold on men of all degrees of education through more than two thousand years, and that they have stood the test of translation into languages of totally different genius and structure—perhaps

[1] A. H. Layard, *Discoveries in Nineveh and Babylon*, N. Y., 1853, ρ. 663.

[2] Eccles viii. 16–17.

the most striking case of persistence in all the history of literature. Assuming, as always, the fact of inspiration, we may wonder how any medium of expression can be capable of conveying the same ideas to men of such different ages and stages of culture. The seeming paradox of the permanence of such works as these books of Hebrew wisdom may remind us that, after all, the power of abstract reasoning is only a small part of the faculties of our minds. To quote Professor James again: " Over immense departments of our thought we are still, all of us, in the savage state. Similarity operates in us, but abstraction has not taken place. We know what the present case is like, we know what it reminds us of, we have an intuition of the right course to take, if it be a practical matter. But analytic thought has made no tracks, and we cannot justify ourselves to others. In ethical, psychological, and æsthetic matters, to give a clear reason for one's judgment is universally recognized as a mark of rare genius." [1] In other words, underneath the purely intellectual faculties on which we moderns plume ourselves there lies the far greater and richer mass of our emotional and instinctive faculties. Even in the most highly civilized races instinct and emotion constitute all the deeper parts of the mental life; and it

[1] James, *Psychology*, II, 365.

is in this larger and fuller realm of consciousness that the Hebrew wisdom has its roots. By putting its thoughts in concrete words, which name always palpable things, and by clothing its words with poetical form, it gained the same permanence of meaning that the sensations and emotions themselves have, and will have until many ages have evolved man into an animal very different from us. The permanent place of these books in our literature would be proof enough, if proof were needed, that intuition without reasoning reaches deeper and more permanent truths than does reasoning alone, and of the further truth that if such deep and permanent truths are to be bodied forth in any language it must be concrete in its terms and endowed first of all with the power of expressing emotion. We read these books with the constant sense of the justness with which they sum up experience even for us to-day; but they do not even tend to inosculate with our modern efforts to unravel the mysteries of the universe. They trust wholly to intuition, and through this trust arrive at glimpses of the verities which lie behind the mask of experience.

CHAPTER V

THE EPISTLES OF THE NEW TESTAMENT

I

IF one, after reading in the Old Testament, passes on directly into the first three gospels one finds almost no change of literary atmosphere: in their mode of thought and of expression they belong to the Oriental world. The narrative, as we have seen, has almost the same concreteness of vocabulary and simplicity of sentence structure; and the apparatus of connectives between the parts is almost as limited. Even the literary form of the teachings of Jesus is closely like that of kindred forms in the Old Testament. If we make a rough classification of these teachings into aphorisms, practical injunctions, prophetic sayings, and parables we shall find each of these four forms paralleled in the Old Testament. For the aphorisms compare a passage from *St. Matthew*,

No man can serve two masters: for either he will hate the one, and love the other; or else he will hold to the one, and despise the other.   Ye cannot serve God and mammon.[1]

with one from *Proverbs*,

But the path of the just is as the shining light, that shineth more and more unto the perfect day.

The way of the wicked is as darkness: they know not at what they stumble.[2]

For the practical injunctions compare

Give not that which is holy unto the dogs, neither cast ye your pearls before swine, lest they trample them under their feet, and turn again and rend you,[3]

with that saying in *Proverbs* which was quoted by St. Paul in *Romans*:

If thine enemy be hungry, give him bread to eat; and if he be thirsty, give him water to drink:

For thou shalt heap coals of fire upon his head, and the Lord shall reward thee.[4]

For the prophetic denunciations compare these utterances of Jesus,

But woe unto you, scribes and Pharisees, hypocrites! for ye shut up the kingdom of heaven against men: for ye neither go in yourselves, neither suffer ye them that are entering to go in.

Woe unto you, scribes and Pharisees, hypo-

[1] Matt. vi. 24.   [2] Prov. iv. 18–19.
[3] Matt. vii. 6.   [4] Prov. xxv. 21–22.   Cf. Rom. xii. 20.

crites! for ye devour widows' houses, and for a pretence make long prayer: therefore ye shall receive the greater damnation.

with the following from *Isaiah*:

Woe unto them that call evil good, and good evil; that put darkness for light, and light for darkness; that put bitter for sweet, and sweet for bitter!

Woe unto them that are wise in their own eyes, and prudent in their own sight!

Woe unto them that are mighty to drink wine, and men of strength to mingle strong drink:

Which justify the wicked for reward, and take away the righteousness of the righteous from him! [2]

Finally, in using the parables as the vehicle of his teaching, Jesus was again making use of a form already familiar to the Jews from their own scriptures. Everyone knows the parable of the one ewe lamb which the prophet Nathan told to David.[3] Here are two more examples: the first is the little apologue of Jotham in the story of Abimelech:

And when they told it to Jotham, he went and stood in the top of mount Gerizim, and lifted up his voice, and cried, and said unto them, Hearken unto me, ye men of Shechem, that God may hearken unto you.

The trees went forth on a time to anoint a king

[1] Matt. xxiii. 13–14.   [2] Isa. v. 20–23.   [3] 2 Sam. xii.

over them; and they said unto the olive tree, Reign thou over us.

But the olive tree said unto them, Should I leave my fatness, wherewith by me they honour God and man, and go to be promoted over the trees?

And the trees said to the fig tree, Come thou, and reign over us.

But the fig tree said unto them, Should I forsake my sweetness, and my good fruit, and go to be promoted over the trees?

Then said the trees unto the vine, Come thou, and reign over us.

And the vine said unto them, Should I leave my wine, which cheereth God and man, and go to be promoted over the trees?

Then said all the trees unto the bramble, Come thou, and reign over us.

And the bramble said unto the trees, If in truth ye anoint me king over you, then come and put your trust in my shadow; and if not, let fire come out of the bramble, and devour the cedars of Lebanon.[1]

This second one is from the prophet Isaiah:

Now will I sing to my wellbeloved a song of my beloved touching his vineyard. My wellbeloved hath a vineyard in a very fruitful hill:

And he fenced it, and gathered out the stones thereof, and planted it with the choicest vine, and built a tower in the midst of it, and also made a

[1] Judges ix. 7–15.

winepress therein: and he looked that it should bring forth grapes, and it brought forth wild grapes.

And now, O inhabitants of Jerusalem, and men of Judah, judge, I pray you, betwixt me and my vineyard.

What could have been done more to my vineyard, that I have not done in it? wherefore, when I looked that it should bring forth grapes, brought it forth wild grapes?

And now, go to; I will tell you what I will do to my vineyard: I will take away the hedge thereof, and it shall be eaten up; and break down the wall thereof, and it shall be trodden down:

And I will lay it waste: it shall not be pruned nor digged; but there shall come up briers and thorns: I will also command the clouds that they rain no rain upon it.

For the vineyard of the Lord of hosts is the house of Israel, and the men of Judah his pleasant plant: and he looked for judgment, and behold oppression; for righteousness, but behold a cry.[1]

Thus all of these forms of discourse which Jesus made use of in his teaching are closely akin to forms found in the Old Testament. So far as literary classification goes these teachings of the Gospel cannot be separated from the Old Testament literature.

This likeness of the external form springs from a likeness in the forms of thought. In these sayings of Jesus we may trace the characteristics which I have

[1] Isa. v. 1–7.

already pointed out in the wisdom literature of the Old Testament. He states a fact or declares a precept, and leaves it with no attempt to develop its relations or draw out its implications. His discourses, like the poetical wisdom of the Old Testament, deal only with the solid and unanalysed facts of existence; consequently they have the same entire objectivity which we have found to be a trait of the Hebrew wisdom. In these teachings there are no secondary causes: God watches over the fall of a sparrow just as he created the universe and established laws and ordinances for men to obey. Therefore, though the language from which we get these teachings is Greek, the forms and the thought which they express are those of the Oriental world.

II

When we pass on, however, to the Fourth Gospel and to the epistles of St. Paul, we find a striking change. In the Fourth Gospel, though the sentences are almost as simple as in the first three, the thought is continuous through long passages. For example, in the story of the healing of the blind man the miracle, simply and briefly told, leads on to the examination of the man and his parents by the Pharisees, at the end of which

The man answered and said unto them, Why herein is a marvellous thing, that ye know not from whence he is, and yet he hath opened mine eyes.

Now we know that God heareth not sinners: but if any man be a worshipper of God, and doeth his will, him he heareth.

Since the world began was it not heard that any man opened the eyes of one that was born blind.

If this man were not of God, he could do nothing.

Then after Jesus has sought him out, and has spoken the discourse on the True Shepherd, the story comes back to its original starting point:

There was a division therefore again among the Jews for these sayings.

And many of them said, He hath a devil, and is mad; why hear ye him?

Others said, These are not the words of him that hath a devil. Can a devil open the eyes of the blind?[1]

The author of this gospel shows here as elsewhere a sense of structure and development for which one may look in vain in the first three gospels.

In the epistles of St. Paul and in *Hebrews* we get still farther away from the merely agglutinative coherence of the Old Testament, for here we find a rich and varied apparatus of words, phrases, and

[1] John ix–x.

clauses to express the reasoned sense of the transition
from one subject to another, and of the relations between them. *Romans* is full of such passages as,
" Therefore being justified by faith," or " Likewise
the Spirit also helpeth our infirmities "; and in *Hebrews* occurs such a passage as this:

> Now of the things which we have spoken this is
> the sum: We have such an high priest, who is set
> on the right hand of the throne of the Majesty
> in the heavens;
> A minister of the sanctuary, and of the true
> tabernacle, which the Lord pitched, and not man.[1]

Here the author consciously and explicitly brings to
an end a considerable stretch of reasoning by summing it up into an abstraction; and he uses his con-
nective clause, " Now of the things which we have
spoken this is the sum," to give notice of his purpose.
Such phrases and clauses express states of mind and
acts of thought which are not expressed at all in the
Old Testament. This conscious, defined sense of the
relations between ideas is as necessary and almost as
palpable a part of the stream of thought for us as are
our sensations of light or our perceptions of men and
animals; and the particles and phrases which express
them are therefore an inseparable part of our modern
language. To write on science or history or philos-

[1] Heb. viii. 1–2.

ophy without them would be like building a wall of brick without mortar; and their presence in these epistles is in itself enough to put the latter into another region of literature from that of the Old Testament and the first three gospels.

In the same way we find that the sentences of the Fourth Gospel and of the epistles are more complex and longer than those of the other gospels. In *St. John* one finds such sentences as this:

And as Moses lifted up the serpent in the wilderness even so must the Son of man be lifted up:

That whosoever believeth in him may have eternal life.[1]

In St. Paul, especially in the somewhat imperfect translation of the Authorised Version, the complexity of sentences is sometimes so great that the main thought is lost in its modifications and amplifications:

Unto me, who am less than the least of all saints, is this grace given, that I should preach among the Gentiles the unsearchable riches of Christ;

And to make all men see what is the fellowship of the mystery, which from the beginning of the world hath been hid in God, who created all things by Jesus Christ:

To the intent that now unto the principalities

[1] John iii. 14–16.

and powers in heavenly places might be known
by the church the manifold wisdom of God,

According to the eternal purpose which he
purposed in Christ Jesus our Lord:

In whom we have boldness and access with confidence by the faith of him.[1]

Such sentences body forth a far more complex state
of mind than the simple sentences of the Old Testament. Even in the simpler sentence which I have
just quoted from *St. John* the objective facts—
Moses, and the serpent in the wilderness, and Christ
crucified—are subordinated to the perception, now
clearly defined and abstracted, of the faith which
leads to salvation. This is a kind of writing, therefore, whose chief aim is to express not the solid realities of the external world, but to bring out the relations set up between them by thought; and such
sentences as these which we are considering com-
bine and recombine these facts in an endless variety
of ways in order to make clear these relations. We
have seen that in Hebrew a sentence could sometimes be complete without a verb: in this kind of
writing the verb and the grammatical structure of
the sentence may be the most important part of the
expression.

In like manner as one passes on from *St. Luke*

[1] Ephes. iii. 8–12.

into *St. John* one sees that the words are used with a new kind of significance:

> In him was life; and the life was the light of men. And the light shineth in darkness; and the darkness comprehended it not.[1]

Here *life* and *light* and *darkness* obviously have meanings far beyond their mere literal denotation: their force now is no longer merely in their physical signification; it is rather in their suggestions and implications. Their objective and every-day meaning is lost in their indefinably suggestive power. So all through this gospel, in *the well of water springing up into everlasting life, the good shepherd, the bread of life,* the unstudied similitudes of the other gospels have given place to suggestions of illimitable thoughts which trail clouds of mystical glory through the pages. In the epistles we meet still another class of words, which have even less counterpart in the Old Testament. Such words as *predestination, concupiscence, heresy, immutability* did not exist in the old Hebrew; yet in these writings of the New Testament such abstract words, like the complex sentences, are a necessity of expression. The epistles of St. Paul and *Hebrews* could not have been written in the vocabulary of *Proverbs* and *Job.*

[1] John i. 4–5.

Thus in the case of the words as in that of the structure of the chapters and of the sentences, the meaning is no longer, as in the Old Testament, limited to the statement of single propositions and injunctions resting on objective fact: the language is now pregnant with intellectual meanings, and it is used by writers who must strive to set forth these meanings clearly and exhaustively.

This difference between these epistles and the rest of the Bible is so essential that I will venture further to illustrate it. *Proverbs* has the verse:

> He that spareth the rod hateth his son: but he that loveth him chasteneth him betimes.[1]

St. Paul uses a closely related idea as follows:

> Now I say, That the heir, as long as he is a child, differeth nothing from a servant, though he be lord of all;
> But is under tutors and governors until the time appointed of the father.
> Even so we, when we were children, were in bondage under the elements of the world:
> But when the fulness of the time was come, God sent forth his Son, made of a woman, made under the law,
> To redeem them that were under the law, that we might receive the adoption of sons.

[1] Prov. xiii. 24.

And because ye are sons, God hath sent forth the Spirit of his Son into your hearts, crying, Abba, Father.

Wherefore thou art no more a servant, but a son; and if a son, then an heir of God through Christ.[1]

When we compare the two passages we see that the Hebrew sage stopped short with the utterance of the obvious truth, without searching out its consequences. St. Paul, on the other hand, had to search out and extract what is for his present purpose the essential attribute of the heirship, the state of dependence before the full inheritance. This sharp and controlling sense of the relation between the facts, distinct from the facts themselves, he could not have expressed in the downright directness of the Old Testament style.

For a second example we may consider the manner in which the author of *Hebrews* uses the ordinances of *Exodus* and *Leviticus* about the sacrifice and the building of the tabernacle. The priestly writers who filled in these portions of the Pentateuch with their great mass of precise and minute details were wholly preoccupied with the proper ordering of present realities. The reason for all their carefulness they assumed: they were planning a ritual which

[1] Gal. iv. 1–7.

should be worthy of the Lord God of Hosts. The writer of *Hebrews,* on the other hand, must find in these services a deeper and hidden meaning.

Then verily the first covenant had also ordinances of divine service, and a worldly sanctuary.

For there was a tabernacle made; the first, wherein was the candlestick, and the table, and the shewbread; which is called the sanctuary.

And after the second veil, the tabernacle which is called the Holiest of all;

Which had the golden censer, and the ark of the covenant overlaid round about with gold, wherein was the golden pot that had manna, and Aaron's rod that budded, and the tables of the covenant;

And over it the cherubims of glory shadowing the mercyseat; of which we cannot now speak particularly.

Now when these things were thus ordained, the priests went always into the first tabernacle, accomplishing the service of God.

But into the second went the high priest alone once every year, not without blood, which he offered for himself, and for the errors of the people:

The Holy Ghost this signifying, that the way into the holiest of all was not yet made manifest, while as the first tabernacle was yet standing:

Which was a figure for the time then present, in which were offered both gifts and sacrifices, that could not make him that did the service perfect, as pertaining to the conscience;

> Which stood only in meats and drinks, and divers washings, and carnal ordinances, imposed on them until the time of reformation.[1]

For such a thinker the external ordinances were overshadowed by the meaning of the symbols. His object of thought was no longer confined to the exact fulfillment of certain prescribed forms: he was concerned rather with implications, conclusions, and inferences drawn from a study of the objective facts of the old dispensation by abstraction and generalization.

It is the dominance in these epistles of the New Testament of this whole new range of thought and mental action that makes the wisdom literature of the Old Testament seem by comparison so remote and so primitive. Two fields of literature could hardly be more different; and the difference is due to the difference in interests, in thought, and in outlook between two ages of the world. In a word, when we pass from *Proverbs* and *Job* to *St. John* and *Romans* and *Hebrews* we have passed from the world of Solomon to the world of Socrates.

St. Paul himself summed up this whole difference in mental constitution between the Jews and the world of Western thought when he wrote in *1 Corinthians*:

[1] Heb. ix. 1–10.

> For the Jews require a sign, and the Greeks seek after wisdom:
>
> But we preach Christ crucified, unto the Jews a stumbling block, and unto the Greeks foolishness.[1]

To the Jews the crucifixion was a stumbling block because it destroyed all supernatural sanction of the new law. For their minds the new law which Jesus proclaimed could draw its authority only from his own personal authority and from the mighty works with which it was accompanied: as is said in *St. John ii. 23*, " many believed in his name when they saw the miracles which he did." When what had seemed to some of them such a supernatural sanction was shattered by the miserable death of Jesus on the cross they could see no reason to accept him as the Messiah. To the Greeks, on the other hand, the crucifixion was foolishness because it led nowhere; because in itself it gave them no new understanding of the nature of this new dispensation which should illuminate it and make it its own sanction. To them the death of Jesus was merely futile, for it gave them no new insight into the secrets of the universe, and brought no new means of understanding life. St. Paul's special mission was the translation of a gospel which had been first delivered in terms of Jewish and Oriental thought into terms of

[1] 1 Cor. i. 22–23.

Greek and modern thought; and to fulfil this mission he had to write in a manner very different from that of *Proverbs* and *Job*: men trained in the philosophy of Socrates would never have accepted as an explanation of the world such a collection of random and heterogeneous aphorisms as that contained in the former, or a series of hardly connected poems like the latter. Such a wisdom could give no aid to men who were trying to define the nature of goodness, for it offered no new means of harmonizing the universe and ordering the welter of experience into an intellectual system. The Greek mind therefore would have little interest in the new religion unless it offered a new and deeper understanding of the world and so carried its own sanction for the new and revolutionary laws of conduct which followed from it.

Thus these epistles had something of the universal aim of philosophy. St. Paul, especially in polemic passages where he is defending and justifying the gospel of Christ, felt the necessity of harmonizing the old dispensation with the new. He must show that there was no " catastrophe," as the geologists would say, in the way the old faith had been swallowed up to make place for the new. His effort was to prove that the new dispensation was an outgrowth and fulfillment of the old.

Know ye therefore, that they which are of faith, the same are the children of Abraham.

And the scripture, foreseeing that God would justify the heathen through faith, preached before the gospel unto Abraham, saying, In thee shall all nations be blessed.

So then they which be of faith are blessed with faithful Abraham.

For as many as are of the works of the law, are under the curse: for it is written, Cursed is every one that continueth not in all things which are written in the book of the law to do them.

But that no man is justified by the law in the sight of God, it is evident: for, The just shall live by faith.

And the law is not of faith: but, The man that doeth them shall live in them.

Christ hath redeemed us from the curse of the law, being made a curse for us: for it is written, Cursed is every one that hangeth on a tree:

That the blessing of Abraham might come on the Gentiles through Jesus Christ; that we might receive the promise of the Spirit through faith.[1]

His mode of reasoning he took over from the somewhat literal allegorizing of the Jewish rabbis and the mystical allegorizing of the Hellenistic Jews, for he was a Jew to the core; but where they allegorized the past history of Israel to find fantastic similitudes for present facts, or for doctrines which

[1] Gal. iii. 7–14.

were already formulated (as Philo found in the Pentateuch an allegorical statement of all the achievements of Greek philosophy), St. Paul uses such similitudes as a means of symbolizing and bodying forth glimpses of larger and pregnant truths which can be suggested but not defined:

> Which things are an allegory: for these are the two covenants; the one from the mount Sinai, which gendereth to bondage, which is Agar.
>
> For this Agar is mount Sinai in Arabia, and answereth to Jerusalem which now is, and is in bondage with her children.
>
> But Jerusalem which is above is free, which is the mother of us all.[1]

The difference is similar to that between metaphysics and poetry: the former strives to define absolute principles of the universe and of existence; the latter stirs the imagination to seeing them by intuition. The rabbinical learning was occupied with establishing and justifying doctrines which were already known: St. Paul sets forth new truths in the terms of the history of Israel. Always, however, his aim was to find a way in which the new and the old might be brought together into a single principle which would unify and harmonize them. He had, in part at any rate, the instinct for understanding

[1] Gal. iv. 24–26.

his universe which is so distinct from being satisfied with mere obedience to the law and the prophets.

This spontaneous desire to bring diverse facts into a single system of thought, and to show an inherent connection between the objects of experience through an underlying unity of idea, appears even more clearly in the *Gospel According to St. John* and *Hebrews*, works which show the deep influence of St. Paul and of his ways of thought. *Hebrews* shows the way in which the new covenant given through the Son superseded the old:

> But now hath he obtained a more excellent ministry, by how much also he is the mediator of a better covenant, which was established upon better promises.
>
> For if that first covenant had been faultless, then should no place have been sought for the second.
>
> For finding fault with them, he saith, Behold, the days come, saith the Lord, when I will make a new covenant with the house of Israel and with the house of Judah:
>
> .   .   .   .   .   .
>
> In that he saith, A new covenant, he hath made the first old. Now that which decayeth and waxeth old is ready to vanish away.[1]
>
> And every priest standeth daily ministering and offering oftentimes the same sacrifices, which can never take away sins:

[1] Heb. viii. 6–8, 13.

But this man, after he had offered one sacrifice for sins for ever, sat down on the right hand of God;

From henceforth expecting till his enemies be made his footstool.

For by one offering he hath perfected for ever them that are sanctified.[1]

Here theology has definitely begun, for this writer is consciously expounding a system in which the relations of the old and the new shall be made clear and rational, and in which both the teachings of the law and the prophets and the new revelation through Jesus shall have their ordered and recognisable places.

The same impelling need to make the gospel bring order out of an otherwise unintelligible universe appears in the prologue to *St. John*:

In the beginning was the Word, and the Word was with God, and the Word was God.

The same was in the beginning with God.

All things were made by him; and without him was not any thing made that was made.

In him was life; and the life was the light of men.[2]

Here the universal principle by which the whole universe could be thought into a single system is found in the mystical idea of Christ as the Word.   This is a philosophical and metaphysical operation of

[1] Heb. x. 11–14.   [2] John i. 1–4.

thought; and this step taken, Christian thinkers are on the same ground as the philosophers of Greece, for now they can apprehend the universe as a single whole.

When we turn to the moral teachings of St. Paul we see that as a necessary consequence of this difference in thought they differ in form from the teachings in the first three gospels and those of the *Epistle of St. James*. In these the teachings take the form of independent precepts, ordinarily not based on any other reason than the obvious sanction of the divine command. St. Paul, on the other hand, always shows that the new rules of life which he is enforcing are necessary results of the new conception of the world which underlies the gospel. In *Colossians* he declares:

> If ye then be risen with Christ, seek those things which are above, where Christ sitteth on the right hand of God.
>
> Set your affection on things above, not on things on the earth.
>
> For ye are dead, and your life is hid with Christ in God.[1]

In the first three gospels peace and forgiveness are a matter of divine injunction. "If thy brother trespass against thee, rebuke him; and if he repent

[1] Col. iii. 1–3.

forgive him." St. Paul, summing up in *Galatians* the practical and positive side of Christianity, declares:

> But the fruit of the Spirit is love, joy, peace, longsuffering, gentleness, goodness, faith,
>
> Meekness, temperance: against such there is no law.
>
> And they that are Christ's have crucified the flesh with the affections and lusts.
>
> If we live in the Spirit, let us also walk in the Spirit.[1]

Everywhere in his epistles he shows that the new life of the Christian follows of necessity from the new truths which he has accepted. In other words his writings show the mental workings of the abstract reasoner, not merely that of the intuitive thinker.

III

Nevertheless, one would never put St. Paul's writings in the same class with those of modern philosophy or theology, and this not merely because he was a Jew, or because of the difference in power of inspiration and of the freshness and importance of the message; for though he uses the forms of speech which belong to modern thought he uses them

[1] Gal. v. 22–25.

in a very different way. His epistles, except perhaps *Romans,* show little predetermined plan: their progress from one idea to another seems often to follow the impulse of the moment rather than a single and firmly grasped idea. His sentences, as we have seen, frequently run away with themselves and end in a manner that he could hardly have foreseen when he started them; and the vocabulary, though containing many abstract words, is even more generally characterized by the figurative use of concrete words. Indeed, the most striking characteristic of his style is the way in which passages of reasoning soar away into bursts of splendid eloquence which have far more of the nature of poetry than of scientific precision. Thus in *Romans,* after the careful exposition of the life of the flesh and the life of the spirit and predestination, he suddenly breaks away into the triumphant declaration of faith:

Who shall separate us from the love of Christ? shall tribulation, or distress, or persecution, or famine, or nakedness, or peril, or sword?

As it is written, For thy sake we are killed all the day long; we are accounted as sheep for the slaughter.

Nay, in all these things we are more than conquerors through him that loved us.

For I am persuaded, that neither death, nor life,

nor angels, nor principalities, nor powers, nor
things present, nor things to come,

Nor height, nor depth, nor any other creature,
shall be able to separate us from the love of God,
which is in Christ Jesus our Lord.[1]

Again in *1 Corinthians*, after the exposition of the
church as the mystical body of Christ, his style rises
unconsciously to the more poetical and heightened
diction of the chapter on charity:

Though I speak with the tongues of men and of
angels, and have not charity, I am become as
sounding brass, or a tinkling cymbal.

And though I have the gift of prophecy, and
understand all mysteries, and all knowledge; and
though I have all faith, so that I could remove
mountains, and have not charity, I am nothing.

And though I bestow all my goods to feed the
poor, and though I give my body to be burned,
and have not charity, it profiteth me nothing.

Charity suffereth long, and is kind; charity
envieth not; charity vaunteth not itself, is not
puffed up,

Doth not behave itself unseemly, seeketh not her
own, is not easily provoked, thinketh no evil;

Rejoiceth not in iniquity, but rejoiceth in the
truth;

Bareth all things, believeth all things, hopeth
all things, endureth all things.[2]

[1] Rom. viii. 35–39.   [2] 1 Cor. xiii. 1–7.

And in the most eloquent passage in all his writings, the great proof of immortality, the style, beginning at a level which even for St. Paul is distinguished by a certain restrained intensity of feeling, rises gradually until it breaks forth into the sheer cry of exultation at the end:

> So when this corruptible shall have put on incorruption, and this mortal shall have put on immortality, then shall be brought to pass the saying that is written, Death is swallowed up in victory.
>
> O death, where is thy sting? O grave, where is thy victory?
>
> The sting of death is sin; and the strength of sin is the law.
>
> But thanks be to God, which giveth us the victory through our Lord Jesus Christ.[1]

If theology be a science this constant falling back on the figurative to express his ideas removes St. Paul from the ranks of the theologians; for it shows that he was setting forth glimpses of truths too great and transcendent to be reduced to system. He trusts to the emotional implications of things rather than to the cool and abstract inferences drawn from them by rigidly logical processes. We have seen that the use of concrete words carries with it inevitably some appeal to the emotions, and it is only as abstraction

[1] Cor. xv. 54–57.

approaches the rarefaction of mathematics or of pure logic that all element of the emotional is stripped away. With St. Paul so much of the expression lies in the marvellous power of the figures of speech, that we seem to be turning our backs on modern thought, and reverting to the methods of thought and of expression of the Old Testament. In this same great chapter of *1 Corinthians* he makes no pause to sum up his thought in abstractions:

But some man will say, How are the dead raised up? and with what body do they come?

Thou fool, that which thou sowest is not quickened, except it die:

And that which thou sowest, thou sowest not that body that shall be, but bare grain, it may chance of wheat, or of some other grain:

But God giveth it a body as it hath pleased him, and to every seed his own body.

. . . . . .

There is one glory of the sun, and another glory of the moon, and another glory of the stars: for one star differeth from another star in glory.

So also is the resurrection of the dead. It is sown in corruption; it is raised in incorruption:

It is sown in dishonour; it is raised in glory: it is sown in weakness; it is raised in power:

It is sown a natural body; it is raised a spiritual body. There is a natural body; and there is a spiritual body.

And so it is written, the first man Adam was made a living soul; the last Adam was made a quickening spirit.[1]

Here the great truths lie rather in the connotation of the words, in their implications, associations and uplifting suggestions, than in their literal meaning; and if these clouds of feeling were stripped away the value and stimulating power of the passage would fall dead.

IV

All this is merely another way of saying that the language of St. Paul is largely mystical; and in this respect his writings go with portions of *Hebrews*, and especially with the *Gospel according to St. John* and the *Epistles of St. John*. The word *mystical*, however, is so vague a description that we must come to a closer understanding of its significance. And a clearer understanding and definition of the mystical habit of thought and expression will help us to define more exactly the literary character of these portions of the New Testament and so to appreciate better their place and importance in English literature. Here, as in the last chapter, we shall get light on our problem from the modern understanding of the faculty of reasoning.

[1] 1 Cor. xv. 35–38, 41–45.

I have shown that reasoning rests on the ability first to break up the concrete facts of experience into the various attributes and qualities by which we know them, and then to see that a similarity which has been vaguely apprehended by intuition springs from the necessary concomitants of some one of these attributes. To take a simple example from our own subject, reasoning about the composition of the Pentateuch proceeded first by the extraction of certain common attributes and qualities, such as abstractness, formal precision, and an interest narrowed to matters of ecclesiastical organization and chronology; these attributes once extracted led to the assumption of a document marked throughout by these attributes which could be separated from the rest of the work; then by following up the consequences of these attributes it became evident that this document must come from a school of priests late in the history of Israel. The final inference depends on the ability to do two things: first, to single out and define the attributes in such a way that they can be referred to without ambiguity wherever they occur; and second, the ability to follow out their consequences without allowing feeling or other extraneous considerations to creep in and confuse the result.

When we apply this test to these semi-mystical writings of the New Testament we shall find that they are not the products of a strictly defined reasoning. At most they show the ability to see that the similarity between ideas is significant and pregnant, and to make a partial analysis and a vague application of its results and further consequences. In this partial power of reasoning they show a more developed form of thought than that reflected by the wisdom books of the Old Testament: but still a form of thought which stops short of the precision and definiteness of modern scientific reasoning.

A comparison of a passage from *St. Matthew* with one from *St. John* based on a similar figure will make clearer what I mean. In *St. Matthew* we read:

> Ye are the light of the world. A city that is set on an hill cannot be hid.
> Neither do men light a candle, and put it under a bushel, but on a candlestick; and it giveth light unto all that are in the house.
> Let your light so shine before men, that they may see your good works, and glorify your father which is in heaven.[1]

With this consider the following from the prologue to *St. John*:

> In him was life; and the life was the light of men.
> And the light shineth in darkness; and the darkness comprehended it not.[2]

[1] Matt. v. 14–16. [2] John i. 4–5.

And also the following:

> Then Jesus said unto them, Yet a little while is
> the light with you. Walk while ye have the light,
> lest darkness come upon you: for he that walketh
> in darkness knoweth not whither he goeth.
>
> While ye have light, believe in the light, that
> ye may be the children of light.[1]

In these two passages though the figure is the same,
the treatment is entirely different: in the former we
have a simple form of the parable, in the latter a
typical case of the symbolism by which the mystical
way of thought proceeds, but also simple. In the former the similarity between the light of the candle
and the example of the righteous man is felt intui-
tively, but not analysed at all: both sides of the similarity consist of concrete experience, of experience
in the round, as it were. In the other case the concrete fact of the candle has disappeared and given
place to a single attribute, the light. This attribute
leads directly to further consequences; following this
attribute, light, one is pointed on to the way in which
Christ has in like manner altered the world by his
coming; and this aspect of his manifestation is in
part explained and made clearer by the train of
thought. To put the matter in another way, in the
parable the similarity between diverse things which is

[1] John xii. 35–36.

the substance of most thought is assumed as a simple
and obvious fact; there is no effort to analyse it, to
see the nature of the likeness, no effort to develop it
in order to see what further consequences are involved in the likeness. In the symbolic use of *St.
John*, on the other hand, the points of likeness seem
to be detached from the total sensation and stated as
a single attribute; on this attribute the attention is
then fixed, so that the resemblance is seen to go
deeper and farther. The latter represents, then, a
more developed form of thought, one which sees more
points differentiated in its objects, as it were, more
perspective, more consequences in them. And getting a glimpse of these further resemblances and consequences it comes to a more or less vague feeling of
the nature of the similarity which binds the facts together, and a more or less vague feeling of the
further results which follow on that special nature.
It differs from the older, Oriental mode of thought
in that it has a partial idea of the nature of the
single character which it analyses out, and a partially
defined idea of the directions in which it leads. It
differs from modern, Western thought in that neither
the exact nature of the attribute nor the exact nature
of its consequences is reached. If we should recur to
Socrates's search for the essential nature of justice
we should see how deeply this mystical thought dif-

fers from really abstract reasoning. It may be conceived as lying half-way, as it were, between the
Oriental, purely intuitive habit of thought and the
modern, thoroughly analytical. It is by no means
isolated: St. Paul's contemporary, Philo Judæus,
carried the mysticism to fantastic results; and some
of the works of Plato and even of Aristotle run off
into such figurative forms as to be hardly distinguish-
able from myths or allegories. Such cases probably
mean that intuition ran away from reasoning, and
gave glimpses of deep underlying truths too vast or
too nebulous to be seized and made definite by the analytic reason.

The kind of scientific man whose chief boast is
his hard-headedness would probably compare mysticism and all its works to the rumored feat of the
Hindoo magicians, who, we are told, standing on the
bare and packed earth of a market place throw an end
of rope into the air, and then climbing up it hand
over hand disappear into the void of heaven: so mysticism, starting from the similitudes of real things,
in a moment eludes our grasp and loses itself in
clouds where it is vain to try to follow it. The figure
would have much truth, especially if we recognize
its inadequacy to suggest the whole truth. The appeal of mysticism is of necessity limited, and for most
of us very narrowly so; in this respect, as I shall

point out in the chapter on the apocalypses, it is like the appeal of music. Sooner or later it loses itself in a region which is for almost everyone an unprofitable void. On the other hand, as Professor James has shown in his *Varieties of Religious Experience*, the hither borders of this region are also those of all religious and spiritual experience; and what value mysticism has it derives from its ability to lift the soul to the certitude of such experiences. The capacity of men for such spiritual experiences differs; and in consequence each one of us sets a different estimate on the profitableness of mysticism. But these writings of the New Testament will be a witness, except to the kind of man of science who swallows his Herbert Spencer whole, that the things of the spirit lie part way at any rate within the confines of another order of experience.

Coming back to a somewhat more sober way of looking at the subject, and considering it from the side of the style, we can see that the chief distinction between this mystical reason and the modern analytical reasoning is that in the former there is a large and inseparable element of the emotional. Psychologists to-day, as we have seen, hold that feeling is inseparable from the sensations; and it is a truth in literature that the appeal to the emotions must be made through the concrete. It is only as the abstract approaches the rarefaction of the mathematical or of pure logic that all element of the emotional is stripped away. Now since the mystical reasoning is so largely figurative, it is couched in terms of the concrete, and therefore retains the strong emotional coloring which goes with the concrete. In the end it is still bound to terms which are more than half constituted of the non-rational element of feeling. In the figure of the light which is so dear to the author of the Fourth Gospel one feels that the connotation of the figure,—all the cloud of feelings and associations which throng about our idea of light,—is more important than the actual denotation. If the idea were made really abstract its value and stimulating power would fade away. Mysticism is like poetry in that without emotion it would be a contradiction in terms.

Here again, then, we get back to the same truth which lies behind the wisdom books of the Old Testament: from the point of view of literature power lies in the capacity of the written word to stir up feeling. Therefore in literature Bacon's apothegm, "Dry light is ever the best," has no place. The sensations and emotions of man, which do not change with the ages, are the permanent foundation of the mental life: the glory of the sun and the moon and the stars affects us in the same way that it did St. Paul; and we to-day at the call of his words rise on similar uprushes of feeling to a region above the dust and turmoil of the present life. He had the genius for expressing these inexpressible thoughts; and he does so now by the pregnant figure of the sowing of the grain, now by a pure ejaculation of the triumph of the soul over matter, as in the cry, "O death, where is thy sting? O grave, where is thy victory?"

We can go a step farther, I think, without stepping out of a strictly literary study of these great masterpieces of expression into the field of theology: we can say that St. Paul was compelled to be partly mystical in the sense in which I have used the word here. If the message which was burned into his soul on the road to Damascus was of eternal significance, if it concerned the inscrutable things of God, it could not be reduced to the definiteness which some philosophers vainly hope to reach. At best man can attain only to glimpses of such truths, and then necessarily by intuition, not by reasoning; and such glimpses of supernatural truths can be communicated to other men through words only by such nobly figurative language as St. Paul had the genius to use: for by such language alone can the imagination be set soaring. The history of all literature will bear out the conclusion that follows from the study of the Bible, its greatest monument in English, that reasoning is

here impotent.   It is only by virtue of the deep infusion of feeling which always goes with knowledge
attained by intuition that the human mind can soar
to the eternal and the infinite.   St. Paul himself has
said it once for all: " Now we see as in a glass,
darkly ": and these shadowy glimpses of the transcendent realities can be brought within the powers of
language only by the adumbrations and kindling figures of a half-poetic speech.

CHAPTER VI

THE PROPHECY

I

WE have seen in discussing the other forms of the Biblical literature that the narrative, except for a small portion of the *Acts of the Apostles*, is extremely simple in style, and that it has neither complications nor subtleties of construction; that the poetry, with an equal simplicity, sets forth directly, through powerful and concrete imagery, the fundamental and lasting emotions of mankind, but that, like the narrative, it never arrived at the point of creating characters and situations; that the wisdom literature of the Old Testament, limited like the narrative and the poetry by the nature of the Hebrew language, never arrived at reasoning in the modern sense, but stopped content with the truths which can be reached by intuition: and that it is not until we reach the Fourth Gospel and the epistles of St. Paul that we pass over to the mental life of the modern

world. Even here, however, we found that the most
stirring passages revert to intuition, since they deal
with matters where man's reason flags helpless. With
the prophecy we come back to the Old Testament,
and to a form which as literature is the most typically
and distinctively Biblical of all.

Of all the writings in the English Bible these
oracles of the prophets are the most foreign and the
least like anything that we have in modern literature: as they appear here they belong to a vanished
past. Men are still born who have glimpses of the
everlasting verities to communicate to other men; but
they deliver them in forms wholly different. The
prophet of the Old Testament was at once preacher
and statesman, seer of visions and guide in the affairs
of the nation, reformer of religion, moralist, and
poet. The prophecies contain deliverances on all subjects, from new revelations of the nature of Jehovah
to the practical questions of tithes or the keeping of
the Sabbath. Yet through them all, as we have seen,
the normal form is poetical, and they all show the
parallelism of the Hebrew poetry. At the very beginning of *Isaiah* there is a good example:

> Hear, O heavens; and give ear, O earth: for the
> Lord hath spoken, I have nourished and brought
> up children, and they have rebelled against
> me.

The ox knoweth his master, and the ass his master's crib: but Israel doth not know, my people doth not consider.

Ah sinful nation, a people laden with iniquity, a seed of evildoers, children that are corrupters: they have forsaken the Lord, they have provoked the Holy One of Israel unto anger, they are gone away backward.[1]

A statesman nowadays in public utterances betakes himself to extended and orderly exposition: the statesman-prophets of Israel often saw their messages as a vision, and they summed up the pith of the situation in a brief oracle in highly poetic form. Nowadays poets are men apart from the multitude, whose writings rarely touch public opinion. To understand the position of Amos and Isaiah and Jeremiah we must think of them as poets whose words had practical force on the life of their times, whose utterances swayed public opinion, and guided the action of kings.

The prophets themselves as they appear in different parts of the Old Testament were of the greatest variety of character. The highest type were farseeing statesmen; yet they passed under the same name as the " sons of prophets " who were sometimes, so far as we can tell, not very different from the der-

[1] Isa. i. 2–4.

vishes of to-day. An incident in the story of Saul
shows the range of the word in these ancient times:

> And he went thither to Naioth in Ramah: and
> the Spirit of God was upon him also, and he went
> on, and prophesied, until he came to Naioth in
> Ramah.
> And he stripped off his clothes also, and prophe-
> sied before Samuel in like manner, and lay down
> naked all that day and all that night. Wherefore
> they say, Is Saul also among the prophets?[1]

This is a long way from the dignity of Isaiah before
Hezekiah. We know directly very little about the
prophets; but it is significant that the same word is
used for so dervish-like an action as this and for the
lofty utterances of the greatest statesmen and thinkers of Israel. It seems to have implied some sort of
abnormal or supernormal state of mind. The phrase
which the prophets use themselves is perhaps as definite a description of this state of mind as we can get:
" the hand of the Lord was upon me." I do not
know that modern psychology adds much by explain-
ing that the message must have surged up from the
subliminal portion of the consciousness, and that it
took the form of automatic speech. Such a description only says in a more elaborate way that the mes-

[1] 1 Sam. xix. 23–24.

sage came to the prophet through no volition of his own, and that in the moulding of the message his conscious thought played no part. In the New Testament the visions of St. Paul belong to the same class of phenomena:

> It is not expedient for me doubtless to glory. I will come to visions and revelations of the Lord.
>
> I knew a man in Christ above fourteen years ago, (whether in the body, I cannot tell; or whether out of the body, I cannot tell: God knoweth;) such an one caught up to the third heaven.
>
> And I knew such a man, (whether in the body, or out of the body, I cannot tell: God knoweth;)
>
> How that he was caught up into paradise, and heard unspeakable words, which it is not lawful for a man to utter.[1]

We may suppose that the prophets of the Old Testament received their messages in a like state of exaltation, when the depths of the soul overflowed the ordinary bounds of consciousness and floated them into a higher region of illumination.

We have seen that the wisdom of the Hebrews never passed beyond the stage of intuition to that of abstract reasoning. This prophecy is therefore an even more typical part of the Old Testament literature, since here the conscious effort of the prophet contributed nothing. In the prophecies we

[1] 2 Cor. xii. 1–4.

meet a form of literature which has no kindred in our modern world. The self-induced trances of the dervishes are modern examples of a phenomenon which has come down unchanged from a remote antiquity in the East; and though such inarticulate trances are a long way from the inspired utterances with which we are dealing, they help us to understand the broken utterance and the incoherence of thought in a prophet like Hosea. Nowadays and in our Western world we have an instinctive distrust of a man whose mental equilibrium is uncertain. We forget too much perhaps that such great geniuses of our modern world as Cæsar and Napoleon I were subject to emotional upsets of a form which doctors describe as epileptoid. And in the New Testament the writings of St. Paul, which seem so near our own day, are the work of a man who, as we have just seen by his own testimony, was subject to trances. Like the prophets of the Old Testament he saw visions and was wrapt out of himself into a state in which his mind was opened wide to the messages from the unseen world. In this matter of the prophecy he may furnish for us the connecting link between the Old Testament and the New.

At the same time it must be borne in mind that though the prophecy is the most Oriental and foreign of all the forms of literature with which we deal, yet it is the portion of the literature through which the Jewish nation had its strongest influence on the thought of the world. Through the prophets were delivered the great messages by which this small and forlorn nation changed the course of civilization. Amos and Hosea and Isaiah first proclaimed the doctrine that Jehovah, the God of Israel, was the God who ruled all the nations of the earth; and two centuries later by a direct and necessary development of this teaching, the great unknown prophet whom we may call the Isaiah of the Exile, advancing to a higher plane of truth, proclaimed Jehovah as the one God, who made the heavens and the earth, beside whom the gods of the heathen were silly stocks and stones. And in the apocalypse, which developed naturally out of the prophecy, the Jews advanced to the doctrine of the future life and of the immortality of the soul. Thus in these forms which we are considering in this chapter we are dealing with the form of utterance in which more than in any other was uttered forth the heart and the soul of the Jewish race.

II

The prophecy is, however, harder to study than any other portion of the Bible since as it stands in our Bible it is wholly disordered. The Jews of the Exile and of the next centuries gathered the fragments of the prophecy which remained to them into four great books, which came to have the names *Isaiah, Jeremiah, Ezekiel,* and *the Twelve.* Of these *Ezekiel* is the only book which is confined to the prophecies of a single prophet. *Isaiah* is almost more miscellaneous in contents than is the book of the *Twelve*; into it were gathered fragments of prophecy and prophetic writing which dated from a generation before Isaiah, before 750 B.C., to the end of the Persian period and the beginning of the Greek, about 300 B.C.: and these are all thrown together without regard to chronology or authorship. Any thorough understanding of the books of the prophets is therefore dependent on a careful study of them with the help of some manual of Biblical introduction. In this way only can one sort out the different fragments and arrange them in something like a chronological order. The study is worth the effort, for the oracles of these ancient prophets have a rugged grandeur and elevation which set them apart as almost the highest peak in all the writings of men; and the individual prophets have characteristics which can only be brought out by recognizing the period from which their utterances spring. At the same time there is no more inspiring passage in all history than the way in which the prophets of this small people, a helpless buffer state between the great empires of the Nile and the Euphrates, at each crisis in their history rose triumphant above the limitations of temporal weakness and distress. In such a study as this, however, I must assume the fruits of this study and discuss only the larger outlines of its results.

With the chronological order of the prophecies once restored, one can see a regular development of the literary forms which is curiously analogous to that of other literatures. It seems to be a general law that any school of literature rises to its climax when the power of thought and the power of feeling are justly balanced, when the writer has a clear and firm perception of facts and their meaning, and at the same time when this perception of fact is fired and fused by the heat of feeling and imagination; when the intellectual faculties, cooler and more controlled, study the facts and formulate their meaning, and the emotional faculties, warmer and more impulsive, add momentum and intense feeling to this understanding and by the spontaneous and unforeseen leap of intuition rise to the apprehension of new truths and to the feeling for overtones of meaning often only imperfectly articulate. As such a school breaks up, these two forces tend to split apart and to produce two schools, in one of which the intellectual faculties predominate and in the other the emotional. The

Shakspere period is the most notable example in English literature. Shakspere beyond any other writer in English joined to the grasp on the solid and concrete facts of life and the keenest and most penetrating perception of their meaning a power of feeling and a charm of form which fused and transfigured the facts into a stream of living beauty. It is hard to say whether one thinks first of the firm and definite outline of his characters or of the glowing beauty of his poetry and its rich halo of suggestiveness. In the generation succeeding him these two constituents of the poetic power fall apart. On the one hand there is the school of Drayton, of Brown, of Wither and the Fletchers, and the other mellifluous poets of the post-Elizabethan time, whose verse has the flowing and gracious beauty that belongs to a golden age, yet whose thought is so thin and reflected as to leave little lasting impression on one's mind. On the other hand there is the school of Donne and the so-called metaphysicians, whose intensity of thought lost itself in subtle intricacies and involution and who lacked the power of clothing their thought with clear and beautiful words. A like differentiation might be made out for the poets of the nineteenth century, starting with the great school of Wordsworth, Coleridge, Shelley, Keats, and Byron, which splits in our own time into the two tendencies shown by Tennyson and

Browning, of flowing beauty of form on the one hand, and rugged and whimsical intricacy of thought on the other. We are too near these latter poets to work out the parallel in detail; but the history of English literature clearly establishes the law. In a school of poetry the decay and breaking up come as the forces of thought and of feeling separate from each other.

A development closely akin to this appears in the external form of these books of the prophecy. The first great prophets show the penetrating and statesmanlike understanding of fact fused by the intensity of their emotion and transfigured to words of glowing fire. Two hundred years later, in the prophets of the time of the Exile one finds the firm and earnest perception of fact on the one hand in Ezekiel, Haggai and Malachi, and on the other the soaring imagination and emotion of the Isaiah of the Exile, and the mystical visions of Zechariah; but by this time we find no example of the two forces fused into one.

This change in the outward manifestation of the gift I will set forth at some little length, then I will return to the general characteristics of all the prophets and discuss what seems to be the essence of their character in our literature. In the next chapter we shall see how the prophecy developed naturally into another form of literature, known as the apocalypse, which gave to the New Testament its climax in *Rev-*

elation. It is significant of the character of all the literature we are studying that the element of the prophecy which thus rose up into new life is that which embodies emotion and intuition, and that as it soared to its highest reaches, more and more it cut loose from the trammels of fact and the limitations of time and space.

The writings of the prophets as we have them begin with Amos, Hosea, and Isaiah, in the middle of the eighth century B.C., the time when under Jeroboam II of Northern Israel and Azariah of Judah, the two little kingdoms flickered up into a final period of prosperity and apparent independence before the great power of the Euphrates aroused itself and extended its borders once more to meet those of Egypt. Of these we may take the prophecies of Amos and Isaiah as examples of the prophecy at its strongest and noblest.

The first appearance of Amos, a rough herdsman from the hills of Judah, before the wealthy and cultivated nobles of Samaria, men grown fat with riches and luxury, is a most dramatic incident. He begins with a series of denunciations against their hereditary enemies:

> Thus saith the Lord; For three transgressions of Damascus, and for four, I will not turn away the punishment thereof ; because they have

threshed Gilead with threshing instruments of iron:

But I will send a fire into the house of Hazael, which shall devour the palaces of Ben-hadad.

I will break also the bar of Damascus, and cut off the inhabitant from the plain of Aven, and him that holdeth the sceptre from the house of Eden: and the people of Syria shall go into captivity unto Kir, saith the Lord.[1]

Then he follows with denunciations of Gaza and Ashdod, of Tyrus, of Edom because " he did pursue his brother with the sword, and did cast off all pity, and his anger did tear perpetually, and he kept his wrath for ever ", of Ammon, and of Moab, " because he burned the bones of the king of Edom into lime." Then when his hearers are lulled by these satisfying denunciations of their enemies, suddenly and without warning he turns on them:

Thus saith the Lord; For three transgressions of Israel, and for four, I will not turn away the punishment thereof; because they sold the righteous for silver, and the poor for a pair of shoes;

That pant after the dust of the earth on the head of the poor, and turn aside the way of the meek:

.   .   .   .   .   .

And they lay themselves down upon clothes laid to pledge by every altar, and they drink the

[1] Amos i. 3–5.

wine of the condemned in the house of their god.[1]

Here we have the prophecy at its best; the sharp perception of the concrete facts is fused by imagination into a message of the deeper meaning which underlies it. Amos always shows this combination: both his descriptions of the oppressive luxury of the nobles and the imagery in which he denounces the punishment of them are extraordinarily vivid:

Ye that put far away the evil day, and cause the seat of violence to come near;

That lie upon beds of ivory, and stretch themselves upon their couches, and eat the lambs out of the flock, and the calves out of the midst of the stall;

That chant to the sound of the viol, and invent to themselves instruments of music, like David;

That drink wine in bowls, and anoint themselves with the chief ointments; but they are not grieved for the affliction of Joseph.[2]

And for the punishment:

And I also have given you cleanness of teeth in all your cities, and want of bread in all your places: yet have ye not returned unto me, saith the Lord.

And also I have withholden the rain from you, when there were yet three months to the harvest: and I caused it to rain upon one city, and caused

---

[1] Amos ii. 6-8.　　　　　[2] Ibid., vi. 3-6.

it not to rain upon another city: one piece was rained upon, and the piece whereupon it rained not withered.

So two or three cities wandered unto one city, to drink water; but they were not satisfied: yet have ye not returned unto me, saith the Lord.[1]

And again:

Thus saith the Lord; As the shepherd taketh out of the mouth of the lion two legs, or a piece of an ear; so shall the children of Israel be taken out that dwell in Samaria in the corner of a bed, and in Damascus in a couch.

Hear ye, and testify in the house of Jacob, saith the Lord God, the God of hosts,

That in the day that I shall visit the transgressions of Israel upon him I will also visit the altars of Beth-el: and the horns of the altar shall be cut off, and fall to the ground.

And I will smite the winter house with the summer house; and the houses of ivory shall perish, and the great houses shall have an end, saith the Lord.[2]

In all his declaration of the new and unwelcome truth, that Jehovah would punish his chosen people for their unrighteousness as well as reward them for their good deeds, Amos has the sharpest and strongest sense of the actual evil for which the punishment

[1] Amos iv. 6–8.   [2] Ibid., iii. 12–15.

would come and the imagination and feeling which clothed those facts with spiritual power.

So in the same way with Isaiah, a younger and greater contemporary of Amos. He is the most notable of all the prophets, for he more than any of them shows this complete balance of the unfailing grasp of fact and the power of the imagination which fuses the fact into an expression of the higher truths which lie behind. In all his prophecies one feels the statesmanship of a man who, looking beyond the mountains of Judah to the movements of the great world outside, recognized that Assyria was irresistible and that the only hope for Judah was to bow before the storm and trust in the Lord God. Moreover, one finds in Isaiah's prophecies what one does not find in those of the other prophets, a firm confidence that they will have weight: one recognizes that here is a man who impressed his own high and inspired purpose on the actions of weak and unwilling kings.

What I wish to emphasize now, however, is the solid and vivid appreciation of fact and the high imagination of his messages. Of the grasp of fact one can find many instances. His warning to Hezekiah not to intrigue with Egypt, not only shows the statesman's insight into the situation, but recreates the situation for us:

Woe to the rebellious children, saith the Lord, that take counsel, but not of me; and that cover with a covering, but not of my Spirit, that they may add sin to sin:

That walk to go down into Egypt, and have not asked at my mouth; to strengthen themselves in the strength of Pharaoh, and to trust in the shadow of Egypt!

Therefore shall the strength of Pharaoh be your shame, and the trust in the shadow of Egypt your confusion.

For his princes were at Zoan, and his ambassadors came to Hanes.

They were all ashamed of a people that could not profit them, nor be an help nor profit, but a shame, and also a reproach.

The burden of the beasts of the south: into the land of trouble and anguish, from whence come the young and old lion, the viper and fiery flying serpent, they will carry their riches upon the shoulders of young asses, and their treasures upon the bunches of camels, to a people that shall not profit them.

For the Egyptians shall help in vain, and to no purpose: therefore, have I cried concerning this, Their strength is to sit still.[1]

And he describes the state of Judah as follows:

Your country is desolate, your cities are burned with fire: your land, strangers devour it in your

[1] Isa. xxx. 1–7.

presence, and it is desolate, as overthrown by strangers.

And the daughter of Zion is left as a cottage in a vineyard, as a lodge in a garden of cucumbers, as a besieged city.[1]

Indeed, all the great prophets of the earlier time described the conditions under which they lived so definitely that modern historians find in their utterances much of the material from which to reconstruct the history of the period.

The imagery of Isaiah's prophecies shows this same vivid consciousness of actual fact. Before the war against Pekah and Rezin he declares:

And in that day it shall come to pass, that the glory of Jacob shall be made thin, and the fatness of his flesh shall wax lean.

And it shall be as when the harvestman gathereth the corn, and reapeth the ears with his arm; and it shall be as he that gathereth ears in the valley of Rephaim.

Yet gleaning grapes shall be left in it, as the shaking of an olive tree, two or three berries in the top of the uppermost bough, four or five in the outmost fruitful branches thereof, saith the Lord God of Israel.[2]

When Judah is threatened by Assyria, he declares:

And my hand hath found as a nest the riches of the people: and as one gathereth eggs that are

[1] Isa. i. 7–8.   [2] Ibid., xvii. 4–6.

left, have I gathered all the earth; and there was none that moved the wing, or opened the mouth, or peeped.

Shall the axe boast itself against him that heweth therewith? or shall the saw magnify itself against him that shaketh it? as if the rod should shake itself against them that lift it up, or as if the staff should lift up itself, as if it were no wood.

Therefore shall the Lord, the Lord of hosts, send among his fat ones leanness; and under his glory he shall kindle a burning like the burning of a fire.[1]

And in an undated prophecy there is the well-known passage:

Whom shall he teach knowledge? and whom shall he make to understand doctrine? them that are weaned from the milk, and drawn from the breasts.

For precept must be upon precept, precept upon precept; line upon line, line upon line; here a little and there a little:

For with stammering lips and another tongue will he speak to this people.

To whom he said, This is the rest wherewith ye may cause the weary to rest; and this is the refreshing: yet they would not hear.

But the word of the Lord was unto them precept upon precept, precept upon precept; line upon line, line upon line; here a little and there a little; that they might go, and fall backward, and be broken, and snared, and taken.[2]

[1] Isa. x. 14–16.   [2] Ibid., xxviii. 9–13.

Such examples illustrate the unfailing concreteness of Isaiah: whatever the message which came to him to express he had figures of speech sometimes of almost startling homeliness by which to stamp it into the hearts of his people. Yet no matter how homely the figure his earnestness and his elevation of thought and the power of his message forestall any effect of triviality.

Even more characteristic of Isaiah's style, however, are the figures of speech which he draws from the great forces of nature; and here again the language is vividly concrete:

> Therefore as the fire devoureth the stubble, and the flame consumeth the chaff, so their root shall be as rottenness, and their blossom shall go up as dust: because they have cast away the law of the Lord of hosts, and despised the word of the Holy One of Israel.

> Therefore is the anger of the Lord kindled against his people, and he hath stretched forth his hand against them, and hath smitten them: and the hills did tremble, and their carcasses were torn in the midst of the streets. For all this his anger is not turned away, but his hand is stretched out still.[1]

> Woe to the multitude of many people, which make a noise like the noise of the seas; and to the rushing of nations, that make a rushing like the rushing of mighty waters !

[1] Isa. v. 24–25.

The nations shall rush like the rushing of many waters; but God shall rebuke them, and they shall flee far off, and shall be chased as the chaff of the mountains before the wind, and like a rolling thing before the whirlwind.

And behold at eveningtide trouble; and before the morning he is not. This is the portion of them that spoil us, and the lot of them that rob us.[1]

Anyone can pile up figures of speech drawn from floods and fire and lightning and thunder; but Isaiah applied them so that a single phrase expresses all the terrors that lie in these mighty forces; and, what is more, he used them in a way which always justified the superlative. In the later writers who filled in the prophetic books with imaginations of their own the effort to wield these resounding phrases is painfully apparent. But with Isaiah whether the figure be homely or remote, it is always concrete, and so apt that each time one comes back to the reading one is struck with fresh surprise at the power. Always one feels with Isaiah, as with the earlier poets of Israel, that he is drawing his imagery from things which he himself has felt and seen and heard, and not from a store-house of inherited literature. His speech springs from the experiences of

[1] Isa. xvii. 12–14.

his own life; it never suggests that its phrasing comes second or third hand from reality.[1]

On the other hand, the quality which is even more characteristic of Isaiah than his solid consciousness of fact is the high moral and spiritual elevation of his prophecies. The keynote of his message by some shrewd instinct of the compiler is set at the very beginning of the book:

> Ah sinful nation, a people laden with iniquity, a seed of evil doers, children that are corrupters: they have forsaken the Lord, they have provoked the Holy One of Israel unto anger, they are gone away backward.
>
> . . . . . .
>
> To what purpose is the multitude of your sacrifices unto me? saith the Lord: I am full of the burnt offerings of rams, and the fat of fed beasts; and I delight not in the blood of bullocks, or of lambs, or of he goats.
>
> When ye come to appear before me, who hath required this at your hand, to tread my courts?
>
> Bring no more vain oblations; incense is an abomination unto me; the new moons and sabbaths, the calling of assemblies, I cannot away with; it is iniquity, even the solemn meeting.
>
> Your new moons and your appointed feasts my soul hateth: they are a trouble unto me; I am weary to bear them.

[1] See Isa. xxiv. 16-23; Jere. l-li., both very late additions to the prophetical books.

> And when ye spread forth your hands, I will hide mine eyes from you: yea, when ye make many prayers, I will not hear: your hands are full of blood.
>
> Wash you, make you clean; put away the evil of your doings from before mine eyes; cease to do evil;
>
> Learn to do well; seek judgment, relieve the oppressed, judge the fatherless, plead for the widow.[1]

And the essence of his warning to Judah against the power of Samaria and Damascus is the following passage:

> For the Lord spake thus to me with a strong hand, and instructed me that I should not walk in the way of this people, saying,
>
> Say ye not, A confederacy, to all them to whom this people shall say, A confederacy; neither fear ye their fear, nor be afraid.
>
> Sanctify the Lord of hosts himself; and let him be your fear, and let him be your dread.[2]

This is the lesson which gives grandeur to the prophecies of this period. Amos and Hosea had already in the generations before Isaiah declared that the power of Jehovah transcended the little boundaries of Israel; Isaiah reinforced the lesson and lifted it to even a higher plane. Everywhere his understanding of the fate of his people is fused and

---

[1] Isa. i. 4; 11–17.   [2] Ibid., viii. 11–13.

transfigured by his intense and soaring imagination.
His message was of surpassing grandeur; and he
clothed it with a language marked by profusion and
splendor of imagery, and by compression and intensity of feeling. Thus his prophecy everywhere shows
the combination which I have spoken of, the combination of vividness and concreteness of thought
and clear insight into fact, with the burning and
inspired earnestness of feeling which transmutes the
facts and endows them with an instant and lasting
effect on the imagination. Isaiah, more than any
other of the prophets, shows in the highest degree
these two qualities and the perfect balance between
them.

Let us now, passing down a century into the bitter
time during which Judah followed the kingdom of
North Israel to political extinction, come to the
utterances of Jeremiah, the "weeping prophet."
This very name "weeping prophet" indicates the
direction in which the prophetic literature is passing.
The emotion is already surging to the front, though
with Jeremiah not so much so as to obscure the sense
of fact. He describes the conditions of the Judah of
his day as distinctly as does Isaiah the conditions of
a century before. One of his prophecies against the
weak and silly kings of Judah in his day may serve
as an example. Here is that against Jehoiakim:

Woe unto him that buildeth his house by unrighteousness, and his chambers by wrong; that
useth his neighbour's service without wages, and
giveth him not for his work;

That saith, I will build me a wide house and
large chambers, and cutteth him out windows;
and it is cieled with cedar, and painted with ver-
milion.

Shalt thou reign, because thou closest thyself
in cedar? did not thy father eat and drink, and do
judgment and justice, and then it was well with
him?

He judged the cause of the poor and needy; then
it was well with him; was not this to know me?
saith the Lord.

But thine eyes and thine heart are not but for
thy covetousness, and for to shed innocent blood,
and for oppression, and for violence, to do it.

Therefore thus saith the Lord concerning Jehoiakim, the son of Josiah king of Judah; They shall
not lament for him, saying, Ah, my brother! or,
Ah sister! they shall not lament for him, saying,
Ah, Lord! or, Ah his glory!

He shall be buried with the burial of an ass, drawn
and cast forth beyond the gates of Jerusalem.[1]

Jeremiah had as strongly as had Isaiah the unblurred
insight into the facts and the conditions of his day.
In his case the word " Jeremiad " does not mean a
vague and unthinking abuse of conditions which he

[1] Jere. xxii. 13–19.

did not himself grasp. He was a preacher of repent-
ance and of the wrath to come; but he recognized his
impotence in the councils of the kings, and he knew
that his efforts to rouse the people to their desperate
state were vain. With him the sense of fact has not
begun to decay.

On the other hand, as I have said, the name which
is given to him of the " weeping prophet " points to
the change which is coming over the prophecy. With
him the emotion is more noticeable than the grasp of
fact. One of his own utterances points to this breaking down of the equilibrium. " I am full of the fury
of the Lord, I am weary with holding in "; and the
following passage shows how his feeling was getting to the verge of control:

> Oh that my head were waters, and mine eyes a
> fountain of tears, that I might weep day and
> night for the slain of the daughter of my
> people!
>
> Oh that I had in the wilderness a lodging place of
> wayfaring men; that I might leave my people and
> go from them! for they be all adulterers, an assem-
> bly of treacherous men.
>
> And they bend their tongues like their bow for
> lies: but they are not valiant for the truth upon the
> earth; for they proceed from evil to evil, and they
> know not me, saith the Lord.[1]

[1] Jere. ix. 1–3.

Indeed the keynote to his message may be found in the words:

> A wonderful and horrible thing is committed in the land;
> The prophets prophesy falsely, and the priests bear rule by their means; and my people love to have it so: and what will ye do in the end thereof? [1]

The vehemence and distress of the prophet has risen to a point in which words begin to be impotent. We no longer feel with him as with Isaiah that the vivid sense of fact is in perfect balance with the power of feeling and imagination. Now the feeling and emotion tend to reduce the prophet to helpless despair. Both elements of the prophecy still exist, but the feeling is beginning to overshadow the intellectual grasp.

As we pass on into the next generation, the two great prophets of the Exile show the differentiation already well begun. On the one hand Ezekiel's prophecies have earnestness and sincerity, but in form they are painstaking rather than inspired. With the great unknown prophet, the Isaiah of the Exile, on the other hand, facts become vague and uncertain: from him we get no help for the reconstruction of the history; but his imagination soars on the wings of his spiritual emotion to heights where the vision of man loses itself in the clouds of heaven.

[1] Jere. v. 30–31.

Let us consider Ezekiel first. His style at times has almost a legal precision and repetitiousness. In Chapter xviii the proverb, " The fathers have eaten sour grapes and the children's teeth are set on edge," is elaborated into a series of formal and detailed judgments on the fate of a just man's son that is a robber and a shedder of blood, and of the robber's son " that seeth all his father's sins which he hath done, and considereth, and doeth not such like." In such writing we have come far from the impassioned oracles of Amos, and Isaiah, and Jeremiah. It has little relation to poetry, but belongs rather to the formal elaborations of doctrine by the later writers of the Deuteronomic and priestly schools.

Ezekiel's visions at first sight seem to break up our classification. The description of " the appearance of the likeness of the glory of the Lord " at the beginning of the book seems at first sight to be purely mystical; but it has been pointed out that the figures of the cherubim and of the wheels are borrowed somewhat literally from the sculptures of the Babylonian temples; as compared with the vision of Isaiah in *Isaiah vi* this vision of Ezekiel has a painstaking literalness that points rather to poverty of imagination than to a superabundance of it. Ezekiel was by no means destitute of poetic power, as is sufficiently shown in the lamentations inserted in his prophecies. The vision of the Valley of Dry Bones, one of the most striking passages in all the Bible, will give a fair idea both of his power and of his limitations:

The hand of the Lord was upon me, and carried me out in the spirit of the Lord, and set me down in the midst of the valley which was full of bones,

And caused me to pass by them round about: and, behold, there were very many in the open valley; and, lo, they were very dry.

And he said unto me, Son of man, can these bones live? And I answered, O Lord God, thou knowest.

Again he said unto me, Prophesy upon these bones, and say unto them, O ye dry bones, hear the word of the Lord.

Thus saith the Lord God unto these bones; Behold, I will cause breath to enter into you, and ye shall live:

And I will lay sinews upon you, and will bring up flesh upon you, and cover you with skin, and put breath in you, and ye shall live; and ye shall know that I am the Lord.

So I prophesied as I was commanded: and as I prophesied, there was a noise, and behold a shaking, and the bones came together, bone to his bone.

And when I beheld, lo, the sinews and the flesh came up upon them, and the skin covered them above: but there was no breath in them.

Then said he unto me, Prophesy unto the wind,

prophesy, son of man, and say to the wind, Thus
saith the Lord God, Come from the four winds, O
breath, and breathe upon these slain, that they
may live.

So I prophesied as he commanded me, and the
breath came into them, and they lived, and stood
upon their feet, an exceeding great army.[1]

Here is imaginative power of a high order: but the
imagination flags and becomes pedestrian in the application of the vision:

Then he said unto me, Son of man, these bones
are the whole house of Israel: behold, they say,
Our bones are dried, and our hope is lost: we are
cut off for our parts.

Therefore prophesy and say unto them, Thus
saith the Lord God; Behold, O my people, I will
open your graves, and cause you to come up out
of your graves, and bring you into the land of
Israel.

And ye shall know that I am the Lord, when I
have opened your graves, O my people, and brought
you up out of your graves.

And shall put my spirit in you, and ye shall live;
and I shall place you in your own land: then shall
ye know that I the Lord have spoken it, and performed it, saith the Lord.[2]

Such an ending hardly justifies the indefinitely suggestive power of the vision: nor has it the overwhelm-

[1] Ezek. xxxvii. 1–10.   [2] Ibid., 11–14.

ing rush of feeling of the earlier prophets. One no longer feels one's self in the presence of a man who was impelled by the very intensity of his feeling to the utterance of his message; one no longer feels that the message surged up, spontaneously and inevitably, from the depth of the prophet's consciousness. Beside Amos and Elijah, the wild prophets of the desert, Ezekiel seems a cultivated man of the study with high moral insight, reasoning out the words which he is called upon to deliver. It is as if he were writing out ordinances with a careful, almost scholarly scrutiny of the form which they would take, and a painstaking care for the exact statement of fact. The long vision at the end of the book is in substance, and at times in manner, closely akin to the later chapters of *Exodus* and the earlier chapters of *Leviticus* and of *Numbers*. It shows Ezekiel as the student of the law, absorbed in working out and codifying the prescriptions for the liturgy and ritual of the temple. He brings the prophecy into close relations with the legal portions of the Pentateuch; though with him the absorption in details is always relieved by imaginative insight into their symbolic meaning. There is much in his prophecy in which the poetic form seems an outer shell rather than an organic part of the message. In Ezekiel, in contrast to the earlier prophets, the sense of fact is no longer fused and transfigured by the tense heat of the imagination and feeling.

With Ezekiel's younger and greater contemporary, the Isaiah of the Exile, the case is just the opposite. The very fact that his name is lost seems symbolic of the relative unimportance of specific facts in his writing. His message is a message of comfort and of spiritual uplifting. His people are hopelessly subdued and political action has no meaning for them or for him. We know from his prophecy that Judah is captive in Babylon; but his prophecies contain almost no description of the condition under which the people lived; and the promises of comfort to them are vaguely large and figurative. The promises of unalloyed bliss in the later chapters of the book made to the people apparently after the return to Jerusalem, when their miserable state must have been a bitter contrast to their jubilant hopes, seem to be heightened almost in proportion to their present despair. We shall see later what a long step this soaring into visions of a vague and unfixed future is toward the apocalyptic literature which succeeded the prophecy in the next century or two.

On the other hand no portion of the literature of the Old Testament is more individual in style and thought or more gloriously uplifting in expression than the oracles of this great prophet of the Exile.

He rises to a new level of faith with the indomitable
buoyancy which was the genius of Israel at each crisis
of its religion. The ancestral idea that Jehovah
would protect them in all events against the gods of
the heathen was finally shattered; but this new seer
boldly declares that Jehovah is the God of the whole
earth:

> Have ye not known? have ye not heard? hath it
> not been told you from the beginning? have ye
> not understood from the foundations of the earth?
> It is he that sitteth upon the circle of the earth,
> and the inhabitants thereof are as grasshoppers;
> that stretcheth out the heavens as a curtain, and
> spreadeth them out as a tent to dwell in.[1]

> I am the Lord, and there is none else, there is
> no God beside me: I girded thee, though thou hast
> not known me:
> That they may know from the rising of the sun,
> and from the west, that there is none beside me.
> I am the Lord, and there is none else.
> I form the light, and create darkness: I make
> peace and create evil: I the Lord do all these
> things.
> Drop down, ye heavens, from above, and let the
> skies pour down righteousness: let the earth open,
> and let them bring forth salvation, and let right-
> eousness spring up together; I the Lord have
> created it.[2]

[1] Isa. xl. 21–22.   [2] Ibid., xlv. 5–8.

This triumphant exultation in the omnipotent power of Jehovah is the keynote of his message.

Nevertheless this characteristic and jubilant elevation only emphasizes the disturbance of the equilibrium which we found in Amos and Isaiah. The Isaiah of the Exile is not a statesman charged with the responsibility for the political actions of his nation. He bears a message of comfort and of hope; but he proclaims a future whose details are not unveiled. Isaiah always had his feeling in firm control; and though it rise to white heat, it only gives the words of his oracle a stronger motion without changing their character. The Isaiah of the Exile in contrast is carried away into lyrical utterances which almost become pure rhapsody.

> Sing, O heavens; and be joyful, O earth; and break forth into singing, O mountains: for the Lord hath comforted his people, and will have mercy upon his afflicted.[1]

> Awake, awake; put on thy strength, O Zion; put on thy beautiful garments, O Jerusalem, the holy city: for henceforth there shall no more come into thee the uncircumcised and the unclean.

> Shake thyself from the dust; arise, and sit down, O Jerusalem: loose thyself from the bands of thy neck, O captive daughter of Zion.

> .   .   .   .   .

> How beautiful upon the mountains are the feet

[1] Isa. xlix. 13.

> of him that bringeth good tidings; that publisheth
> peace; that bringeth good tidings of good, that
> publisheth salvation; that saith unto Zion, Thy
> God reigneth!
>
> Thy watchmen shall lift up the voice; with the
> voice together shall they sing: for they shall see
> eye to eye, when the Lord shall bring again Zion.
>
> Break forth into joy, sing together, ye waste
> places of Jerusalem: for the Lord hath comforted
> his people, he hath redeemed Jerusalem.
>
> The Lord hath made bare his holy arm in the
> eyes of all the nations; and all the ends of the earth
> shall see the salvation of our God.[1]

Such passages are wholly different from the grave
and terse utterances of Isaiah and his stern consciousness of fact. By the side of the prophet of the exile,
Isaiah seems more austere and more remote, a figure
isolated in antiquity: and beside Isaiah the prophet
of the Exile seems carried away by emotion and imagination, and uncontrolled by the stern sense of fact.

An even more striking example of this tendency of
one school of the later prophecy to break over into
rhapsodical utterance may be found in the striking
passage in *Isaiah xxi* which comes from some other
unknown prophet of the Exile:

> My heart panted, fearfulness affrighted me:
> the night of my pleasure hath he turned into fear
> unto me.

[1] Isa. lii. 1–2, 7–10.

Prepare the table, watch in the watchtower, eat, drink: arise, ye princes, and anoint the shield.

For thus hath the Lord said unto me, Go, set a watchman, let him declare what he seeth.

And he saw a chariot with a couple of horsemen, a chariot of asses, and a chariot of camels; and he hearkened diligently with much heed:

And he cried, A lion: My lord, I stand continually upon the watchtower in the day time, and I am set in my ward whole nights:

And, behold, here cometh a chariot of men, with a couple of horsemen. And he answered and said, Babylon is fallen, is fallen; and all the graven images of her gods he hath broken unto the ground.

O my threshing, and the corn of my floor: that which I have heard of the Lord of hosts, the God of Israel, have I declared unto you.[1]

Here the wild incoherence of the message and the swift flashing of its imagery seem to point to an intensity of feeling which has broken away from any sober control and consideration of facts. Here, even more than in the Isaiah of the Exile, the emotional power predominates.

Thus the prophecy has lost its perfect balance and fusion. In the Isaiah of the Exile the messages show a dominance of emotion and a relaxing grasp of fact; his utterances tend to rhapsody; the promises of hope have become vague, and though they are more

[1] Isa. xxi. 4-10.

soaring they tend in the direction of the mystical. With Ezekiel on the other hand we found that the sense of fact was in the dominant and that the emotional force had lost its momentum. Thus in these two prophets of the Exile, who were almost contemporaneous, we may see the breaking down begun. This process I have not space to trace out. Suffice it to say that with Haggai and Malachi, earnest and sincere as they were, one feels the limitation to the perception of a narrow range of fact, and a corresponding weakening of the imaginative power. In Zechariah an increasing interest in the vision and increasing reliance on vague and mystical suggestions go with a corresponding insignificance of fact. So the prophecy gradually passed away. On the one hand, it was drying up, as it were, in the words of earnest men whose feeling and imagination were too weak to burn their words into the life of their contemporaries; on the other hand, it was floating off into the clouds of the mystical kingdom of God and losing its hold on the realities of human life.

III

If after this brief sketch of the gradual change in the character of the prophetic literature, we attempt to define its chief characteristics as part of the

English Bible we shall find its determining attribute in the fact that the prophet spoke always as the mouthpiece of Jehovah: he was possessed by the hand of the Lord, and the words which emerged from his lips were the immediate utterance of God. Sometimes Jehovah speaks directly in the first person:

When Israel was a child, then I loved him, and called my son out of Egypt.

As they called them, so they went from them: they sacrificed unto Baalim, and burned incense to graven images.

I taught Ephraim also to go, taking them by their arms; but they knew not that I healed them.

I drew them with cords of a man, with bands of love: and I was to them as they that take off the yoke on their jaws, and I laid meat unto them.[1]

Sometimes the prophecy passes from such direct discourse to a description of the message which is committed to the prophet, as in the case of the fine dialogue which has been incorporated in the book of the prophet Micah:

Hear ye now what the Lord saith; Arise, contend thou before the mountains, and let the hills hear thy voice.

Hear ye, O mountains, the Lord's controversy, and ye strong foundations of the earth: for the

[1] Hosea xi. 1–4.

Lord hath a controversy with his people, and he will plead with Israel.

O my people, what have I done unto thee? and wherein have I wearied thee? testify against me.

For I brought thee up out of the land of Egypt, and redeemed thee out of the house of servants; and I sent before thee Moses, Aaron, and Miriam.

O my people remember now what Balak king of Moab consulted, and what Balaam the son of Beor answered him from Shittim unto Gilgal; that ye may know the righteousness of the Lord.

Wherewith shall I come before the Lord, and bow myself before the high God? shall I come before him with burnt offerings, with calves of a year old?

Will the Lord be pleased with thousands of rams, or with ten thousands of rivers of oil? shall I give my firstborn for my transgression, the fruit of my body for the sin of my soul?

He hath showed thee, O man, what is good; and what doth the Lord require of thee, but to do justly, and to love mercy, and to walk humbly with thy God? [1]

But always these oracles of the prophets differ from anything else in the Old Testament in the fact that the man who utters them feels that the words spring from his lips completely formed, without volition of his own. This consciousness of detachment appears strikingly in the account of how Amaziah, the priest of the sanctuary at Beth-el, tried to silence Amos:

[1] Micah vi. 1–8.

Also Amaziah said unto Amos, O thou seer, go flee thee away into the land of Judah, and there eat bread, and prophesy there:

But prophesy not again any more at Beth-el: for it is the king's chapel, and it is the king's court.

Then answered Amos, and said to Amaziah, I was no prophet, neither was I a prophet's son; but I was an herdman and a gatherer of sycomore fruit:

And the Lord took me as I followed the flock, and the Lord said unto me, Go, prophesy unto my people Israel.[1]

Here Amos, unlike Isaiah and Jeremiah and most of the other prophets, seems to feel little responsibility for results: it is as if he felt his function to be fulfilled when he had thrust his message on the unwilling attention of his hearers. In the *Psalms* and in *Job* the passionate faith or distress of the individual Jew rings through the verses and imparts the note of poignant feeling which makes them kin to the whole world. In the prophets, even in the yearning love which shines through the messages of Hosea or the bitter and burning despair of Jeremiah, there are always a larger thought and a majesty which befit the words of the Lord God of Hosts.

As a result of this sense of possession by the hand of Jehovah the prophetic writings show a feeling for

[1] Amos vii. 12–15.

the proportions of things which makes them the best possible foundation for a study of modern literature. It is easy for a student of any form of art to get into the frame of mind of Walter Pater, that sublimated sentimentalist, and feel that the only effort worth a refined man's attention is to free himself from the turmoil and dust of life, and dwell in a half-ascetic, half-æsthetic Olympus of beautiful words and beautiful things. To a student of these books of the prophets such an attitude is impossible, for they continually occupy themselves with the solid realities of history and human fate. With them it is not a question of whether an individual man shall taste the last drop of sweetness or wisdom from this world's cup, or even, as with Shakspere at his highest, of how the tangle of character and circumstance in man's fate shall work itself out into clear portrayal: the prophets are concerned with the fulfillment of the will of God, and with bringing his chosen people to a compelling sense of the righteousness that shall regenerate the world. And their indomitable faith in the enduring purpose of Jehovah makes the controlled hedonism and agnosticism of *Ecclesiastes* seem pusillanimous. Even in the case of Haggai this absorption in the service of the God of the whole earth lends dignity and power to the narrowing interest of the message.

This largeness of interest is reinforced by the special virtues of the Old Testament poetry. We have seen that the Hebrew language was limited to the solid and concrete realities of life, and that the Hebrew poetry as it is translated in the English of our Bible added to the higher expressiveness of poetry the freedom and the undisturbed naturalness of prose. These virtues are shared by the prophecies; and they in consequence reinforce the high seriousness and the large and noble sense of proportion by a robustness and weighty power which again distinguishes them in our literature. Finally, the inmost essence of their power lies in its spiritual elevation. To these prophets, to Amos and Hosea and Isaiah, to Jeremiah, Ezekiel and the Isaiah of the Exile, to Joel and Malachi and Zechariah, with all their unknown contemporaries and coworkers, it was given to touch the realities of the world of this life with the vivifying force of the unseen. Their oracles were phrased in the words of the things which men can see and hear and feel, but they are filled with the palpable breath of the things which lie beyond our present capacities to comprehend. More than the other writings of the Old Testament they spring from what, because it is inexplicable, we call genius.

CHAPTER VII

THE APOCALYPSE

I

THE prophecy did not pass away, however, without sowing the seeds of a type of writing, which in thought was to rise still higher, and finally to bear fruit in one of the books of the New Testament; this was the work of the apocalyptic writers, who gradually succeeded to the place of the prophets in the last centuries of the old era, and who in the first century of the new produced the book of *Revelation.* The outward form of the apocalypses is sometimes fantastic, almost trivial; but the faith which produced them ennobled this outward form into the vehicle of the most elevated thought yet attained by the Jewish race.

The apocalyptic writing sprang naturally out of the prophecies; for the Jews of the Exile and of the succeeding wretched centuries took literally the many promises of the restoration of power and happiness to Israel and of punishment for their enemies which they read in the books of the prophets. The Isaiah of the Exile has many such passages of hope as the following:

> Thus saith the Lord, the Redeemer of Israel, and his Holy One, to him whom man despiseth, to him whom the nation abhorreth, to a servant of rulers, Kings shall see and arise, princes also shall worship, because of the Lord that is faithful, and the Holy One of Israel, and he shall choose thee.

> Thus saith the Lord, in an acceptable time have I heard thee, and in a day of salvation have I helped thee: and I will preserve thee, and give thee for a covenant of the people, to establish the earth, to cause to inherit the desolate heritages;

> That thou mayest say to the prisoners, Go forth; to them that are in darkness, Shew yourselves. They shall feed in the ways, and their pastures shall be in all high places.

> They shall not hunger nor thirst; neither shall the heat nor sun smite them: for he that hath mercy on them shall lead them, even by the springs of water shall he guide them.

> And I will make all my mountains a way, and my highways shall be exalted.

> Behold, these shall come from far: and, lo, these from the north and from the west; and these from the land of Sinim.[1]

With such promises of restoration for Israel go cor-

[1] Isa. xlix. 7–12.

responding denunciations of the woe to come for the enemies of Israel:

> Shall the prey be taken from the mighty, or the lawful captive delivered?
>
> But thus saith the Lord, Even the captives of the mighty shall be taken away, and the prey of the terrible shall be delivered: for I will contend with him that contendeth with thee, and I will save thy children.
>
> And I will feed them that oppress thee with their own flesh; and they shall be drunken with their own blood, as with sweet wine: and all flesh shall know that I the Lord am thy Saviour and thy Redeemer, the Mighty One of Jacob.[1]

From these and similar prophecies had developed the idea of a day of the Lord when the heathen should be brought to judgment and confusion, and the way prepared for the return of Israel.

As time went on and the Jews became hopelessly insignificant as a nation, instead of letting go their hope of the fulfillment of these prophecies they merely postponed it to a vaguer and more distant future. The later prophetic writings show a corresponding largeness and vagueness of outline, of which examples may be found in *Joel*:

> Let the heathen be wakened, and come up to the valley of Jehoshaphat: for there will I sit to judge all the heathen round about.

[1] Isa. xlix. 24–26.

Put ye in the sickle, for the harvest is ripe: come, get you down; for the press is full, the fats overflow; for their wickedness is great.

Multitudes, multitudes in the valley of decision: for the day of the Lord is near in the valley of decision.

The sun and the moon shall be darkened, and the stars shall withdraw their shining.

The Lord also shall roar out of Zion, and utter his voice from Jerusalem; and the heavens and the earth shall shake: but the Lord will be the hope of his people, and the strength of the children of Israel.

So shall ye know that I am the Lord your God dwelling in Zion, my holy mountain: then shall Jerusalem be holy, and there shall no strangers pass through her any more.[1]

Scattered through the books of the prophets there is a considerable body of writing of this large and vague character which unveils the destiny of Israel and its enemies in an undetermined future. The considerable passage in *Isaiah xxiv–xxvii*, which comes probably from the end of the fourth century B.C. or later, is an example. Here are two specimens from it:

And in this mountain shall the Lord of hosts make unto all people a feast of fat things, a feast of wines on the lees, of fat things full of marrow, of wines on the lees well refined.

[1] Joel iii. 12–17.

And he will destroy in this mountain the face of the covering cast over all people, and the vail that is spread over all nations.

He will swallow up death in victory; and the Lord God will wipe away tears from off all faces; and the rebuke of his people shall he take away from off all the earth: for the Lord hath spoken it.[1]

In that day the Lord, with his sore and great and strong sword shall punish leviathan the piercing serpent, even leviathan that crooked serpent; and he shall slay the dragon that is in the sea.

In that day sing ye unto her, A vineyard of red wine.

I the Lord do keep it: I will water it every moment: lest any hurt it, I will keep it night and day.

Fury is not in me: who would set the briers and thorns against me in battle? I would go through them, I would burn them together.

Or let him take hold of my strength, that he may make peace with me; and he shall make peace with me.

He shall cause them that come of Jacob to take root: Israel shall blossom and bud, and fill the face of the world with fruit.[2]

This type of the apocalyptic writing is little different in external form from the prophecy of the earlier centuries. It is not often as sustained as *Joel*, which is the finest example of it; and it is not infrequently

[1] Isa. xxv. 6–8.   [2] Ibid., xxvii. 1–6.

broken by passages which cannot be distinguished from psalms, as in *Isaiah xxiv–xxvii*. In subject matter it is often characterized by a revelling in grim pictures of the annihilation of the heathen, after the manner of Ezekiel in his prophecies against the semi-mystical " Gog, the land of Magog, the chief prince of Meshech and Tubal " :

> For in my jealousy and in the fire of my wrath have I spoken, Surely in that day there shall be a great shaking in the land of Israel;
> So that the fishes of the sea, and the fowls of the heaven, and the beasts of the field, and all creeping things that creep upon the earth, and all the men that are upon the face of the earth, shall shake at my presence, and the mountains shall be thrown down, and the steep places shall fall, and every wall shall fall to the ground.
> And I will call for a sword against him throughout all my mountains, saith the Lord God: every man's sword shall be against his brother.
> And I will plead against him with pestilence and with blood; and I will rain upon him, and upon his bands, and upon the many people that are with him, an overflowing rain, and great hailstones, fire, and brimstone.
> Thus will I magnify myself, and sanctify myself; and I will be known in the eyes of many nations, and they shall know that I am the Lord.[1]

[1] Ezek. xxxviii. 19–23.

And, thou son of man, thus saith the Lord God:
Speak unto every feathered fowl, and to every beast
of the field, Assemble yourselves, and come; gather
yourselves on every side to my sacrifice that I do
sacrifice for you, even a great sacrifice upon the
mountains of Israel, that ye may eat flesh, and
drink blood.

Ye shall eat the flesh of the mighty, and drink
the blood of the princes of the earth, of rams, of
lambs, and of goats, of bullocks, all of them fat-
lings of Bashan.

And ye shall eat fat till ye be full, and drink
blood till ye be drunken, of my sacrifice which I
have sacrificed for you.

Thus ye shall be filled at my table with horses
and chariots, with mighty men, and with all men
of war, saith the Lord God.

And I will set my glory among the heathen, and
all the heathen shall see my judgment that I have
executed, and my hand that I have laid upon them.

So the house of Israel shall know that I am the
Lord their God from that day and forward.[1]

This idea of the great and dreadful day of the Lord
is repeated with many slight variations in *Joel* and
in a number of late additions to the books of the
prophets, such as *Jeremiah l–li, Isaiah xxiv–xxvii,
Zechariah ix–xiv.* Where the imagination of the
writer was weak and dependent as in *Jeremiah l–li*
the denunciation and promise are labored and repeti-

[1] Ezek. xxxix. 17–22.

tious; where it was strong and soaring the message is eloquent and stirring. Always its source and its support lay in the inextinguishable confidence of these later generations of Jews that the promises of Jehovah through his prophets could not pass unfulfilled. Postponement of the fulfilment has only the effect of heightening the colors of the final retribution and adding grandeur to its scope.

II

It was in another direction, however, that this late, post-prophetic writing brought forth the type of the apocalypse which is most commonly thought of as such, that which appears full fledged in the visions of *Daniel* and comes to its culmination in *Revelation*, and in the Apocrypha in *2 Esdras*. Outwardly this type of the apocalypse may be described as a kind of writing in which the events of the immediate past and of the present are set forth in elaborate imagery as the visions of a seer of a time long past. *Daniel,* which can be dated more definitely than any other book of the Old Testament, comes from the year 164 B.C. when the Jews had been saved from total extinction by the miraculous victories of Judas Maccabæus and the temple had just been rededicated after the desecrations of Antiochus Epiphanes. It sums up

the history of the preceding centuries in the vision of
the four beasts, which stand for the empires of Assyria, Chaldea, Persia, and Greece, and symbolises
the war between the Ptolemies and the kings of
Syria and the persecutions of Antiochus Epiphanes
in the vision of the ram and the he-goat and the
little horn of the he-goat which

> waxed great, even to the host of heaven; and it
> cast down some of the host and of the stars to
> the ground, and stamped upon them.
>
> Yea, he magnified himself even to the prince of
> the host, and by him the daily sacrifice was taken
> away, and the place of his sanctuary was cast down.
>
> And an host was given him against the daily
> sacrifice by reason of transgression, and it cast
> down the truth to the ground; and it practised, and
> prospered.[1]

In *2 Esdras* this imagery is developed in a somewhat different way in the form of the feathers of the
eagle which is declared to be the " kingdom which
was seen in the vision of thy brother Daniel."

> Then I beheld, and, lo, in process of time the
> feathers that followed stood up upon the right side,
> that they might rule also; and some of them ruled,
> but within a while they appeared no more:
>
> For some of them were set up, but ruled not.
>
> After this I looked, and, behold, the twelve

[1] Dan. viii. 10–12.

feathers appeared no more, nor the two little feathers:

And there was no more upon the eagle's body, but three heads that rested, and six little wings.

Then saw I also that two little feathers divided themselves from the six, and remained under the head that was upon the right side: for the four continued in their place.

And I beheld, and, lo, the feathers that were under the wing thought to set up themselves, and to have the rule.

And I beheld, and, lo, there was one set up, but shortly it appeared no more.[1]

In *Revelation* the same machinery appears in the beast with seven heads and ten horns:

And I stood upon the sand of the sea, and saw a beast rise up out of the sea, having seven heads and ten horns, and upon his horns ten crowns, and upon his heads the name of blasphemy.

And they beast which I saw was like unto a leopard, and his feet were as the feet of a bear, and his mouth as the mouth of a lion: and the dragon gave him his power, and his seat, and great authority.

And I saw one of his heads, as it were wounded to death; and his deadly wound was healed: and all the world wondered after the beast.

And they worshipped the dragon which gave power unto the beast: and they worshipped the beast,

[1] 2 Esdras xi. 20–26.

saying, Who is like unto the beast? who is able to make war with him? [1]

It is to be noted, however, that the author of *Revelation* subordinates this special type of imagery. It is hardly more than an incident in a very great profusion of images of many kinds. In comparison, *Daniel* and even *2 Esdras* seem to dwell on the somewhat cumbrous machinery of their visions to the point almost of weariness. It is as if, especially in the case of *Daniel*, the imagination of the writer had not power and heat enough to burn away the dross of the form. In all three of these apocalypses, however, the device is so transparent that it is wholly innocent; and scholars have found much exercise for learning and ingenuity in unravelling the puzzle so artfully constructed in order to get at the exact date of the given apocalypse.

Nor is there anything essentially new in the machinery. Ezekiel, whose influence on later writers was so great, used elaborate figures to describe present conditions in a way which needed only a moderate extension to provide all the machinery of the apocalypses. He sets forth the fate of Assyria, then recently accomplished, in the figure of a parable spoken to Pharaoh, king of Egypt:

[1] Rev. xiii. 1–4.

Behold, the Assyrian was a cedar in Lebanon with fair branches, and with a shadowing shroud, and of an high stature; and his top was among the thick boughs.

The waters made him great, the deep set him up on high with her rivers running round about his plants, and sent out her little rivers unto all the trees of the field.

Therefore his height was exalted above all the trees of the field, and his boughs were multiplied, and his branches became long because of the multitude of waters, when he shot forth.

All the fowls of heaven made their nests in his boughs, and under his branches did all the beasts of the field bring forth their young, and under his shadow dwelt all great nations.

Thus was he fair in his greatness, in the length of his branches: for his root was by great waters.

The cedars in the garden of God could not hide him: the fir trees were not like his boughs, and the chestnut trees were not like his branches; nor any tree in the garden of God was like unto him in his beauty.

I have made him fair by the multitude of his branches: so that all the trees of Eden, that were in the garden of God, envied him.

Therefore thus saith the Lord God; Because thou hast lifted up thyself in height, and he hath shot up his top among the thick boughs, and his heart is lifted up in his height;

I have therefore delivered him into the hand of the mighty one of the heathen; he shall surely deal with him: I have driven him out for his wickedness.

And strangers, the terrible of the nations, have cut him off, and have left him: upon the mountains and in all the valleys his branches are fallen, and his boughs are broken by all the rivers of the land; and all the people of the earth are gone down from his shadow, and have left him.

.   .   .   .   .

I made the nations to shake at the sound of his fall, when I cast him down to hell with them that descend into the pit: and all the trees of Eden, the choice and best of Lebanon, all that drink water, shall be comforted in the nether parts of the earth.[1]

Here though the description is still of the nature of a laboriously expanded figure of speech, it borders on the nature of conscious allegory.

In *Zechariah i–viii* also the preponderant importance of the visions points to an increasing elaboration in the outward form of the prophecy, which must have helped to prepare the way for the visions of the apocalypses:

And I turned, and lifted up mine eyes, and looked, and, behold, there came four chariots out from between two mountains; and the mountains were mountains of brass.

In the first chariot were red horses; and in the second chariot black horses;

Ezek. xxxi. 3–12, 16.

And in the third chariot white horses; and in the fourth chariot grisled and bay horses.

Then I answered and said unto the angel that talked with me, What are these, my lord?

And the angel answered and said unto me, These are the four spirits of the heavens, which go forth from standing before the Lord of all the earth.

The black horses which are therein go forth into the north country; and the white go forth after them; and the grisled go forth toward the south country.

And the bay went forth, and sought to go that they might walk to and fro through the earth: and he said, Get you hence, walk to and fro through the earth. So they walked to and fro through the earth.

Then cried he upon me, and spake unto me, saying, Behold, these that go toward the north country have quieted my spirit in the north country.[1]

Here though the vision itself has great suggestive power, the message conveyed through it is disappointing, for it is concerned only with the choice of a high priest and his aides for the rebuilding of the Temple. So also the great vision of Ezekiel of the rebuilding of the Temple shows how deliberately the form of the vision can be used for a purely expository

[1] Zech. vi. 1–8.

purpose. It is only a short step from these half
consciously elaborated visions from the time when
the prophecy was fading away to the laboriously
invented visions of *Daniel* and *Esdras*.

III

On the other hand the apocalypses in their purpose
and in the ideas which they brought into effective
bearing on the life of the Jews kept alight the torch
of faith handed down by the prophets. As a class
the apocalypses sprang from persecution. They
brought comfort to Jews, and in later times to
Christians, in the bitter throes of distress, strengthening their spirit by the promise of recompense in the
everlasting bliss of paradise. This background of
suffering is more explicitly outlined in *2 Esdras* than
in either *Daniel* or *Revelation*:

> And after seven days so it was, that the thoughts
> of my heart were very grievous unto me again,
> And my soul recovered the spirit of understand-
> ing, and I began to talk with the most High again,
> And said, O Lord that bearest rule, of every
> wood of the earth, and of all the trees thereof,
> thou hast chosen thee one only vine:
> And of all lands of the whole world thou hast
> chosen thee one pit: and of all the flowers thereof
> one lily:

And of all the depths of the sea thou hast filled thee one river: and of all builded cities thou hast hallowed Sion unto thyself:

And of all the fowls that are created thou hast named thee one dove: and of all the cattle that are made thou hast provided thee one sheep:

And among all the multitudes of people thou has gotten thee one people: and unto this people, whom thou lovedst, thou gavest a law that is approved of all.

And now, O Lord, why hast thou given this one people over unto many? and upon the one root hast thou prepared others, and why hast thou scattered thy only one people among many?

And they which did gainsay thy promises, and believed not thy covenants, have trodden them down.

If thou didst so much hate thy people, yet shouldest thou punish them with thine own hands.[1]

For thou seest that our sanctuary is laid waste, our altar broken down, our temple destroyed;

Our psaltery is laid on the ground, our song is put to silence, our rejoicing is at an end, the light of our candlestick is put out, the ark of our covenant is spoiled, our holy things are defiled, and the name that is called upon us is almost profaned: our children are put to shame, our priests are burnt, our Levites have gone into captivity, our virgins are defiled, and our wives ravished; our righteous men carried away, our little ones

[1] 2 Esdras v. 21-30.

destroyed, our young men are brought in bondage, and our strong men are become weak;

And, which is the greatest of all, the seal of Sion, hath now lost her honour; for she is delivered into the hands of them that hate us.[1]

Such a situation of apparent despair for their religion all these seers of the later time faced in the same manner as Amos and Hosea and Isaiah faced the overwhelming of Israel by the Assyrians, and as the Isaiah of the Exile faced the casting down of the hope of Judah by the Babylonians. Just as they rose above the dilemma on which their religion seemed inevitably wrecked to a higher and larger truth, so did these seers of the later time rise to the perception of immortality and the blessing of paradise. *Daniel* declares:

And many of them that sleep in the dust of the earth shall awake, some to everlasting life, and some to shame and everlasting contempt.

And they that be wise shall shine as the brightness of the firmament; and they that turn many to righteousness as the stars for ever and ever.[2]

And the book describes in terms of mystical splendor the glories of the kingdom of heaven:

I beheld till the thrones were cast down, and the Ancient of days did sit, whose garment was white

[1] 2 Esdras x. 21–23.   [2] Dan. xii. 2–3.

as snow, and the hair of his head like the pure wool; his throne was like the fiery flame, and his wheels as burning fire.

A fiery stream issued and came forth from before him; thousand thousands ministered unto him, and ten thousand times ten thousand stood before him: the judgment was set, and the books were opened.

.   .   .   .   .

I saw in the night visions, and, behold, one like the Son of man came with the clouds of heaven, and came to the Ancient of days, and they brought him near before him.

And there was given him dominion, and glory, and a kingdom, that all peoples, nations, and languages, should serve him: his dominion is an everlasting dominion, which shall not pass away, and his kingdom that which shall not be destroyed.[1]

Here the full organ music of such words as " his throne was like the fiery flame " and the " thousand times ten thousand," and the half apprehensible imagery stir the imagination with intimations of the immortal world.

That *Revelation* belongs to the same class of literature as *Daniel*, is obvious, but as I have already pointed out, though it has in part the same imagery, it shows greater richness of imaginative power and less literal prolixity in the use of the machinery of the

[1] Dan. vii. 9–10, 13–14.

visions. The general scheme of the unfolding of the seventh seal into the seven trumpets, and of the seven trumpets preparing the way for the seven vials, in spite of a certain superficial confusion resulting from the rush of the writer's feeling, is carried out to a conclusion. At each stage the author, before passing on to the judgment on the powers of evil, pauses to declare a glorious vision of God and the blessedness of the saints and martyrs; and the seventh seal and the seventh trumpet involve all that follows them. Into this structure the author has worked earlier oracles and visions, and their diversity accounts for the effect of overwhelming confusion that is apt to be one's first impression of the book. The dominant idea, however, is the final blessedness and reward of the saints and martyrs; and the description of the New Jerusalem is the actual climax towards which the whole book leads.

In language *Revelation* is clothed with associations gathered from almost all parts of the Old Testament, and especially from the largest and most suggestive passages of the prophets. The vision of God in Chapter iv is based on the visions of *Isaiah vi* and *Ezekiel i* and *x*; the four living beings are taken over directly from *Ezekiel i*; the four horsemen in the first four seals in Chapter vi lead back to the four chariots in the passage which I have just quoted from *Zechariah*; and the judgment in Chapter vi described in terms of storm, earthquake and volcano, recalls many passages like *Isaiah ii* and *Zephaniah* and *Joel*. Again, the language and the imagery of Chapter xiv are almost wholly taken from the prophets: " Babylon is fallen " from *Isaiah xxi,* the cup of the wrath of the Lord from *Jeremiah xxv,* the putting in of the sickle from *Joel iii*; and much of the imagery of the New Jerusalem is drawn from Ezekiel and from the Isaiah of the Exile. In spite of all these borrowings, however, the author of *Revelation* welds all that he has taken into the expression of his own purpose; he has his own vision of the struggle of the powers of this world against the Lord of hosts; and though he uses the words and figures of other men to shadow it forth, he does so without letting their words draw him aside from his own purpose. Accordingly there is no effect of patchwork, of a man of a less power using the work of greater men than himself; the greater power is here and the borrowings are fused by the heat of the writer's own thought. On the other hand, the connotation of this imagery for all Jewish Christian readers would have included all the holiest associations of their religion, just as for us it helps to fuse Old Testament and New into a single memory. Thus the power of the most exalted and spiritual parts of the Old Testament clothes as with a halo of richly colored light these new hopes and promises of the Christian faith; and *Revelation* becomes, as it were, a summary of the spiritual force of the Old Testament, brought together into a single book with a new and even more exalted meaning.

IV

Yet when one considers these descriptions of Heaven and of the Almighty carefully and tries to visualize what is described, one sees that there is no real hold on concrete and present fact: all that most touches one's imagination resolves itself into a vague blaze of glory which defies every effort to distinguish its outlines. Even the great Italian painters failed when they put such descriptions as these into visual form. *Daniel* itself asserts the ineffableness of this glory:

And I Daniel alone saw the vision: for the men that were with me saw not the vision; but a great quaking fell upon them, so that they fled to hide themselves.

Therefore I was left alone, and saw this great vision, and there remained no strength in me: for my comeliness was turned in me into corruption, and I retained no strength.[1]

[1] Dan. x. 7-9.

So in *Revelation*, though the descriptions seem so specific, yet it is impossible to visualize them. The picture of the New Jerusalem, which is seemingly phrased in terms of sight, cannot be put together:

> And the twelve gates were twelve pearls; every several gate was of one pearl: and the street of the city was pure gold, as it were transparent glass.
>
> And I saw no temple therein: for the Lord God Almighty and the Lamb are the temple of it.
>
> And the city had no need of the sun, neither of the moon, to shine in it: for the glory of God did lighten it, and the Lamb is the light thereof.[1]
>
> And he showed me a pure river of water of life, clear as crystal, proceeding out of the throne of God and of the Lamb.
>
> In the midst of the street of it, and on either side of the river, was there the tree of life, which bare twelve manner of fruits, and yielded her fruit every month: and the leaves of the tree were for the healing of the nations.
>
> .   .   .   .   .
>
> And there shall be no night there; and they need no candle, neither light of the sun; for the Lord God giveth them light: and they shall reign for ever and ever.[2]

No effort to make a mental picture of these splendors will leave any definite impression: the effect is only of an overwhelming glory and of a blessedness which

[1] Rev. xxi. 21–23.   [2] Ibid., xxii. 1–2, 5.

passes man's understanding. In spite of the fact that the imagery is material, the effect is wholly immaterial and ideal.

In this power of the prophecies and the apocalypse to communicate the sense of glories which are real, and yet impalpable, to give us a fleeting glimpse of unseen realities beyond the apprehension of our present faculties, we come, I think, to the inner essence and power of this biblical literature of which the prophecy and the apocalypse are the most typical portion. When one thinks of the serenity of the Greek representations of the gods beside these visions of the Hebrew and Christian seers, the latter at first may seem confused and turgid. Then as one thinks it over the very clarity and definiteness of outline in those wonderful marbles stand out as a limitation: in comparison with these vague and mystical imaginings of the Christian seers the representations of Greek art are impotent. In the end the Greek statue of a god, for all its gracious beauty, is only a glorified and idealized man. The visions of the apocalypse, on the other hand, transcend once for all the limitations of human nature: and frankly soaring away from the capacities of human thought, they are enabled to give such glimpses of the other world as are possible for beings who must for the present see through a glass darkly. Thus even in literature one feels that the prohibition, " Thou shalt not make unto thee any graven image, or any likeness of anything that is in heaven above or that is in the earth beneath, or that is in the water under the earth," produced unique results; for the Jewish mind and the Christian mind have never limited the godhead to visible form.

V

A student of literature cannot go far in the explanation of such illimitably suggestive power of infinite things as has made these visions of *Revelation* so fitting a climax to our Bible; but I may recall the fact that I pointed out in my discussion of the poetry of the Old Testament, that the expression of emotion depends largely on a concrete vocabulary, and still more on the rhythmical and musical attributes of style. This conclusion is borne out by the most eloquent parts of St. Paul's epistles, where as we have seen he rises spontaneously and inevitably into figurative language, and thus is enabled to record the glimpses of ineffable truths and blessedness which are so characteristic of him. Now when we examine the language of these passages of *Revelation*, we find that they also are full of words for the great forces of nature before which man is impotent:

And the temple of God was opened in heaven, and there was seen in his temple the ark of his testament: and there were lightnings, and voices, and thunderings, and an earthquake, and great hail.

And I looked, and behold a pale horse: and his name that sat on him was Death, and Hell followed with him. And power was given unto them over the fourth part of the earth, to kill with sword, and with hunger, and with death, and with the beasts of the earth.

And thus I saw the horses in the vision, and them that sat on them, having breastplates of fire, and of jacinth, and brimstone: and the heads of the horses were as the heads of lions; and out of their mouths issued fire and smoke and brimstone.

By these three was the third part of men killed, by the fire, and by the smoke, and by the brimstone, which issued out of their mouths.[1]

All the explanations of science cannot raise mankind above the terrors of such powers as these: reason is futile in the presence of sudden death; and the words which bring it vividly before us meet a response which is all the more powerful in that it is instinctive.

In another class of words used in both *Revelation*

[1] Rev. xi. 19; vi. 8; ix. 17–18.

and by St. Paul the force depends even less on any definable meaning. Consider the following passages:

> There are also celestial bodies, and bodies terrestrial: but the glory of the celestial is one, and the glory of the terrestrial is another.
> There is one glory of the sun, and another glory of the moon, and another glory of the stars: for one star differeth from another star in glory.
> So also is the resurrection of the dead.[1]

> And all the angels stood round about the throne, and about the elders and the four beasts, and fell before the throne on their faces, and worshipped God,
> Saying, Amen: Blessing, and glory, and wisdom, and thanksgiving, and honour, and power, and might, be unto our God for ever and ever. Amen.[2]

That part of the meaning of the words which counts in such bursts of eloquence cannot be set forth in a dictionary, for their denotation,—their absolute and tangible meaning,—is as nothing beside their connotation,—the cloud of implications, associations, suggestions, which float through our minds at their call. They stand for purely emotional affections of the mind, for large and deep stirrings of the soul which are as real and as indefinable as the soul itself. If there be a man whose soul does not respond to such

[1] 1 Cor. xv. 40–42.　　　　[2] Rev. vii. 11–12.

words as *honor*, *noble*, *glory*, one can do nothing to help him: such emotions are even less rational than other emotions, and therefore less susceptible of explanation or proof; and being so they lie at the roots of human nature.

This illimitably suggestive power of the words is made even more deeply and largely expressive by the music of the style; not only in the English but also in the Greek and in the Latin, the most impressive passages of *Revelation* are dominated by the same general sounds, the long, open vowels and the liquid, singing consonants.   Here is an example from *Revelation,* in the English and in the Latin:

> And the four beasts had each of them six wings about him; and they were full of eyes within: and they rest not day and night, saying, Holy, holy, holy, Lord God Almighty, which was, and is, and is to come.
>
> And when those beasts give glory and honour and thanks to him that sat on the throne, who liveth for ever and ever,
>
> The four and twenty elders fall down before him that sat on the throne, and worship him that liveth for ever and ever, and cast their crowns before the throne, saying,
>
> Thou art worthy, O Lord, to receive glory and honour and power: for thou hast created all things, and for thy pleasure they are and were created.[1]

[1] Rev. iv. 8–11.

Et quatuor animalia, singula eorum, habebant
alas senas, et in circuitu et intus plena sunt oculis;
et requiem non habebant die ac nocte, dicentia:
Sanctus, Sanctus, Sanctus, Dominus Deus omnip-
otens, qui erat, et qui est, et qui venturus est.

Et cum darent illa animalia gloriam et honorem,
et benedictionem sedenti super thronum, viventi
in sæcula sæculorum,

Procidebant viginti quatuor seniores ante seden-
tem in throno, et adorabant viventem in sæcula
sæculorum, et mittebant coronas suas ante
thronum dicentes:

Dignus es, Domine Deus noster, accipere gloriam,
et honorem et virtutem, quia tu creasti omnia, et
propter voluntatem tuam erant, et creata sunt.

These passages, with many others like them in the
prophets, in *Daniel* and in *Revelation*, illustrate the
truth of literature which has been set forth by Professor James in his discussion of mysticism:

" In mystical literature such self-contradictory
phrases as ' dazzling obscurity,' ' whispering silence,'
' teeming desert,' are continually met with. They prove
that not conceptual speech, but music rather, is the
element through which we are best spoken to by mystical truth. Many mystical scriptures are indeed little
more than musical compositions." Then after quoting
an unintelligible passage from Madame Blavatsky he
goes on, " These words, if they do not awaken laughter
as you receive them, probably stir chords within you
which music and language touch in common. Music

gives us ontological messages which non-musical criticism is unable to contradict, though it may laugh at our foolishness in minding them. There is a verge of the mind which these things haunt; and whispers therefrom mingle with the operations of our understanding, even as the waters of the infinite ocean send their waves to break among the pebbles that lie upon our shores." [1]

VI

With these fine words we may take our leave of the different types of literature in the Bible, before passing on to consider how such large and noble qualities as we have been considering not only survived the process of translation, but in our English Bible almost gained new power. But before so passing on it is worth while to stop for a moment to point out in how real a way *Revelation* embodies and exemplifies the attributes and qualities which in English literature are peculiarly biblical.

We have seen that in the narrative the especial virtues, which have been so marvellous a preservative against the inroads of oblivion, are the simplicity and the concreteness; that in these stories solid fact follows solid fact with no intrusion of the writer's interpretation of their meaning. So likewise with the po-

[1] W. James, *Varieties of Religious Experience*, p. 421.

etry: what distinguishes that from everything else in English literature is the undiluted concreteness which it took from the Hebrew, and which makes it the immediate expression of the emotions; and this expressiveness is reinforced by the strong rhythm and music, which are an even more direct expression of emotion. The wisdom of the Old Testament we have seen to be wholly intuitive, and therefore dependent on feeling rather than on intellectual processes; and even in the epistles of the New Testament, where we come nearest to the rigorously abstract reasoning of the modern world, the most memorable parts, for literature at any rate, are the bursts of eloquence which soar off in impassioned figures to regions where reason must give place to intuition. The prophecy at its height shows the complete fusion of understanding and feeling, the latter expressed in the strong rhythm of the poetical form and in the nobly figurative language of the oracles. Then as the outward form of the prophecy broke up, where the element of feeling faded out the gift of prophecy itself seems to have failed: where the feeling preponderated prophecy merged insensibly into the apocalypse, through which its spirit was perpetuated into Christianity. In all these forms, therefore, the appeal is through the feelings and by way of intuition to our perception of the deeper and larger truths which defy delimitation by the intellectual processes of reasoning.

Revelation surpasses all the other books of the Bible in its frank self-abandonment to the great realms of feeling and instinctive reactions which surround on every side the little region of experience which has been mapped by the intellect. Its language has no meaning to the type of mind which must find a literal and consistent meaning in all it reads. Scholars find in the beast with the seven head and ten horns data which enable them to settle with some certainty the period of the book; and in the great red dragon and in some other parts of the imagery a transfiguration of the mythology of Assyria and Chaldea and the primitive ancestors of the Jews. But a minute's consideration will show that the cool and dispassionate study which has rescued such facts as these from so tumultuous a rush of mystical emotion is a very different frame of mind from that of the reader who, abandoning all idea that the book is explicable in the terms of this present world, bathes his soul in its portrayal of the glories of the new heavens and the new earth. To take the book and all its imagery literally, on the other hand, would be like attempting to recite in a literal sense such a hymn as "There is a fountain filled with blood," or even "Onward, Christian soldiers":

religious emotion is not expressed by the denotation of words, but by their higher connotations, and by the purely sensuous qualities of music. Undoubtedly there are people, and deeply religious people, whom *Revelation* leaves cold and unmoved; for there are many people whose temperaments incline them toward the cooler services of the Puritan churches rather than to the rich and luxuriant liturgies of the medieval church and of the Church of Rome to-day. Even such people, however, can intellectually apprehend how the deepest appeal of the Bible, from the side of literature at any rate, is through the super-rational feelings of awe and reverence. The hold of all great religious literature is on the emotional side of human nature, and the exclusively religious temperament seems always to have a large strain of mysticism. Our English Bible would not be what it is if it did not in all its parts through the large suggestions and associations of its vocabulary and the surging music of its style enrich its message with these overtones of meaning; and in *Revelation* for those who have ears to hear these illimitable meanings dominate all others.

CHAPTER VIII

THE TRANSLATION

I

So far we have been considering the distinct types of literature which are to be found in the English Bible; in discussing them I have tried to throw light on their form and other characteristics by some of the facts that have been gathered concerning their probable source and history. These facts, which have been collected and arranged by the science which is technically known as the Introduction to the Old Testament and the New Testament or as the Higher Criticism, show that the various books of the Bible, especially those of the Old Testament, are of various origin, and sometimes of a kind of compilation unknown to us to-day. To understand how much perspective there is in these books and how illuminating that perspective is one must follow out a considerable course of study in this subject: in such an essay as this I have been able only to refer to results which scholars have reached after long and devoted labor. Now, in order to lead on to a study and understanding of the literary character of the English Bible as a whole I must sketch first the processes by which all these separate books became one book; and then the various stages of translation and revision which ended in the Authorised Version, otherwise known as the King James Bible. This is for English literature, in our times at any rate, the form in which the Bible stands as the great monument of English literature.

To understand the literary character of this great translation we must not forget that it is a translation, and that at the same time it has, what one hardly looks for in a translation made to-day, unequalled vitality and freshness of expression. It is one of the few examples in English of a translation which is complete on both sides; for it renders not only the meaning of the single words and sentences, for the most part with great accuracy, but it communicates to us also the spirit and vigor of the original. In other words, it not only gives us the denotation of the books which it translates, but it clothes its own language with the rich connotation of the original and with the less definable but no less potent expressive power of sound. Our study of the power of the Bible in English literature would be incomplete if we did not at least make an effort to find some of the causes for this especial success of the Authorised Version.

I will begin the consideration of this part of the subject by bringing together a few facts about the collection of the original books into a single book, and then, before going on to discuss the actual translation into English, consider briefly two intermediate translations which have had some influence on the present form of the English.

II

The collection of the books of the Old Testament and of the New Testament, which were so varied in origin and date and character, into a single book thought of as " the Scriptures " occupied a considerable length of time and was the result of processes which can be traced only vaguely. We know that by the end of the first century A.D. the Jews of Palestine accepted the books of the Old Testament as we read them in the English Bible, and that by the end of the second century A.D. the books of the New Testament, nearly as we have them, were accepted by the Christians. In the case of the Old Testament the Greek-speaking Jews admitted more books into the Scriptures than did the Jews of Palestine, and in the case of the New Testament the Eastern and

Western Churches differed on the acceptance of *Revelation* and some of the Catholic Epistles. But the idea of a closed list of books which alone should be considered the inspired word of God, and in the main the list of the books which were to be so accepted, were established at these dates.

In the case of the Old Testament this acceptance of a definite set of books to the exclusion of all others came about in three stages of growth which are reflected in the well-known phrase " The Law, the Prophets, and the Writings." The first stage in this acceptance of certain books as an authoritative statement of the will of Jehovah above and beyond all other books goes back ultimately to the discovery and promulgation of the original Deuteronomy by Josiah in 621 B.C. When that book was once accepted as authoritatively stating the covenant between Jehovah and his people, it undoubtedly acquired a veneration different from that of all other books. It was now thought of as " the Law." During the Exile this idea of a definite statement by Jehovah of the Law which his chosen people were to fulfil was developed and crystallized by the priests; and after the reforms of Ezra and Nehemiah *Deuteronomy* was merged in the larger, more comprehensive, and more fully developed book of law and history which we know as the Pentateuch. Henceforth the Law became the central and dominant fact in the religion of the Jews and in their Scriptures. The Pentateuch, which arose from the amalgamation of the history of the world and of the people of Israel down to the final giving of the Law through Moses, was known to the Jews as the " five-fifths of the Law "; and it maintained a sanctity and authority above all other parts of the Scriptures.

The other two layers of the canon, as the technical term is, gradually came into existence through a process of growth which we can understand only by inference from a few scattered facts. We know that by the second century B.C. the Jews were accustomed to speak of " the Law and the Prophets," and that the books of the prophets were quoted by a formula which implied that they were now recognised as part of the Scriptures. These books of the prophets included for the Jews the Former Prophets, which are our books of *Joshua, Judges, Samuel,* and *Kings,* and the Latter Prophets, which are our books of the prophets—*Isaiah, Jeremiah, Ezekiel,* and *The Twelve.* The reason that these historical books were included in " The Prophets " lay in the fact that their composition was controlled by the prophetic theory of history set forth by *Deuteronomy.* All these books must have assumed their place beside the Law because they were looked on either as illustrations of the working of the Law in the history of Israel or else as parallel and equally direct declarations of the will of Jehovah. Thus they too came to be considered as standing apart from all other books and possessed of a peculiar and sacred authority.

The final stage in the building up of the Old Testament is even more obscure in its history: we know little more than the fact that by the time the New Testament books were written the Jews commonly used the phrase " the Law, the Prophets and the Writings." It is probable that the addition of this third layer to the canon was quite as informal and natural a process as that which put the Former and the Latter Prophets beside the Law. Certain books, such as *Psalms* and *Proverbs*, were venerated because of their traditional association with David and with Solomon, the founder of the kingdom and the builder of the temple; and for the inclusion of *Psalms* there was the added reason of their daily use in the services of the temple. The inclusion of other books, such as *Esther*, the *Song of Solomon*, and *Ecclesiastes*, was disputed until the end of the first century A.D. Soon after that time, however, the leading rabbis seem to have united on the list of the books which should be included in the Scriptures, and the canon of the Old Testament was complete so far as the Hebrew was concerned. Even then, however, the Greek translation of the Scriptures, commonly known as the Septuagint, which was the Bible of Greek-speaking Jews and Christians in the first Christian centuries, included a number of books which were not accepted by the Jews of Palestine. The growth of the Old Testament canon must therefore have been gradual and by no means uniform. One can understand why pious men among the Jews should have felt that such books as *Esther*, the *Song of Solomon*, and *Ecclesiastes* had no place in the sacred scriptures, but we know vaguely only the reasons which finally caused their inclusion,—in the case of the two latter pretty clearly the traditional association with Solomon, in the case of *Esther* through a supposed explanation of the feast of Purim.

The canon of the New Testament seems to have been formed by an analogous process of natural selection. The epistles of St. Paul were probably the first of the New Testament books to be known and read in their present form. While the original apostles were still living it is probable that the stories and teachings of the gospel were largely transmitted by word of mouth. When these first disciples gave place to the second generation, however, and as the gospel, enlarging its field, was spread more and more through the catechists who had learned the stories and teachings from them, oral transmission must have tended to give way to written. The common material in the first three gospels points, it is now generally held, to the existence of two documents or perhaps sets of documents, one of which contained a life of Jesus in a form very much like our *St. Mark*, the other the body of his sayings, but in a form not yet wholly fixed, as can be seen by the differing use of them in *St. Matthew* and *St. Luke*. The existence of extra-canonical gospels such as those of *The Hebrews* and of *St. Peter* seems to show that these materials were brought together in still other combinations than those which we have in the canonical gospels. If the first three gospels had come into their present shape not later than ten or fifteen years after the destruction of Jerusalem in 70 A.D., it is probable that for something less than a century they were more or less in competition with other gospels based on the same or like materials combined in a somewhat different way; and that our three gospels finally established themselves by their own superiority to the others. The *Gospel according to St. John*, which is in intention much more an interpretation of the facts than a statement of them, probably was written by the end of the first century. The *Acts of the Apostles*, which is by the same author as *St. Luke*, must have been written about the same time as that gospel. The *Epistles of St. John*, like the gospel, would have come before the end of the first century; the other epistles, even the pseudonymous epistle of *2 Peter*, must have been written not later than the middle of the second century; and by the last quarter of the second century we know that the fathers of the church were making lists of the New Testament books which should be authoritatively accepted.

In the meantime the Old Testament had been the scriptures of the Christian church as well as of the Jewish church. Thus by the beginning of the third century the term " Scriptures " had a fixed denotation. For the Jews of Palestine it meant the books which are now included in our Old Testament; and all other Jews must soon have accepted this limitation. For the Greek-speaking Jews and for most of the Christians the Scriptures included not only the books of our Old Testament but also those of our Apocrypha and the books of the New Testament as we have them. Thus early in the first Christian centuries " the Scriptures " meant a limited number of books, on which the faith of the church could be based. The first stage, therefore, in the creation of our Bible was now complete. The processes which we have to trace henceforward have to do first with certain versions which were the forerunners of the translation into English and then with that translation itself.

III

The first translation which bears in any important way on our English Bible was the translation into Greek made for the use of the Alexandrian Jews during the last three centuries of the old era: it is commonly known as the Septuagint. The bearing of this version on the English is chiefly through the Vulgate and therefore indirect. It gave some of the books the names which we use to-day; and it established the order of the books of the Old Testament as we have them in the English. As it was in some sense a collection of national literature it included such pious tales as *Tobit* and *Judith*, *2 Esdras*, a Jewish apocalypse written after the destruction of Jerusalem in 70 A.D., later books of wisdom like *Ecclesiasticus* and the *Wisdom of Solomon*, the latter of which could not have been expressed in Hebrew, such legendary matter as the stories of Susanna and of Bel and the Dragon, which were added to *Daniel*, and finally such later history as the two books of *Maccabees*. Though all these were more or less closely analogous to kindred books of the Palestinian canon they were not accepted as authoritative by the Jews of Palestine. The order of the books also was altered. Where the Hebrew canon arranged the books according to the chronological growth of the canon,

" the Law, the Prophets and the Writings," the Septuagint rearranged them by a literary classification, putting the books of history in the chronological order of the events which they narrate, then the books of poetry and wisdom, then the Prophets. This arrangement was followed by the English translators in the sixteenth century, though they translated from the original Hebrew.

More important, however, than this change in the order of the books and the giving of a few names was the influence of the language of this Greek version on the Greek of the New Testament. Since the Septuagint was the Bible of Greek-speaking Jews and Christians, the effect of its language on the writers of the New Testament may be compared to the effect of our English Bible on Bunyan's *Pilgrim's Progress*. Out of one hundred and sixty direct quotations from the Old Testament in the New Testament almost all come from the Septuagint; and many familiar phrases came into the New Testament by quotation from this Greek version of the Old Testament. Such phrases as " a day of darkness," " the day of the Lord," " the birds of heaven," " enter into thy closet," " where their worm dieth not and their fire is not quenched," in the Greek New Testament were all direct quotations from this Greek Old Testament. Its influence has been summed up in these words: " Not the Old Testament only, but the Alexandrian version of the Old Testament, has left its mark on every part of the New Testament, even in chapters and books where it is not directly cited. It is not too much to say that in its literary form and expression the New Testament would have been a widely different book had it been written by authors who knew the Old Testament only in the original, or who knew it in a Greek version other than that of the Septuagint." [1]

Though this version was not the basis for the translation of any of the canonical books in our English Bible, its influence cannot be left out of account. Not only did it strongly affect the phrasing of the Greek New Testament, but it also furnished us with the books of the Apocrypha, and they are for literary purposes nearly as important as the regular books of the Bible. Moreover it was in large part the basis of the Latin Bible of the Middle Ages, commonly known as the Vulgate.

IV

The Vulgate again is a version of the Bible which, like the Septuagint, is not in the direct line of ancestry of our English Bible. Nevertheless, unlike the

[1] H. B. Swete, *Introduction to the Old Testament in Greek*, p. 404.

Septuagint, it had direct influence on the language of the English version; and indirectly it contributed a good deal which helped to make the English Bible a great work of literature as well as the foundation of religion. The first translators of our English Bible, Tindale, Coverdale, Rogers and the rest, were churchmen who grew up in a time when the Scriptures could be known only in the Latin. They must have known their Vulgate Bible in the way that our fathers knew their English Bible; and from the freedom with which the Vulgate is quoted all through the sixteenth century and even to the time of Francis Bacon we may feel confident that the minds of these first translators were saturated with its phrases and their ears ringing with its rhythms and tones. On the other hand, when the original Greek was first made generally accessible by Erasmus' New Testament, the *Novum Instrumentum* of 1516, the obvious corruptness of the text of the Vulgate helped to send Luther and Tindale to the preparation of new and accurate translations from the original. This incentive was strengthened by the fact that the words and phrases of the Vulgate had been overlaid with fantastic allegorical interpretations, and even more by the fact that on the ecclesiastical connotations of such words as *pœnitentia, ecclesia, presbyter,* and the like were based many of the most oppressive and unspiritual practices of the church of that period. Moreover, in the history of literature the Vulgate is of great importance for its own sake. It was the Bible for all Europe down to the Reformation, and the only source of knowledge of the Scriptures; and all references to the Bible in mediæval and Renaissance literature to go back to it. In itself, besides being one of the two or three best translations ever made of the Scriptures, it is a work of extraordinary vigor, beauty, and individuality of character. A modern writer says of it, " we may gladly echo the words of the ' translator ' to the readers in our own Authorised Version that Jerome performed his task ' with that evidence of great learning, judgment, industry, and faithfulness, that he hath for ever bound the Church unto him in a debt of special remembrance and thankfulness.' " [1]

In text the Vulgate is a curious conglomerate of fresh translation from the Hebrew and the Greek and thorough or partial revision of what is known as the Old Latin text. When Latin gradually became the language of the Western civilized world, translations of the Septuagint were made into Latin, so that by the middle of the third century A.D. there was a complete Latin Bible, though not necessarily in

[1] H. J. White, Article "Vulgate," *Hastings' Dictionary of the Bible.*

a single text. In 383 A.D. Damasus, who was then Pope, commissioned Jerome to prepare a revised and authoritative version of the New Testament in Latin.

Jerome was singularly well qualified for the work. Beginning life with the best education the time afforded in literature, rhetoric, and Greek, he was converted from worldly things when a little past thirty years old and gave the rest of his life to asceticism and study. He was an excellent Latin scholar, with a pure and vigorous Latin style of his own, a good Greek scholar, and later in life a good Hebrew scholar. He seems to have had the rare combination of thorough and laborious scholarship with ardor of temperament and command of style, a combination that we shall find also in William Tindale. He was thus able to fuse the products of his learning and give to the style of his version a flow and rhythm which translations usually lack.

Jerome began his work with a thorough revision of the gospels. The rest of the New Testament he revised also from the Greek, but much less thoroughly. After this he turned his attention to the Old Testament, beginning with the *Psalter* and revising this and some other books from the Septuagint. By this time it became apparent to him, however, that he must go to the Hebrew; and accordingly through the instruction of a Jew who came secretly to him at night, he perfected his knowledge of that language. Then in irregular order he translated most of the books of the Old Testament from the Hebrew and certain of the apocryphal books from the Chaldee. The *Wisdom of Solomon, Ecclesiasticus* and probably *1* and *2 Maccabees* he did not revise; they stand in the Vulgate in the form which they held in the Old Latin. Thus this work, which was to have so potent an influence, left its maker in a curiously composite form. It came into general circulation in the place of the Old Latin only very gradually; and like all other works of the Middle Ages, being handed down by copying, its text gradually became corrupted, at first by familiar phrases from the Old Latin which were written in by sleepy copyists, later on by carelessness and the invasion of marginal notes. Various efforts were made to restore the original text, notably by Alcuin on the commission of Charlemagne, but it was not until printing was invented in the fifteenth century that the text became anything like settled. Even then there were notorious divergencies in reading in many places; and when, in 1590, Pope Sixtus Quintus issued an edition which he decreed should be accepted as the " true, lawful, authentic, and indubitable " Vulgate, as prescribed by the Council of Trent for use in all the churches of the Christian world, it was found to have so many errors that a revised edition was issued by authority in 1592. Some of the divergencies of the Vulgate from the Hebrew and the accepted Greek text it should be said, however, go back to variant readings in early manuscripts which are of considerable importance for the restoration of the text.

In his discussion of the canon in his various prefaces Jerome pointed out explicitly that the books which appear in our English Bible in the Apocrypha were not found in the Hebrew; and he made the distinction, which was taken up by the English Church, that " the Church doth read these books for example of life and instruction of manners; but yet doth it not apply them to establish any doctrine," as it is put in the Thirty-Nine Articles. Nevertheless the Council of Trent in 1547 included these books as part of the sacred and canonical scriptures; and until the time that Luther had gone back to Jerome's declaration, no one seems to have thought of distinguishing between these books and the others.

The direct influence of the Vulgate on the text and vocabulary of the English Bible I will refer to later. For the present I will confine myself to pointing out certain qualities and attributes which it possesses in common with our English Bible and which it seems not unreasonable to think the latter gained in part at any rate by reflection from the Vulgate. This indirect influence on the style and general expressiveness of our English Bible is a difficult matter to estimate, and it can never be weighed with any exactness. Nevertheless, as I have said, Tindale and his successors must have been steeped in the language of the Vulgate; and since its style has strongly marked qualities which fit it for expressing spiritual truths and deep and earnest feeling, we may reasonably suppose that it had considerable influence on the style of our English versions.

To begin with, the Latin of the Vulgate is very far from the finished and rhetorical language of Cicero or even of Cæsar. The Latin of Jerome's time was more or less broken down in syntax, and like all languages in their decay its vocabulary was much contaminated by local and colloquial forms, some of which went back to the Latin of several centuries before. As a matter of fact, this Latin of the Vulgate is nearer to English in its constructions and order of words than it is to the classical Latin. It shows the direct influence of the Hebrew in the Old Testament and of Greek considerably affected by the Hebrew in the New Testament. A few examples will make clear the comparative resemblance of this Latin of the Vulgate to our modern English:

> Adæ vero dixit: Quia audisti vocem uxoris tuæ, et comedisti de ligno, ex quo præceperam tibi, ne

comederes, maledicta terra in opere tuo: in labori-
bus comedes ex ea cunctis diebus vitæ tuæ.

Spinas et tribulos germinabit tibi, et comedes
herbam terræ.

In sudore vultus tui vesceris pane, donec rever-
taris in terram de qua sumtus es: quia pulvis es,
et in pulverem reverteris.

And unto Adam he said, Because thou hast
harkened unto the voice of thy wife, and hast
eaten of the tree, of which I commanded thee,
saying, Thou shalt not eat of it: cursed is the
ground for thy sake; in sorrow shalt thou eat of it
all the days of thy life;

Thorns also and thistles shall it bring forth to
thee; and thou shalt eat the herb of the field;

In the sweat of thy face shalt thou eat bread,
till thou return unto the ground; for out of it wast
thou taken: for dust thou art, and unto dust shalt
thou return.[1]

Ubi eras, quando ponebam fundamenta terræ?
indica mihi, si habes intelligentiam.

Quis posuit mensuras ejus, si nosti? vel quis
tetendit super eam lineam?

Super quo bases illius solidatæ sunt? aut quis
demisit lapidem angularem ejus,

Cum me laudarent simul astra matutina, et
jubilarent omnes filii Dei?

Where wast thou, when I laid the foundations
of the earth? declare, if thou hast understanding.

[1] Gen. iii. 17–19.

Who hath laid the measures thereof, if thou knowest? or who hath stretched the line upon it?

Whereupon are the foundations thereof fastened? or who laid the corner stone thereof;

When the morning stars sang together, and all the sons of God shouted for joy?[1]

Alia claritas solis, alia claritas lunæ, et alia claritas stellarum. Stella enim a stella differt in claritate:

Sic et resurrectio mortuorum. Seminatur in corruptione, surget in incorruptione.

Seminatur in ignobilitate, surget in gloria; seminatur in infirmitate, surget in virtute;

Seminatur corpus animale, surget corpus spiritale. Si est corpus animale, est et spiritale, sicut scriptum est:

Factus est primus homo Adam in animam viventem; novissimus Adam in spiritum vivificantem.

Sed non prius, quod spiritale est, sed quod animale; deinde quod spiritale.

Primus homo de terra, terrenus; secundus homo de cœlo, cœlestis.

There is one glory of the sun, and another glory of the moon, and another glory of the stars: for one star differeth from another star in glory.

So also is the resurrection of the dead. It is sown in corruption; it is raised in incorruption:

It is sown in dishonour; it is raised in glory: it is sown in weakness; it is raised in power:

[1] Job xxxviii. 4–7.

It is sown a natural body; it is raised a spiritual body. There is a natural body, and there is a spiritual body.

And so it is written, The first man Adam was made a living soul; the last Adam was made a quickening spirit.

Howbeit that was not first which is spiritual, but that which is natural; and afterward that which is spiritual.

The first man is of the earth, earthy: the second man is the Lord from heaven.[1]

This close resemblance in the order of the Latin to the natural order of the words in English helps to make it probable that its language affected the translation made by Tindale and Coverdale.

When we turn to the sensuous qualities and attributes which the English has in common with the Vulgate the richness of the music and the expressive beat of the rhythm stand out preëminent. A notable characteristic of our English Bible, as I have pointed out in the chapter on the poetry, is its power to express strong and earnest feeling through the pure sound of the style: through its rhythm and the harmony and mingling of tones its language gives expression to those deeper and diffused moods which for lack of more exact expression we call stirrings of the soul. Since the symbols of style are in the first

[1] 1 Cor. xv. 41–47.

place symbols for the sounds of the human voice, style shares to some degree the power of music to body forth by direct appeal to the ear these feelings which must always elude articulate expression through the meanings of the words. How far this power of music and of the musical sound of language lies in the qualities and successions of the sound and how far in the beat of the rhythm cannot be said, even if it were necessary for our present purpose to know; but it is important to recognise that the sensuous attributes of style are in themselves an expression of an important part of man's consciousness; and that in them style finds much of its power to express the deep and noble emotions which are so large a part of religion. Unconsciously Tindale and his successors recognised this fact, as did all writers of the sixteenth century.

In the Vulgate this music was so rich that it could clothe even the bare, unlovely details of the sacrifices with a beauty of coloring that would make them in the Latin a fit basis for an anthem.

Idcirco ubi immolabitur holocaustum, mactabitur et victima pro delicto: sanguis ejus per gyrum altaris fundetur.

Offerent ex ea caudam et adipem qui operit vitalia:

Duos renunculos, et pinguedinem quæ juxta ilia est, reticulumque jecoris cum renunculis.

Et adolebit ea sacerdos super altare: incensum est Domini pro delicto.

In the place where they kill the burnt offering shall they kill the trespass offering: and the blood thereof shall he sprinkle round about upon the altar.
And he shall offer of it all the fat thereof; the rump, and the fat that covereth the inwards,
And the two kidneys, and the fat that is on them, which is by the flanks, and the caul that is above the liver, with the kidneys, it shall he take away:
And the priest shall burn them upon the altar for an offering made by fire unto the Lord: it is a trespass offering.

In more inspiring passages the Latin indefinitely deepens and enriches the expression and clothes it as with the strong but subdued harmonies of a great organ, as in the psalm I have quoted on p. 123, and in the following passage from *Revelation*:

Et vidi, et audivi vocem Angelorum multorum in circuitu throni, et animalium et seniorum; et erat numerus eorum millia millium,
Dicentium voce magna: Dignus est Agnus, qui occisus est, accipere virtutem et divinitatem, et sapientiam et fortitudinem, et honorem et gloriam, et benedictionem.
Et omnem creaturam, quæ in cœlo est, et super terram et sub terra, et quæ sunt in mari, et quæ

¹ Lev. vii. 2–5.

in eo, omnes audivi dicentes: Sedenti in throno, et
Agno: Benedictio et honor, et gloria et potestas in
sæcula sæculorum.

Et quatuor animalia dicebant: Amen. Et
viginti quatuor seniores ceciderunt in facies suas
et adoraverunt viventem in sæcula sæculorum.

And I beheld, and I heard the voice of many
angels round about the throne and the beasts and
the elders: and the number of them was ten thousand times ten thousand, and thousands of thousands:

Saying with a loud voice, Worthy is the Lamb
that was slain to receive power, and riches, and
wisdom, and strength, and honour, and glory, and
blessing.

And every creature which is in heaven, and on
the earth, and under the earth, and such as are in
the sea, and all that are in them, heard I saying,
Blessing, and honour, and glory, and power, be
unto him that sitteth upon the throne, and unto
the Lamb for ever and ever.

And the four beasts said, Amen. And the four
and twenty elders fell down and worshipped him
that liveth for ever and ever.[1]

The prevalence of such resonant phrases as *vocem
angelorum multorum, honorem at gloriam, in sæcula
sæculorum,* makes this passage almost an anthem as
it stands; and its grave sonorousness is a palpable

---

[1] Rev. v. 11–14.

utterance of the awe and reverence which man feels in the presence of an almighty God. The more that one reads in this splendid Latin Bible the more sure does one become that men who were brought up on it and who knew the Scriptures first in its noble tones must have been deeply influenced in their own translation by its stateliness and music.

That writers of the sixteenth century were able, as we are not to-day, to carry over into English these deeply expressive qualities of the mediæval Latin the *Book of Common Prayer* of the English Church is an even more tangible proof. Cranmer took over most of its collects and prayers from the old service books of the Roman Church, which in turn had gathered them from the writings of the ancient fathers of the Church back to the time of St. Jerome, St. Augustine, and St. Chrysostom. With the genius of his century for translation he transferred to the English not only the meaning of the words, but also the rich sound and rhythm of the mediæval Latin; and that without the use of Latinate words. Here are two examples,—the first the collect for the Fifth Sunday after Easter, the other that for the Twenty-fifth Sunday after Trinity. I give first the English, then the Latin of each.

O Lord, from whom all good things do come; Grant to us thy humble servants, that by thy holy inspiration we may think those things that be good, and by thy merciful guiding may perform the same.

Deus, a quo bona cuncta procedunt, largire supplicibus tuis, ut cogitemus te inspirante quæ recta sunt et te gubernante eadem faciamus.

Stir up, we beseech thee, O Lord, the wills of thy faithful people; that they, plenteously bringing forth the fruit of good works, may of thee be plenteously rewarded.

Excita, quæsumus, Domine, tuorum fidelium voluntates ut, divini operis fructum propensius exequentes, pietatis tuæ remedia majora percipiant.[1]

In these cases, as in so many others in the book, in spite of the small number of Latinate words, one is struck by the similarity of the rhythm and coloring between the English and the Latin. Merely as an achievement in translation this clothing of a non-Latinate style with the organ-like richness of the Latin originals has never been surpassed in English. What is important for us here is the fact that it shows how readily and how fully men of the sixteenth century could transfer to English not only the meaning of the words, but also the rich coloring of the Latin style.

[1] From Campion and Beamont: *The Prayer Book Interleaved*: London, 1888.

In the case of the Bible these same qualities of
sound, the subdued richness, the strong beat of the
rhythm and all the other subtler attributes which
clothe the style with its simple and unconscious earnestness are found both in the Vulgate and in the
English translation. This mediæval Latin, as I have
said, was a language of very different qualities from
the language of Cicero and Cæsar. With the greater
simplicity of structure which it owed ultimately in
the case of the Bible to the simplicity of the Hebrew,
it took over from the Hebrew a certain swiftness and
momentum also; and at the same time through the
dominance of the singing qualities which I have
already referred to in the chapter on the poetry of
the Bible, it had a richness and coloring which have
perhaps never been surpassed, and which suffuse its
words with deep reverence and earnestness. This
earnest reverence is one of the most notable qualities
of our English Bible, and that which most lifts it
above all other books of our literature. Since the
capacity of language to express these ennobling emotions depends largely on its purely musical resources,
and since, as we have seen, Tindale and his successors when they thought of a text of the Bible would
have thought of it first in the richly sonorous form
of the Vulgate, we may safely assume that some
part of the sober earnestness and reverence of our

English Bible is to be ascribed to unconscious reflection from the Latin.

At the same time these intermediate translations into Greek and Latin must have had another, though a more remote and less tangible consequence on the style of the English. We have seen that the original books of the Old Testament came from very different ages and circumstances in the history of the people of Israel, and that this difference is still reflected in the style of the English. So far as the style of the Latin had influence it must have helped to blur and obliterate these differences between the various books and parts of books and brought them nearer to a common type of style. Since none of the translators whether into English or into Greek or Latin had any suspicion of these differences of origin every fresh translation and revision would have helped towards making a single book out of writings which had come into existence in such a variety of ways.

For all these reasons, then, if we would understand the nature and power of the English Bible as a work of literature we must take into account the Vulgate, and even to some extent its forerunner, the Septuagint. We shall find later that the Vulgate made some direct contribution to the phrasing of the Authorised Version, especially through the use made of it by Coverdale both for his own Bible of 1535 and for the Great Bible of 1539–41, and also through the labors of Gregory Martin on the Rhemish New Testament of 1582, on which King James's revisers drew so freely. But besides this direct contribution there is, as I trust that I have made clear, the larger contribution of musical expressiveness, which is even more important from the point of view of literature, since it goes farther towards fixing the individuality and strengthening the power of the book. As in the case of a man the set of the mouth, the carriage of the head, the tones of the voice and the decisiveness or slackness of utterance mould our idea of his character, so with a book: rhythm and harmony can no more be reduced to notation than such indications of character in a man can be recorded by anthropometry; yet they are the ultimate means of expression of feelings and emotions which in the book as in the man are in the deepest sense the essentials of character. Though criticism can make no analysis of such facts, it cannot ignore them; for if they cannot be defined they can in part be described; and even as here a little light can be thrown on their origin and causes. And since in the case of the Bible it is even more true than with most books that the spirit is the life, anything that in any way helps to illuminate these deep-lying realities is worthy of study and record.

V

The first complete translation into English was that of John Wyclif. This, however, it is almost certain, contributed nothing to our present English Bible. In the first place it was a translation of the Vulgate: and one of the reasons which stirred Tindale to his work was the fact that had been made clear by the labors of Erasmus, that the text of the Vulgate was in many places corrupt and untrustworthy. In the second place the English of Wyclif's version in the sixteenth century was already archaic. And finally we have Tindale's express declaration in the Epistle to the Reader subjoined to his first edition of the New Testament, " I had no man to counterfet, nether was holpe with englysshe of eny that had interpreted the same, or soche lyke thinge in the scripture before tyme." Wyclif's version was undoubtedly of importance in preparing the way for the reception of the gospel in English, for many manuscripts of the whole or parts of it persist until to-day; and Foxe in his *Book of Martyrs* cites many cases of prosecutions in the early part of the sixteenth century for owning and reading portions of the Scriptures in English, which must have been copies of Wyclif's translation. It is not clear how widespread this reading was. Foxe's extracts come chiefly from the registers of the dioceses of London and of Lincoln, and it is doubtful if this spirit had spread through many other parts of England. Wyclif's doctrines had become so closely associated with the political and social aberrations of Lollardy, that his translation of the Bible must have become discredited by such dangerous associations.

The impulse which led to Tindale's translation of the Bible into English came with the return of John Colet from Italy shortly before the end of the fifteenth century. He had gone to Italy to study Greek, and he had devoted his study to equipping himself with a knowledge of the New Testament in the original language. Coming back to England, he swept away the monstrous superstructure of subtleties which the ecclesiastical philosophy had built on the text of the Vulgate, and declared that the Scripture was to be understood in its plain and simple sense by anyone who could read the language in which it was written. This treatment of the Scriptures was revolutionary to most men of the times, but enormously stimulating to the men whose minds had been opened to the light of the new learning of the Renaissance. These ideas of Colet's came to their full fruition in the scholarly labors of Erasmus.

The latter had come to England in 1498, already skilled in all the learning of the schoolmen, but now eager to study Greek. From the first his intercourse with Colet seems to have swept away his interest in the hairsplitting of the scholastic fathers; and he gave himself with his whole heart to the study of Greek and the propagation of Colet's reasonable view of religion and of learning. His *Enchiridion Militis Christiani*, or *Dagger of the Christian Soldier*, as the title may be translated, took up the idea already declared by Colet that Christianity was not a matter of the acceptance of dogma or the performance of outward rites and ceremonies so much as a pure, righteous, and self-sacrificing life. Moreover, in his first edition of the Greek New Testament, the *Novum Instrumentum* of 1516, he made a declaration which we know Tindale must have read and which we may suppose helped to start the latter on his life's work:

"I totally dissent from those who are unwilling that the Sacred Scriptures, translated into the vulgar tongue, should be read by private individuals, as if Christ had taught such subtle doctrines that they can with difficulty be understood by a very few theologians, or as if the strength of the Christian religion lay in men's ignorance of it. The mysteries of kings it were perhaps better to conceal, but Christ wishes His mysteries to be published as widely as possible. I would wish even all women to read the Gospel and the Epistles of St. Paul. And I wish they were translated into all languages of all people, that they might be read and known, not merely by the Scotch and the Irish, but even by the Turks and the Saracens. I wish that the husbandman may sing parts of them at his plough, that the weaver may warble them at his shuttle, that the traveller may with their narratives beguile the weariness of the way." [1]

Thus Erasmus passed on with renewed strength the enlightened view of Colet that the Scriptures were simple and clear writings which should be put before the whole people; and he helped forward the work by preparing an edition of the New Testament with a fresh Latin translation which made the original text generally accessible. The force which made inevitable the translation into English seems therefore to have had two sources: on the one hand there was this declaration of a few of the most intelligent and enlightened men of the day that the gospels should be freely opened to all the people of England; on the other hand there was the eager faith of certain of the poorer classes of the people, who, clinging to the teachings of Wyclif and reading fragments of his translation in barns and behind hedges at the risk of persecution, kept alive the desire for the Scriptures and prepared the way for a ready dissemination of

[1] Translated by Rev. R. Demaus in *William Tyndale*, p. 45.

Tindale's New Testaments when they came to England in 1526. The history of the beginnings of the English Reformation is obscure, and it has not yet been made out how widely this latter movement was spread in England. It seems clear, however, that at this time a large part of England would have opposed it, and that it was chiefly confined to the larger towns and to the eastern counties. The history is further complicated by the mingling of religion with politics and personal ambitions; but the desire of Englishmen to read the Scriptures for themselves and to decide each man for himself on its meaning, was one of the chief forces which finally ranged England on the Protestant side.

VI

The actual beginnings of our Authorised Version go back to the printing at Worms in 1525 of Tindale's first edition of the New Testament. As we look back now, we can see that the times and the man met in an agreement hardly possible in English history before or since.

Of William Tindale [1] himself, one of the great

---

[1] I follow the spelling of the name in the only known signature of the great translator. A facsimile of the letter in which it is found is given in Demaus, *William Tyndale, a Biography*, 2nd edition, p. 437.

heroes of the English race, we have grievously little definite information outside his published works. Born probably in Gloucestershire, he graduated B.A. from Oxford in 1512, only a few years after Colet had been delivering his lectures on the Epistles of St. Paul, and while he was still preaching in London. From Oxford he went to Cambridge, probably just missing Erasmus there. But Cambridge must have been as much roused by the ferment brought by Erasmus as Oxford had been a few years before by that brought by Colet. Then Tindale returned to Gloucestershire as tutor in the family of a Sir John Walsh; and we have reports through Foxe of the disturbance he created by his disputes with the unenlightened clergy who came to the table of his patron. It is of this time that Foxe tells the following story of Tindale: " Communing and disputing with a certain learned man in whose company he happened to be, he drove him to that issue that the learned man said we were better be without God's laws than the Pope's. Master Tindale, hearing that, answered him, ' I defy the Pope and all his laws.' And said, ' If God spare my life many years, I will cause a boy that driveth the plough shall know more of the Scripture than thou doest.' "

In this frame of mind he went to London in 1523 for the special purpose of making a translation of the Scriptures into English, and in the hope of doing the work under the patronage of the Bishop of London; but, to quote his own words, he " understood at the last not only that there was no room in my Lord of London's palace to translate the New Testament, but also that there was no place to do it in all England, as experience doth now openly declare." Accordingly departing for the Continent in 1523 or 1524, he soon had his New Testament ready for the press. The first attempt at printing it at Cologne was broken up by the enemies of the Reformation; but he escaped with the printed sheets to Worms, and there, towards the end of the year, finished the first printing of the New Testament in English.

His further work in the publication of the Scriptures was a translation of the Pentateuch from the Hebrew, published in 1530, and a careful revision of this and of his New Testament in 1534 and 1535. Besides these he wrote several polemical works, one of which especially, *The Obedience of a Christian Man*, was a treasured work among the English reformers. He met his death in 1536 at the hands of the authorities of Antwerp, after being betrayed into their hands by an Englishman. Foxe's story brings out most touchingly the simple earnestness and good faith of the man, which made him so easy a prey for treachery. This is the conclusion of the story of his arrest:

"Such was the power of his doctrine and the sincerity of his life that during the time of his imprisonment (which endured a year and a half) it is said he converted his keeper, the keeper's daughter, and others of his household. Also the rest that were with Tyndale conversant in the castle, reported of him that if he were not a good Christian man, they could not tell whom to trust.

"The procurator-general, the Emperor's attorney, left this testimony of him, that he was 'homo doctus, pius, et bonus'—a learned, a good, and a godly man." [1]

Everything that we know of Tindale tells the same story: his whole life was devoted to his mission, but when he was not called on to testify, he was retiring and deeply humble. Simple-minded, trustful, full of the warmest feelings and affections, earnest in his service of God, he clung with a faith which was both broad-minded and single to the simplest and highest truths of the gospel; and the strength and depth of his belief carried him unflinchingly to his death at the stake. In his polemical discussions with Sir Thomas More, he stands out in contrast even with that gentlest and most humorous man of the times for his good sense, for his self-control, for his broad spirit of tolerance and love. For prototypes of him we must go back to the days of the apostles.

[1] Foxe: Acts and Monuments, London, 1838, Vol. V, p. 127.

There is a striking resemblance between the temper of Tindale's own writings and that of the epistles of St. Paul, a likeness in the habit of thought, in the swift passage from argument to exhortation, in the unconscious personal references, in the eagerness to impress the truth upon the minds of his readers: and on the other hand, nowhere does the style of the Bible attain a higher earnestness and pitch of feeling than in the translation of these epistles. It is not fantastic, I think, to argue that this likeness in style is based upon a likeness of character: both were educated men, both were filled with the spirit of God, both were impelled to spread the word of God beyond the limits which had been set by the authorities of the day, both in the end gave their lives for their mission. If there have been apostles since St. Paul's time, Tindale is surely one of them; for he had the single love for mankind, the consuming faith, the insight through accidents to the essentials, that fitted him to be the pioneer in bringing back the power of the gospel to England. Not every man with a love for his fellow-men can do them all the good he would wish; nor do a perfect faith and an insight that cannot be baffled carry with them always the power of bringing light to other men's minds: it was Tindale's endowment for his mission that he added to zeal love, —the quality which in some ways is better expressed by our broader word *charity*,—and to them both a scholarship and soundness of judgment that gave a new life among his own people to the truths by which he was himself so deeply moved.

Of Tindale's scholarship we have ample testimony from his contemporaries. He met Sir Thomas More, the type of the best cultivation of the age, on more than even terms; and More himself wrote of him, " Before he fell into these frenzies he was taken for full prettily learned." And the enemy who interrupted the printing at Cologne spoke of Tindale as " learned, skilful in languages and eloquent." The best proof of his scholarship, however, is in his translations, and especially in the fact that we to-day read by far the greater part of our New Testament and of the historical books of the Old in his words.

At the same time, to the zeal of an apostle and the instinct and training of the scholar he added a notable mastery of English style. Here is an example from his prologue to *Exodus* of the lucidity and simplicity, transfused with contagious energy and warmth of feeling, which characterized his own writing:

If any man ask me, seeing that faith justifieth me, Why I work? I answer, Love compelleth me. For as long as my soul feeleth what love God hath shewed me in Christ, I cannot but love God again, and his will and commandments, and of love work them, nor can they seem hard unto me. I think myself not better for my working, nor seek heaven. nor an higher place in heaven, because of it. For a Christian worketh to make his weak brother perfecter, and not to seek an higher place in heaven. I compare not myself unto him that worketh not. No, he that worketh not to-day, shall have grace to turn, and to work to-morrow; and in the mean season I pity him, and pray for him. If I had wrought the will of God these thousand years, and another had wrought the will of the devil as long, and this day turn and be as well willing to suffer with Christ as I, he hath this day overtaken me, and is as far come as I, and shall have as much reward as I. And I envy him not, but rejoice most of all as of lost treasure found. For if I be of God, I have this thousand year suffered to win him for to come and praise the name of God with me. This thousand years have I prayed, sorrowed, longed, sighed, and sought for that which I have this day found; and therefore I rejoice with all my might, and praise God for his grace and mercy.

The best single example that we have, however, of what Tindale was both as a man and as a writer is to be found in a letter which he wrote from Antwerp to his friend Frith when the latter was in prison in. England, voluntarily awaiting martyrdom for the truth: I know of no more noble or beautiful piece of English prose. Here is a portion of it:

Brother Jacob, beloved in my heart! there liveth not in whom I have so good hope and trust, and in whom my heart rejoiceth, and my soul comforteth herself, as in you; not the thousandth part so much for your learning, and what other gifts else you have, as because you will creep alow by the ground, and walk in those things that the conscience may feel, and not in the imaginations of the brain; in fear, and not in boldness; in open necessary things, and not to pronounce or define of hid secrets, or things that neither help nor hinder, whether it be so or no; in unity, and not in seditious opinions: insomuch that if you be sure you know, yet in things that may abide leisure, you will defer, and say (till others agree with you), 'Methinks the text requireth this sense or understanding.' Yea, and if you be sure that if your part be good, and another hold the contrary, yet if it be a thing that maketh no matter, you will laugh and let it pass, and refer the thing to other men, and stick you stiff and stubbornly in earnest and necessary things. And I trust you be persuaded even so of me: for I call God to record against the day we shall all appear before our Lord Jesus, to give a reckoning of our doings, that I never altered one syllable of God's word against my conscience, nor would this day, if all that is in the earth, whether it be pleasure, honour, or riches, might be given me. Moreover, I take God to record to my conscience, that I desire of God to myself in this world no more than that without which I cannot keep his laws.

Finally, if there were in me any gift that could help at hand, and aid you if need required, I promise you I would not be far off, and commit the end to God. My soul is not faint, though my body be weary. But God hath made me evil favoured in this world, and without grace in the sight of men, speechless and rude, dull and slow witted; your part shall be to supply what lacketh in me; remembering that as lowliness of heart shall make you high with God, even so meekness of words shall make you to sink into the hearts of men. Nature giveth age authority, but meekness is the glory of youth, and giveth them honour. Abundance of love maketh me exceed in babbling.

.   .   .   .   .   .

The mighty God of Jacob be with you to supplant his enemies and give you the favour of Joseph: and the wisdom and the spirit of Stephen be with your heart and with your mouth, and teach your lips what they shall say, and how to answer to all things. He is our God, if we despair in ourselves, and trust in him: and his is the glory. Amen.

I hope our redemption is nigh.

WILLIAM TINDALE.[1]

After such words, one can add little. I have shown, I hope, that Tindale's own style at its best rose to the level of that of the English Bible; and his own purpose and character were so noble and devoted that they help to explain the splendid style of his

[1] Foxe: op. cit., Vol. V, p. 133.

translation. His achievement for English prose style reminds one of the passage in *The Virginians* in which Thackeray, speaking of Washington, points out that in the war which began in the backwoods of America, and spread thence over two continents; which divided Europe; which deprived France of all her American possessions, and in the end England of most of hers,—that in all this great war the man who came out with the highest fame and the most glory was the man who fired the first shot. So in the case of Tindale and the art of writing in English prose: after nearly four centuries and all the action and the reaction of time it is still true that the type of prose style which no good writer can forget, and about which all varieties of prose style centre, is the style of the first man who ever made printed English speak to the whole nation. For Tindale fixed the style of the English Bible. The subdued richness, the strong beat of the rhythm, and all the other subtler qualities which clothe the style with its simple and unconscious earnestness, we owe to him, the first translator. His scholarship, his genius for language, fused by the heat of his devotion to his mission and his deep piety, and guided by his passionate desire to bring the gospel into the hands of the common people, wrought out a style which was worthy of the message it was to carry. Though he did not complete the translation of the Old Testament, yet the New Testament and the historical books of the Old Testament which came from him, needed only revision in details. And it is the crowning merit of the line of revisers down to and including King James's companies, that they were wise enough not to attempt to alter the character of the style.

That Tindale did fix the style for the narrative books of the Old Testament and for the New Testament I can make clear by quoting from his Pentateuch of 1530 and his New Testament of 1534 three familiar passages—the first from the story of Joseph and his brethren, the second from *St. Luke,* the third from *1 Corinthians.* For the sake of convenience I modernize the spelling; and to make the comparison clearer I italicize the words that are changed in the Authorised Version.

> *And* Joseph could *no longer* refrain [A. V. himself] before all them that stood *about* him, *but commanded that they should* go *all* out from *him, and that there should be* no man with him, while *he uttered himself* unto his brethren. And he wept aloud, so that the Egyptians and the house of Pharaoh heard *it.* And *he* said unto his brethren: I am Joseph: doth my father yet live? *But* his brethren could not answer him, for they were *abashed* at his presence.
>
> And Joseph said unto his brethren: come near to me [A. V. I pray you], and they came near. And

he said: I am Joseph your brother, whom ye sold into Egypt. *And* now be not grieved *therewith, neither let it seem a cruel thing in your eyes,* that ye sold me hither. For God did send me before you to *save* life. For *this is the second year of dearth* in the land, and five *more are behind in* which there shall neither be earing nor harvest.[1]

And there were in the same *region* shepherds abiding in the field *and watching* their flock by night. And lo, the angel of the Lord *stood hard by* them and the *brightness* of the Lord shone round about them, and they were sore afraid. And the angel said unto them, *Be not afraid.* [A. V. For] behold I bring you [A. V. good] tidings of great joy *that* shall *come* to all *the* people; for unto you is born this day in the city of David a saviour which is Christ the Lord. And *take* this *for* a sign: ye shall find the *child swaddled and laid* in a manger. And *straightway* there was with the angel a multitude of heavenly *soldiers lauding* God, and saying, Glory to God *on high, and peace on the earth: and unto men rejoicing.*[2]

But now is Christ risen from *death* and *is* become the first-fruits of them that slept. For [A. V. since] by *a* man came death *and* by a man came [A. V. also the] resurrection *from death.* For as *by* Adam all die, even so *by* Christ shall all be made alive, *and* every man in his own order. *The first is Christ, then* they that are Christ's at his coming.

[1] Gen. xlv. 1–6.   [2] Luke ii. 8–14.

Then cometh the end when he *hath* delivered up the kingdom to God [A. V. even] the father, when he hath put down all rule, [A. V. and all] authority and power. For he must *rule* till he *have* put all *his* enemies under his feet.

The last enemy that shall be destroyed is death. For he hath put all things under his feet. But when he saith, all things are put under him, it is manifest that he is excepted, which did put all things under him. [A. V. And] When all things *are* subdued unto him: then shall the son also himself be subject unto him that put all things under him, that God may be all in all *things*.[1]

Examples like these may be found almost anywhere in the New Testament or in what Tindale translated of the Old Testament. They show that the style which he set in the beginning all the revisers after him had the discretion to preserve. By one of the curious unfathered traditions which make up so much of the literary history of the sixteenth century Coverdale has been credited with adding the " grace " of style which is said to mark the Authorised Version. " Grace " is not a very happy term for any style so robust and earnest, and Coverdale may well share with the other men who worked over Tindale's words some of the praise for the perfect flexibility and smoothness attained by the final version:

[1] I Cor. xv 20–28.

but it is enough credit to their discretion and literary
sense that they did not blunt the clearness and force
which Tindale left as the crowning virtues of his
noble prose.   To him we may safely ascribe all the
most important qualities of the translation,—the energy, the contagious earnestness, the unassuming dignity and the vividness,—by which it holds its place
in our literature.   He once for all in his version determined the style of the English Bible.

VII

Tindale, however, did not complete the work of the
translation.   After he had prepared his New Testament and his Pentateuch he turned aside from the
work of rendering the Scriptures into English, to
take his part in other ways in advancing the Reformation.   Besides these, however, it is practically certain that the other historical books through *2 Chronicles* in Matthew's Bible of 1537 came from his
hands.   The evidence may be found in any manual of
the history of the English Bible.   A large and important part of the Old Testament, therefore, still
waited for a translator.   The lack was supplied in
Coverdale's Bible of 1535.

Miles Coverdale, to whom we owe the first complete translation of the Bible in English, had a long

and varied career. Beginning under the patronage
of Thomas Cromwell as a useful and willing laborer
in the establishment of the liberal principles which
were Cromwell's political stock in trade, he was at
this period of his life, as his work on the Bible shows,
of a conciliatory temper; in his old age he had so far
advanced in Puritan principles that he was unwilling
to wear a surplice in order to take up again the see
of Exeter, of which he had been deprived in the
reign of Mary. He was entirely humble about his
own capacities as a translator. His Bible, so far as
it is independent of Tindale, is frankly a translation
from secondary sources. The title page of the first
issue declares the book to be " faithfully and truly
translated out of Dutch and Latin into English,"
" Dutch " being the usage of the time for German;
his dedication to the king declares that he had " with
a clear conscience purely and faithfully translated
this out of five sundry interpreters, having only the
manifest truth of the Scripture before mine eyes ";
and in his preface to " the Christian Reader," he
adds: " And to help me herein I have had sundry
translations, not only in Latin, but also of the Dutch
interpreters, whom, because of their singular gifts
and special diligence in the Bible, I have been the
more glad to follow for the most part, according as I
was required." These five sundry interpreters have

been proved to be the Swiss-German or Zürich version
of 1524–29, the Latin translation of Pagninus, Luther's German Bible, the Vulgate, and Tindale so far
as he was available. In the Pentateuch and the New
Testament Coverdale followed Tindale pretty closely,
but with revision by aid of the German versions;
elsewhere his chief dependence was the Swiss-German
Bible. In the Old Testament he had the Vulgate
constantly before him and reproduced in the English text many additions which had crept into its
text in the course of the Middle Ages. An example
of these may be found in verses 5–7 of *Psalm xiv* in
the *Book of Common Prayer*. The *Psalter* here is
from Coverdale's translation in the Great Bible: and
these verses are found in the Septuagint and the Vulgate but not in the Hebrew. In all his work on the
Bible Coverdale treated the Latin text of the Vulgate in this spirit of liberal hospitality. The line
between the Protestants and the Roman Catholics
had not yet been drawn with the subsequent bitter
sharpness: Henry VIII and Cromwell still hoped
that the Church of England, though it was cut loose
from the Pope, might remain a part of the great
Church Catholic; and in matters of minor importance, as were most of these inflations of the text,
Coverdale was ready to follow their lead. Indeed
he went further than this, for in 1538 he published

a New Testament in which he printed in parallel columns the Latin of the Vulgate and a version of the English in which Tindale's language was brought still further into conformity with the text of the Vulgate. His first purpose seems to have been like that of the Zürich version, to reproduce the substance and the spirit of his originals without burdening himself with too much care for scrupulous accuracy of detail. The character of his work may be judged by the *Psalter* of the *Book of Common Prayer*, which is his version as he finally left it in the Great Bible.

Unquestionably Coverdale had an ear for rhythm and for the subtle turn of the phrase, which add the expressive power of music to the words; and the very fact that he did not hold himself closely bound to the letter of the original gave this gift freer play. From him we get many felicitous turns of phrase, such as the following: "Thou canst not make one hair white or black," in place of Tindale's "Thou canst not make one white hair or black"; "she brought forth her first-born son" for Tindale's "first son"; in the account of the transfiguration, "a bright cloud overshadowed them" for Tindale's "shadowed them"; and, for a final example, "is become the headstone in the corner," where Tindale had translated "is set in the principal part of the corner."

In the last case Coverdale himself in the Great Bible brought the passage to the form in which we read it to-day.

A still more important contribution of Coverdale to the translation of the Bible was his service in confirming the principle already asserted by Tindale, that the English Bible should be translated into the language of everyday life and that it should not be cumbered and obscured by learned words. In some places his version seems even more homely than that of Tindale, almost as if he had gone out of his way to keep in touch with the speech of everyday life. For example, in the account of the anointing of Saul to be king he translates, " Then took Samuel a glass of oil and poured it upon his head "; and there is a phrase in *Jeremiah* which has given a popular name to his Bible: " There is no treacle in Gilead."

In general we may consider that Coverdale's special contribution to our English Bible lay in the direction of freedom and of the musical smoothness and flow through which alone language is able to express some of our deepest feelings. In point of accuracy of translation he had little to add, though he undoubtedly made available some renderings in which the Swiss-German and the Vulgate had an advantage, and thus added to the stock of phrasings from which the revisers of 1611 drew. Though the part of the Bible which came from him needed much revision, his influence in strengthening the rhythm and other musical qualities of the English Bible is important. Tindale's work being that of a pioneer, is at times a little abrupt; and the Geneva version of 1560, the next important revision in the history of our Bible, tended to insist on literalism of rendering, sometimes to the injury of the sound. Coverdale's work, both in his own version and in the Great Bible, was a counterbalancing influence in favor of expressiveness in English rather than a slavish rendering of the literal words and order of the Hebrew and Greek. Since the deep and thorough permeation of the English Bible and its language into our literature and our everyday speech is largely due to this exquisite happiness and expressiveness of phrase, Coverdale too must have his niche in the temple of English literature.

The next two versions of the English Bible—that known as Matthew's, published in 1537, and the Great Bible, of which the first two editions are frequently spoken of as Cromwell's and Cranmer's, made no great change in the text. Matthew's Bible was edited by the John Rogers who was the first martyr in Mary's reign. The importance of this version is that in it appears for the first time a new translation of the books from *Joshua* through *2 Chronicles* which it is almost certain was the work of Tindale. John Rogers, who was chaplain to the Merchant Adventurers in Antwerp at the time of Tindale's arrest and trial, was his literary executor and received from him, probably at this time, the manuscript of this translation, which he incorporated in the Bible that he carried through the press the year after Tindale's death. Otherwise the changes made in this version are small and unimportant.

The Great Bible was the first version of the Bible to be made with the open authority of the government. In 1538 Cromwell sent Coverdale to Paris, where there were better printers, to put through the press a version of the Bible which should be officially recognised by the English Church. Coverdale undertook the work in the same spirit in which he had prepared his own version. His scholarship was adequate to enable him to use the Latin and German translations intelligently, but apparently not full enough to send him to the Hebrew and Greek for himself. Nevertheless, with the aid of a new Latin version of the Old Testament made from the Hebrew by Sebastian Münster, Coverdale revised the text of Matthew's Bible, and the result was a version apparently as good as could have been produced without going direct to the originals.

These three versions of the complete Bible,—Coverdale's, Matthew's and the Great Bible,—were produced at a time when feeling on the subject of religion was strong and eager, but before it had risen to the withering heat and bitterness of Elizabeth's reign, when the Church of England stood between the Roman Catholic Church, with the Inquisition looming behind it, on the one side, and the uncompromising doctrinal zeal of the Calvinists on the other. For about twenty years after the appearance of the Great Bible the churchmen of England were too much occupied with other matters to go farther with the translation of the Bible. The latter part of Henry's reign was a period on the whole of reaction, in which the free reading of the Bible by all the people was not an object very dear to the hearts of the authorities. In Edward's reign the Reformation was pushed forward; but especially under Northumberland it was more a device of politics and a cloak for personal greed than the expression of any high spirit of religion. Cranmer, conciliatory in temper and anxious to find a path which all men could follow, was occupied with the government of the Church and with the preparing of the *Book of Common Prayer* from the ancient service books of the church catholic. The printing of the Bible, however, went forward during this period at an immense rate. In the six and a half years of Edward's reign it is said that thirty-five editions of the New Testament and thirteen of the whole Bible were printed in England; but these were all reprints of former versions, without any attempt to remove their imperfections. It was not until the persecution of Mary's reign drove the Protestants out of England and kept them in exile on the Continent that they found time to turn their attention to the preparation of a more accurate version of the Bible.

VIII

Their version was made at Geneva under the inspiration of the strong church of Calvin, and it was made by members of the extreme Calvinist party among the English. In the twenty years which had elapsed since Coverdale's labors, much study had been given to the Bible. A new Latin version of the Old Testament, made from the Hebrew, had been completed by German and French scholars; and the Greek text of the New Testament had been improved by the labors of Robert Stephens, who also for the first time divided the New Testament into verses in his Greek-Latin version of 1551. From Stephens' Greek text Theodore Beza, the friend and successor of Calvin, had made a new Latin version which affected all subsequent revisions of the New Testament.

With these aids a small company of exiles under
the leadership of William Whittingham set to work
at Geneva in the last years of Mary's reign to prepare a version of the Bible which should be before
all things rigorously accurate. To this strict accuracy the Calvinists gave an importance which it did
not have for the broader principles of the English
Church, for they held that the Bible contained within
its covers the whole body of the revelation of God
to man, from which in turn could be deduced every
principle and rule necessary for the guidance of life.
An accurate rendering of the strict letter of the law
was to them therefore of supreme importance. The
position of English churchmen was fairly repre-
sented by Coverdale; for to them the will of God
was also known through the acts of his church, and
the Scriptures were to be interpreted and understood
through the teachings of the church. In their eyes
an anxiously literal translation was of less importance than one which should convey the essential
spirit. The principle of the Genevan revisers is to
our modern views the better, since a version which
only comes somewhere near giving the meaning of
the original cannot become final; and their contribution of laborious accuracy is not to be underestimated.

In this spirit the Genevan revisers went through
both Old and New Testaments word by word and

verse by verse; and, especially in the poetical books
of the Old Testament and in the prophets, their labors
brought the text far nearer to the form in which
we read it to-day than it had been before. In the
New Testament the changes, though numerous, were
generally less important; for Tindale's genius had
brought the translation of the New Testament very
much nearer to perfection than had Coverdale's
labors on the Old Testament. Here again a study of
the history of the English Bible makes clear the
amount of patient scholarship which went to the
perfection of our Bible.

The Genevan version, one must remember, like
Tindale's version, was produced in exile by men who
were driven out of their homes and brought into peril
of their lives by their devotion to their view of religion and their desire to see the Bible read freely by
all their countrymen. This fervor and devotion of
spirit we may well suppose was enough to prevent
their version from being dominated by too literal an
attention to the single words. The Bible was to them
far more than a collection of difficult passages and
words whose idiom did not exactly fit with that of
English: to them it was the living word of God and
the one guide for the upright man in the conduct
of his everyday life. And their labors in bringing
the text of the Bible to greater accuracy set a new

standard: after them no Bible could hold its own
which did not render the original language with the
greatest possible approach to literalness. They established the principle of going direct to the Hebrew
for the text of the Old Testament and to the Greek
for that of the New; and so far as Protestants were
concerned, they removed the corruptions and the di-
versities of readings which make the Vulgate an
unsafe guide for popular understanding of the
Scriptures.

The next version of the Bible in chronological order, the Bishops' Bible, though it was nominally the
basis of the King James Bible, is in reality of less
importance than any of the versions of the sixteenth
century, since its changes made few improvements on
the readings of the Great Bible, and most of these
improvements were taken over from the Genevan
version. Indeed the latter made the Bishops' Bible
necessary by its immediate and wide circulation
which called attention to the many inaccuracies and
imperfections of the Great Bible. Archbishop Parker,
who directed and shared in the revision, committed
different books to various of his colleagues on the
bench and to a few other scholars. The work was
unevenly done and the version never had wide circulation. The eagerness of the publishers to recoup
themselves for the printing of the large and handsome

folio in which most editions of it appeared sufficed to
set it up in a good many churches; but it never attained the popularity of the Genevan version, which
for the rest of the sixteenth century and even for
a dozen or fifteen years after the appearance of the
King James version was the Bible of the great mass
of English people.

The last version which we must consider before
we come to the King James Bible itself is the edition
of the New Testament commonly known as the Rhemish Testament, from the fact that it was made by
members of the Roman Catholic seminary at Rheims.
In the controversies between the Protestants and the
Catholics in Queen Elizabeth's reign the Catholics
had been at a disadvantage because they had had no
version of the Scriptures which they could quote to
the confusion of their opponents.   Accordingly Cardinal Allen, as part of his campaign for the recovery
of England to the old church, authorised Gregory
Martin, who had been a Fellow of St. John's Col-
lege at Oxford, and who was a distinguished scholar
in both Hebrew and Greek, to undertake a translation of the Bible.   It was to be from the Vulgate,
which the Roman Catholic Church had declared to
be the only true text of the Scriptures, and it was to
be translated into a language which should in no way
be stripped of the rich burden of doctrine found by

the Roman Catholic Church in almost every phrase
and sentence both of the Old Testament and the New.
The result is at first glance monstrous. It contains
such examples as the following: in the Lord's prayer,
" Give us to-day our supersubstantial bread "; in
Acts i. 2, Until the day wherein " he was assumpted ";
in *Hebrews xiii. 16*, " Beneficence and communication
do not forget, for with such hosts God is promerited "
(" to do good and communicate forget not, for with
such sacrifices God is well pleased "). The Latin of
the last passage will show the principle on which
Martin worked: *Beneficentiæ autem, et communi-
onis nolite oblivisci: talibus enim hostiis promeretur
Deus.* His purpose was, though making a translation into English, to reproduce slavishly every
word which in the course of the Middle Ages had
acquired any ecclesiastical or theological connotation
or even a suspicion of such connotation. He and his
superiors intended to send the layman continually to
the priest for the interpretation of the Scriptures and
to guard in every possible way against spreading the
opinion that a layman was as competent to understand the Scriptures as was the Church.

If this grotesqueness were all that distinguished
this version from others, we should never have heard
of it except as a literary curiosity. Martin, however,
was not only zealous for the doctrines of his church,

but he was also an admirable scholar in Greek; and where his principle of translation allowed him to be so, he was exquisitely sensitive to the shades of meaning in the English words and the expressiveness of English style. In many cases he found a more exact translation for the Greek word, as in the Parable of the Sower, " and some fell upon a rock " in place of " stones " and " pleasures of this life " for " voluptuous living "; in the Sermon on the Mount, " thy whole body shall be full of darkness," for " all thy body "; in *Hebrews xii. 23*, " and to the spirits of just men made perfect," for " of just and perfect men "; and in the Sermon on the Mount again, " but thou, when thou prayest " for " when thou prayest." In each of these cases the Greek is rendered more accurately or more sensitively. In many other cases Martin by a slight change in the order of the words gave a final fitness to the phrase: for example, " What therefore God hath joined together let not man put asunder," in place of " let not therefore man put asunder that which God hath coupled together "; " the rich he hath sent empty away," for " hath sent away the rich empty "; and in *1 Corinthians xi* " the head of Christ is God," for " God is Christ's head."

Furthermore since this Rhemish New Testament was a translation from the Vulgate, and since it aimed to keep the vocabulary of the Vulgate as far as possible, it brought into the English Bible a considerable number of Latinate words, a good many of which were taken over from this version by the revisers of 1611. Thirty words from the Vulgate which are found in the Authorised Version appear first in the Rhemish New Testament; and in nearly two hundred places words from the Vulgate which took the place of other words, generally not Latinate, have been retained in the Authorised Version. A few such words are *founded, derided, malefactor, clemency, conformed to, contemptible, illuminated, sobriety*. The effect of such words in enriching the tones of our Bible is obvious. If this version had not been made and had not been used so freely by the revisers of 1611, it is certain that our English Bible would have lacked something of its richness of sound.

In itself and for the purpose which it was sent out this Rhemish New Testament accomplished only evil for its makers. Its monstrous obscuration of the plain text of the Scriptures was a strong weapon for the Protestants, and it was almost immediately reprinted by them in parallel columns with the New Testament of the Bishops' Bible, to be used as a patent demonstration of the purpose of the Roman Catholic Church to obscure and obstruct the reading

of the Scriptures. Its only permanent result is thus
a pretty bit of the irony of history. Gregory Martin,
who made the translation, had given himself, in
singleness of mind, in exile, and in hardships com-
parable to those suffered by Tindale, to this work of
making a translation which should help to recover
his fellow-countrymen to what he conceived to be the
true faith; and, like Tindale, he gave up his life to
his work, for he died of consumption at Paris in
October of the year in which his New Testament was
published. Yet the only result of his toil was to im-
prove the version which rendered all his efforts futile; for all that was valuable of his labors was taken
over by the Authorised Version. Practically, then,
the fruits of Gregory Martin's toil and self-sacri-
fice were the furtherance of the cause which he ab-
horred.

IX

The origin of the Authorised Version seems to go
back to an incidental remark made by King James
at a conference of the two wings of the English
Church, called in June, 1604, to consider a petition
of the Puritans against the rights and ceremonies
of the Established Church. Dr. Reynolds, one of
the leaders of the Puritan party, objected to the

inaccuracies of the Bishops' Bible, whereupon the King suggested a new revision, made by authority, which could be accepted by all parties. For some months little was done; but by the end of June a list of scholars who should take part in the revision was ready for submission to James. The revision itself, however, does not seem to have been seriously undertaken till 1607. The rules set for the revisers contemplated six companies of nine scholars each, working at Westminster, Oxford, and Cambridge, one company at each place taking the Old Testament and another the New. The rules prescribed that the basis of the revision should be the Bishops' Bible, but Tindale's, Matthew's, Coverdale's, Whitchurch's (the Great Bible), the Genevan, "to be used when they agree better with the text than the Bishops' Bible"; that each scholar should bring his private notes to a meeting of the company to which he belonged; and that the companies should exchange the results on which each of them had been agreed. The revisers, however, as we have seen, treated their instructions liberally enough to include the Rhemish New Testament among the sources which they used.

The spirit of their work seems to have been large-minded and catholic. There were moderate Puritans engaged in the work with High Churchmen, and all seem to have performed their labors in a sincere de-

sire to reach a conclusion which would be acceptable
to all parties of the Church. They went at their
work seriously and spared no labor to make it perfect. Their own quaint description of their labors
in the address to the Reader is worth quoting:

> Neither did we run over the work with that post-
> ing haste that the *Septuagint* did, if that be true
> which is reported of them, that they finished it in
> seventy two days; neither were we barred or hin-
> dered from going over it again, having once done
> it, like St. *Hierome*, if that be true which himself
> reporteth, that he could no sooner write anything,
> but presently it was caught from him, and published,
> and he could not have leave to mend it: neither, to
> be short, were we the first that fell in hand with
> translating the Scripture into *English*, and con-
> sequently destitute of former helps, as it is written
> of *Origen*, that he was the first in a manner, that
> put his hand to write commentaries upon the
> Scriptures, and therefore no marvel if he overshot
> himself many times. None of these things: the
> work hath not been huddled up in seventy two days,
> but hath cost the workmen, as light as it seemeth,
> the pains of twice seven times seventy two days,
> and more. Matters of such weight and conse-
> quence are to be speeded with maturity: for in a
> business of moment a man feareth not the blame
> of convenient slackness. Neither did we think
> much to consult the translators or commentators,
> *Chaldee, Hebrew, Syrian, Greek*, or *Latin;* no, nor

the *Spanish, French, Italian,* or *Dutch;* neither did we disdain to revise that which we had done, and to bring back to the anvil that which we had hammered: but having and using as great helps as were needful, and fearing no reproach for slowness, nor coveting praise for expedition, we have at the length, through the good hand of the Lord upon us, brought the work to that pass that you see.

So far as can be judged from this quaintly learned address of " the Translators to the Reader," they seem to have been more affected by the attacks of the Catholics on the English versions, especially as set forth in the prefaces and notes of the Rhemish New Testament, than by the scruples of the Puritans. Certainly a much larger portion of their space is given to meeting the arguments of the Roman Catholics. This strong opposition to the principles of translation of the Roman Catholics, however, though important at that time, in the end did not contribute to exactness and uniformity of phrasing. The Roman Catholic Church insisted with all its authority on the literal text of the Vulgate, for on such words as *pœnitentia, hostia, ordines,* and *ecclesia* were built many of its most important doctrines and dogmas; and it held this principle so important that the makers of the Rhemish version marred their work as we have seen by barbarous transliterations of the

Latin words into English. The revisers of 1611, to avoid any danger of such a slavish dependence on the letter of the translation growing up to obscure its real meaning, went out of their way, where variety was not misleading, to use different English words for the same Hebrew or Greek word; and half mockingly they defended their principle in the address to the Reader:

Another thing we think good to admonish thee of, gentle Reader, that we have not tied ourselves to an uniformity of phrasing, or to an identity of words, as some peradventure would wish that we had done, because they observe, that some learned men somewhere have been as exact as they could that way. Truly, that we might not vary from the sense of that which we had translated before, if the word signified the same thing in both places, (for there be some words that be not of the same sense every where) we were especially careful, and made a conscience according to our duty. But that we should express the same notion in the same particular word; as for example, if we translate the *Hebrew* or *Greek* word once by *purpose*, never to call it *intent*; if one where *journeying*, never *travelling*; if one where *think*, never *suppose*; if one where *pain*, never *ache*; if one where *joy*, never *gladness*, &c., thus to mince the matter, we thought to savour more of curiosity than wisdom, and that rather it would breed scorn in the atheist, than

bring profit to the godly reader. For is the kingdom of God become words or syllables? Why
should we be in bondage to them, if we may be
free? use one precisely, when we may use another
no less fit as commodiously? A godly Father in
the primitive time shewed himself greatly moved,
that one of newfangleness called κράββατον, σκίμ-
πους,[1] though the difference be little or none; and
another reporteth, that he was much abused for
turning *cucurbita* (to which reading the people had
been used) into *hedera*.[2] Now if this happen in better times, and upon so small occasions, we might
justly fear hard censure, if generally we should
make verbal and unnecessary changings. We might
also be charged (by scoffers) with some unequal
dealing towards a great number of good *English*
words. For as it is written of a certain great
Philosopher, that he should say, that those logs
were happy that were made images to be worshipped; for their fellows, as good as they, lay for
blocks behind the fire: so if we should say, as it
were, unto certain words, Stand up higher, have a
place in the Bible always; and to others of like
quality, Get ye hence, be banished for ever;
we might be taxed peradventure with St. *James's*
words, namely, *To be partial in ourselves, and judges
of evil thoughts.* Add hereunto, that niceness in
words was always counted the next step to trifling;
and so was to be curious about names too: also

[1] Both words mean *bed*.

[2] *Cucurbita* means a *gourd: hedera* means *ivy*. The reference
is to the vine in Jonah iv. 7.

that we cannot follow a better pattern for elocution than God himself; therefore he using divers words in his holy writ, and indifferently for one thing in nature; we, if we will not be superstitious, may use the same liberty in our *English* versions out of *Hebrew* and *Greek*, for that copy or store that he hath given us. Lastly, we have on the one side avoided the scrupulosity of the Puritans, who leave the old Ecclesiastical words, and betake them to other, as when they put *washing* for *Baptism*, and *Congregation* instead of *Church*: as also on the other side we have shunned the obscurity of the Papists, in their *Azimes, Tunike, Rational, Holocausts, Præpuce, Pasche,* and a number of such like, whereof their late translation is full, and that of purpose to darken the sense, that since they must needs translate the Bible, yet by the language thereof it may be kept from being understood. But we desire that the Scripture may speak like itself, as in the language of *Canaan*, that it may be understood even of the very vulgar.

This principle in most cases had no serious effect. It is responsible for the difference between *a leathern girdle* in *St. Matthew's* account of John the Baptist and *a girdle of a skin* in *St. Marks's*; between *eternal life* in *John iii. 15* and *everlasting life* in the next verse; between *counted unto him for righteousness* in one verse of *Romans iv* and *reckoned to Abraham for righteousness* in another verse. An extreme case is in *James ii. 2–3*: " For if there come into your assembly a man with a gold ring, in goodly apparel, and there come in also a poor man in vile raiment; and ye shall have respect to him that weareth the gay clothing . . .": here *apparel*, *raiment*, and *clothing* all stand for a single noun in the Greek. In most cases such variations are of practically no importance so far as accuracy of rendering is concerned. They tend slightly to obscure the close resemblances in phrasing between corresponding parts of the first three gospels; and in a few cases they may suggest a difference of meaning in the English where there is none in the Greek or Hebrew. On the whole, however, though the principle is departed from in the Revised Version, and rightfully so, purely from the point of view of literature we may hold that the revisers of 1611 showed good judgment. Certainly this freedom in using synonyms must have contributed to greater flexibility of rhythm; for there are innumerable cases where one can see that of two synonyms one would fit more smoothly into the sentence than the other; and in an age when there was so much feeling for euphony and expressiveness of style, such freedom of choice was within its limits an important consideration.

Whether one looks on this principle as conducing to freedom or to license, however, there can be no doubt that this final revision of 1611 was undertaken seri-

ously and according to what were for the time high
standards of accuracy and thoroughness. The final
printing, as has been shown by Dr. Scrivener,[1] was
hurried and careless, so much so that the two issues
of 1611 have distinct sets of errors in matters of
proof-reading. The preparation of the text for the
printers, on the other hand, though uneven was on the
whole thorough and careful. The corrections of the
Revised Version bear testimony rather to the birth
of the science of textual criticism and to a great advance in the knowledge of Hebrew and Greek than
to carelessness or incompetence on the part of the revisers of 1611. The latter used all the sources that
were open to them with independence and discretion.
The substitution of the exquisite phrase, *a man of
sorrows and acquainted with grief*,[2] drawn from *vir
dolorum et expertus infirmitatem* of Pagninus' Latin
translation, for *he is such a man as hath good experience of sorrows and infirmities* of the Bishops' Bible,
and *a man of sorrows and hath experience of infirmities* of the Genevan version, is a strong example,
though not an exceptional one, of the success of
their search for the phrase which should be most
expressive in English as well as a close representative of the original. And the fact that in the climax

[1] F. H. A. Scrivener, *The Authorised Edition of the English
Bible*, 1884.   [2] Isa. liii. 3.

of *1 Corinthians xv,* in the verse, *O death, where is thy sting, O grave, where is thy victory,* the *O* which is called for by the vocative in the Greek, appears for the first time in their version, is high testimony not only to the accuracy of their scholarship but to their fine sense for the purely musical expressiveness of language. Such an essay as this is not the place for a detailed examination of the methods and results of the separate versions: whoever is interested should consult the handbooks on the history of the English Bible. But the result of such study has been to confirm the high estimate of the labors of this band of scholars. Their work was done perhaps at the latest time in which it could represent the hopes and ideas of both the Puritans and the High Church men; and the fact that the two versions from which they drew the greatest number of their improvements on the Bishops' Bible were the Genevan Bible and the Roman Catholic New Testament of Rheims, shows the catholicity of their spirit. All that I shall have to say in the next chapter of the excellencies of our Authorised Version, both as a translation and as a work of literature, will be direct testimony to the value of this latest revision.

So much for the history of the English versions. Even so brief a sketch as this will have made clear the amount of painstaking scholarship and the variety

of sources from which it drew. Beginning with the
devoted and inspired labors of Tindale, through him
it drew on the translations of Jerome, of Erasmus, of
Luther, and through Coverdale and his successors, it
drew on the Swiss-German version of Zürich, on the
Latin translations of Pagninus, of Münster, of Tre-
mellius, of Leo Juda, of Castalio, and of Theodore
Beza, and on the French translations of Lefèvre and
Olivetan, and of the " venerable company of pastors
at Geneva," besides occasional phrases from new
translations into Spanish and Italian. It gathered
its materials wherever they could be found, adopting
here a word and there a phrase in order to arrive
at the closest and most expressive English within
their power. Nothing is more remarkable in the history of our English Bible than this large-minded
and eager search, to which I shall presently recur,
through all the possible sources for anything that
would help towards the best translation into English;
and we may well suppose that this careful scrutiny
of so large a variety of sources, which is not paralleled in the history of any other Bible, did much to
give its permanence to the work of the translators.

CHAPTER IX

I

In a final summing up of the literary characteristics of the Authorised Version there are two aspects in which it must be considered. In the first place we must make some estimate of it as a translation and consider how far the characteristics of the original languages still color the English work, and what skill the translators have showed in rendering the idiom of one language into that of another. In the second place we must try to define the characteristics of the English Bible as a work in English literature apart from its merits or shortcomings as a translation.

Looking at it first as a translation, one must begin by recognising that there are two elements which an adequate translation must render into the new language, on the one hand the literal meanings of the words,—their exact denotation,—on the other hand, the feeling and emotion which suffuses the single words and gives them power. To render the former is a question in part of proper equipment in dictionaries and grammars, in part of patient and enlightened industry in the use of such apparatus. To render the spirit, which is the life, on the other hand, is a question of finding words with apt connotations, associations, and implications, and of so putting them together as to add the expressiveness of sound to the style. For the scholarship and the apparatus of scholarship England in the sixteenth century was well equipped for the time. All manuscripts of the Hebrew are practically identical, and already by the sixteenth century the dictionaries and grammars were so good that Tindale's translation of the clearer parts of the Old Testament stands with little change to-day. The great advance in scholarship has made possible larger improvements in the other books where the original text is more obscure. In the case of the New Testament the foundation work had been laid by Erasmus, and his work was continued by scholars like Robert Stephens and Beza. The science of criticism, however, was not to be born till the beginning of the eighteenth century, and there were many questions of text and preferable readings which it was impossible for the best scholars of the sixteenth century to solve. Hence, as the Revised Version makes clear, in details the Authorised Version needed correction.

On the other hand the infusing of the words of

the translation with the spirit, which gave it its
place as the crowning monument of English literature, could be better accomplished in the sixteenth
century than at any time before or since in English
history. In the first place the state of the language
was at its very best for the purpose. I have pointed
out in the chapter on poetry that the rich coloring of
the Old Testament is largely derived from the fact
that the Hebrew had no words which had not a physical signification, and that they were thus of necessity
clothed with a strength of feeling which can never
be attained by abstract words. The English of the
sixteenth century was more fit to reproduce this character of the Hebrew than it has ever been again.
Since that time English has been enriched chiefly by
the addition of abstract and general words, mostly
from the Latin and Greek, to express the constantly
enlarging range of scientific and philosophical
thought; and we write naturally and necessarily
nowadays in abstract terms from which the figurative force has long since faded out. No one who
has read in the writings of the sixteenth century can
fail to be struck by the picturesqueness which comes
from a figurativeness of language unlike anything
in our language to-day. Even in the statute books
one finds such lively and figurative language as,
" But their vicious living shamelessly increaseth and

augmenteth, and by a cursed custom so rooted and infected that a great multitude of the religious persons in such small houses do rather choose to rove abroad in apostasy than to conform themselves to the true religion "; [1] or in another statute: " Without providing wherefore too great a scope of unreasonable liberty should be given to all cankered and traitorous hearts, willers, and workers of the same." [2] If such language gives color to the legal phraseology of the statute book, one is not surprised to find the language of ordinary books full of vivid and vigorous figures of speech.   Tindale himself in his Epistle to the Reader promises a revision in these words, " and will endeavor ourselves as it were to seethe it better and to make it more apt for the weak stomachs "; and in another place he speaks of " sucking out the sweet pith of the Scriptures."   In the latter case we to-day should probably have written " extract the essence "; and thereby with what is to us the quaintness we should have lost also the eagerness and delight which color Tindale's words with their halo of feeling.   The language of this sixteenth century was lacking in many of our commonest general words, and as a result men used figures of speech more naturally.   Even when we take into account the love of picturesque phrases which effervesced into the affec-

[1] 27 Henry VIII, c. 28.   [2] 26 Henry VIII, c. 13.

tations of euphuism in the latter half of the century and clothed itself in soberer colors in the style of Thomas Fuller a couple of generations later, we must still recognise that all the men who worked on our English Bible, from Tindale to King James's companies of revisers in 1611, must sometimes have adopted figurative forms of expression for the reason that the abstract word had not yet been assimilated in the language. The same change in the character of the everyday language shows in the richer colors of Sir Thomas North's translation of Plutarch as compared with Langhorne's or Clough's, or the liveliness of Shelton's *Don Quixote* and in the warmth and spirit of Florio's translation of Montaigne. The difference lies in each case in the emotional richness of the expression: and that goes back directly to the greater or less degree of concreteness in the vocabulary.

There is still another fact to take into account here. Along with the enrichment of the language through the constant acquisition of new abstract words, and the consequent gain in range and precision of thought, there has gone a considerable increase in the number of words which we use vaguely and lazily. Every general word will for an indolent thinker take the place of several specific words: *move*, for example, in an abstract but vague way, covers the meaning of *run, hop, slide, roll, tumble,* and a host of other specific words. In many cases such abstract words are hardly more definite than gestures: we use such counters of speech as *element, relation, result, effect,* without ever stopping to come to close quarters with their meaning. For several years I have set a class of sophomores to study a textbook in which *elements of style, qualities of style,* and *principles of composition* are used as technical terms; and not three students in a hundred get them straight in their minds on the first reading. This is no doubt an extreme case: but it is safe to say that the general careless use of common abstract terms has largely dulled their expressiveness. Our modern use of language, therefore, tends not only to be less concrete, but also to be vaguer and duller than that of our fathers. This danger obviously makes more difficult the task of modern revisers of the Bible. Unless their scholarship is mated to a keen sense of the expressiveness of words, their revisions will lose both in color and in precision; and even where a writer himself uses these commoner abstract words with entire precision, he cannot always forestall laziness of attention in his readers. We may conclude, therefore, that in so far as any modern version substitutes abstract and general words for concrete, that version misses an essential and invalu-

able part of the message which the Bible has to bring
to us. To use Tindale's phrase, it substitutes " the
imaginations of the brain " for " those things that
the conscience may feel."

Besides the connotation of words we must also
take into account the musical or sensuous qualities
of style. This power it is quite impossible to reduce to notation or to any accurate estimate. We
know that rhythm and a fit sequence of sounds do express feeling, though why or exactly how we cannot
say. The expressive power of rhythm probably has
something to do with the alternate activity and
strength of the attention through which we insensibly
reduce all continuous regularity to alternations. In
all art it means life and feeling. The expressive
power of the pure melody of sounds is even less tangible: yet certain sounds serve to express certain feelings. Ruskin in his description of an English cathe-
dral and of St. Mark's in *The Stones of Venice* used
words in which by actual count one can note that
short vowels and the clicking consonants like g, k, p,
and t express coolness and austerity, and that the
open vowels and the singing consonants, l, m, n, and
r express luxuriant feeling. Why this is so we can
no more explain than we can say why the notes of
the flute can be made to suggest moonlight. We are
here dealing with ultimate facts of experience. The

fact, however, that such ultimate facts are inexplicable does not make them any less potent a force in literature and in human intercourse; and we may suppose that just as a cheerful frame of mind sometimes betrays the most sedate of men into the humming of strange and uncouth sounds, so here in the case of these noblest and most searching of all emotions, the strong coloring of the sounds is at least as important a part of the power of expression as is the use of the single words. Music is a spontaneous and almost universal part of worship; and the power of language to express religious feeling is inseparably bound up with rich coloring of tone and strong beat of rhythm.

Yet unless there be sincere and intense feeling to express, strength of rhythm and rich coloring merely imparts preciosity and affectation to language. In the case of our English translation we have seen that the translators and revisers were stirred to an intensity of feeling on the subject with which they were dealing which has not since been equalled in the history of England. The English Bible was one of the first fruits of the English Reformation, and the history of the successive revisions leading up to the version of 1611 is largely a history of the fluctuations of the Reformation. Tindale gave up his life for the share he had in translating the Bible and in advan-

cing the Reformation; John Rogers, the editor of
Matthew's Bible of 1537, was the first martyr under
the persecution of Mary; the Geneva version was
made by exiles from England during the same persecution, men who belonged to a party for whom the religion of their special sect was the one dominant rule
of life; and the version of 1611 was made at the
beginning of James's reign amidst all the intensity
of feeling aroused by the Gunpowder Plot and the
attempts of the Roman Catholics on the one hand
to reëstablish themselves, and of the Puritans on the
other to assert the domination of their peculiar doctrines. Throughout the three generations in which
the Authorised Version was growing to completion
religious belief was a matter of life and death. And
through a large part of that period men were suffering death and torture even in England for beliefs
which ultimately rested on the language of the Bible.
This intensity of feeling is reflected in the vigorous
rhythm and strong coloring of our English Bible.
The weakness of all modern translations, in spite of
their many advantages in the way of scholarship, is
that they lack this intensity of feeling which is the life
of the Authorised Version. Men in our piping times
of peace cannot have, and therefore cannot impart,
the same burning earnestness which belonged to all
matters of religion in the sixteenth century.

II

Going now beyond the qualities of sixteenth century English, we can ascribe much of the striking picturesqueness of phrase which especially in the Old Testament and in the first three gospels gives the language its vividness to the characteristic concreteness of the Hebrew language. We have seen that in Hebrew every word retains the physical connotation of the original, so that their language had no such abstract words as *principle, relation, contents, explicit,* from which the force of the original figure of speech is wholly evaporated. In consequence Hebrew is a language full of bold figures. The margin of the Authorised Version preserves a few examples of figures which the translators thought too bold for the text. In *Genesis xxxvii. 36* the literal rendering for *captain of the guard* is given in the margin as *the chief of the slaughter-men.* In *Judges xix. 8* the margin gives *till the day declined,* for *until afternoon*; and in verse 9 for *the day groweth to an end, it is the pitching time of day*; in other places *wringer* for *extortioner*; *treaders down* for *oppressors*; *the fields of desire* for *the pleasant fields*; *with one shoulder* for *with one consent.* These are only a few extreme examples of the boldness of figure which has given many familiar phrases to our everyday language:

the fat of the land, the valley of the shadow of death, the end of all flesh, seed of evildoers, a soft answer, son of perdition, all are examples of the necessary and characteristic figurativeness of the Hebrew language. It is hard to estimate the influence of such figures on our everyday English speech, but there can be no doubt that it has helped to keep alive a certain picturesqueness and vividness of phrase which one finds in the great masters of English style.

This picturesqueness of the Hebrew fitted in well with constant figurativeness of English in the sixteenth century of which I have just spoken. In the short passage from the address of the Translators to the Reader which I quoted a few pages back there are such picturesque phrases as *neither did we run over the work with that posting haste, the work hath not been huddled up in seventy two days, bring back to the anvil that which we had hammered*; and the whole address is marked by this simple quaintness of style. One must take into account that the author of this address had grown up in the days of euphuism and must remember also that deliberate picturesqueness of language which characterised Thomas Fuller in the next generation; but apart from any such external influences making for picturesqueness, we must recognise also that the English language of the sixteenth century had more figures of speech and fewer abstract words

than our language of to-day. In this respect also it
was considerably nearer to the Hebrew.

This natural picturesqueness of language which
goes back to the special characteristics of the Hebrew
and of sixteenth century English, is undoubtedly
somewhat heightened for us by the fact that in some
small degree the language of the Authorised Version
is now archaic. Apart from such forms as *saith*
and *prayeth* there are a good many words which,
though still entirely intelligible, are no longer used in
the way that they were used three centuries ago.
Meat no longer means *food*; we no longer use *naughty*
in the sense of *Jeremiah xxiv. 2*, " the other basket
had very naughty figs, which could not be eaten, they
were so bad "; *prevent* no longer means *to go before*
nor *expect* merely *waiting*; *wist* for *knew* has passed
out of usage; and many other forms to a less degree
have dropped out of current speech. Very few of
these words are actually unintelligible, but the forms
are unfamiliar enough to add a certain coloring of
quaintness and remoteness to the language of the
Bible, so that it stands apart from all other works
which are current with us to-day by this difference
in the character of its vocabulary. Part of its literary character is undoubtedly to be ascribed to this
slight flavor of another world which clings to its
words.

It should always be remembered, however, that the concreteness and figurative character of the Bible vocabulary have contributed to maintain the appeal of the Bible not because of their picturesqueness but because such a mode of expression is the only way in which many of the deepest and noblest emotions can be expressed. I have explained at length in the chapter on the poetry how inseparably the expression of the emotions depends on concreteness of phrasing. It is a chief source of strength in our Authorised Version that it has carried over into the English the concreteness of this unfailingly apt imagery and its power to express spiritual truths. The book deals with truths which lie in a region deeper and more universal than can be fathomed by human reason, and which can be expressed only by expressing the sensations which stir up such emotions; and the fact that the sixteenth century English was comparatively so much poorer in words of abstraction, and therefore comparatively so much richer in words which directly expressed emotion, made that period the fittest time for the translation.

Along with this unfailing concreteness and figurative character of the language goes its entire simplicity: of all the books in the language it is the one which can be read with profit and comfort by people of all degrees of intelligence and education. The original books, being written either in the Hebrew language which had no expression for anything but objective facts, or else in Greek which was addressed to a church where the learned were a small minority, were simple in vocabulary and expression. Tindale, taking his inspiration probably from Colet and Erasmus, maintained this simplicity in his own translation and established it as a principle for his successors. The Bible was translated with the purpose of bringing the gospel back to the plain people of England. This principle, joined to the fact that the English of the sixteenth century had not yet been enriched by the great mass of learned words from the Latin, has made the vocabulary of the English Bible very different from the ordinary vocabulary of our own day. A concordance shows in a very striking way how little need the translators of the Bible had for the Latinate words. Among words which appear only once in the Bible are such common words as the following: *amiable, commodious, conquer, constraint, debase, discipline, disgrace, enable, intelligence, modest, quantity, reformation, severity, transferred*. All these words, and they are a small part of the complete list, are among the most familiar in our everyday vocabulary.

It is probable that this principle of keeping inkhorn terms out of the Bible was strengthened by the

contention of the Roman Catholic Church, as declared by the Council of Trent, that the Vulgate was
the only authentic text of the Scriptures, and the
complementary principle that the Scriptures could be
understood only by the initiate.   This principle is
set forth in the preface to the Rhemish New Testament in the following words: " Whereupon, the order
which many a wise man wished for before, was taken
by the deputies of the late famous Council of Trent
in this behalf, and confirmed by supreme authority,
that the Holy Scriptures, though truly and catholicly
translated into the vulgar tongues, yet may not be indifferently read of all men, nor any other except such
as have the express license thereunto of their lawful
ordinaries, with good testimony from their curates or
confessors, that they be humble, discreet and devout
persons, and like to take much good, and no harm
thereby." We have seen that the revisers of 1611
were deeply affected by the efforts of the Roman
Catholic Church to recover England to the old faith,
and it seems clear from the address of the Translators to the Readers in the Authorised Version that
these revisers somewhat overestimated the importance of the Roman Catholic efforts.   Men who are
much given to finding reasons for their actions are
apt to lag behind events.   But in their reaction
from this principle of the old church they were

strengthened in their intention to keep the Scriptures in a language which could be understood by all men. Though there is a slightly greater infusion of Latinate and learned words in the Authorised Version than in any previous version except the Rhemish New Testament, yet it is to be remembered that since the time of Tindale there had been three-quarters of a century of animated and widespread theological discussion, so that some of the Latinate words which would have been unfamiliar to the men of his day would have been generally known in the time of King James.

A comparison of the Bible with almost any other work in the English language will bring out this prevailingly simple character of its vocabulary. Since the concrete things of sensation in which it is so largely phrased are generally expressed in English by words derived ultimately from the Anglo-Saxon, the language of the Bible is far less Latinate than any other work in English. Even *Pilgrim's Progress* seems learned in its vocabulary by the side of the Bible. The influence of this fact in keeping the general style of English simple cannot be overestimated. The fashion of style which we generally think of as Johnsonian is far removed from the vocabulary of the English Bible, but this very remoteness marks its weakness and made certain the reac-

tion which was sure to come to a simpler mode of
speech; and the ideals of style of the nineteenth century stand much nearer to the standard set by the
Bible than did those of the eighteenth century.

Yet in spite of this comparative narrowness in the
range of its vocabulary, the aptness and flexibility
of the style are extraordinary. The revisers of 1611
had a very great stock of readings from which to
draw, not only in English but in Latin, German,
French, and even in Italian and Spanish. Tindale
had set the example of using what aids existed in
his time: he drew with independence and instinctive
sense of style from the Latin of the Vulgate, the
Latin of Erasmus, and the German of Luther; and
we have seen how faithfully later translators and revisers followed his example. Every familiar phrase
in the Bible can be traced to its source, sometimes in
the inspired instinct of one or another of these English translators or revisers, sometimes in one of the
foreign translations which they used. In *Isaiah
liii. 5, the chastisement of our peace* comes directly
from the *castigatio pacis nostræ* of Münster's Latin
translation: the curious rendering in *Job xix. 26, and
though after my skin worms destroy this body* goes
back to the *et post pellem meam contritam vermes
contriverunt hanc carnem* of Pagninus; and we have
seen how freely the valuable results of the Rhemish

Version were appropriated. A study of the constant little changes in the choice and order of words all through the versions of the sixteenth century makes one realise what an immense amount of devoted scholarship, and of weighing words and phrases with a delicate ear for their full expressiveness went into the making of our English Bible. Every chapter of it witnesses to the long and anxious care for both accuracy and expressiveness of rendering.

With this free use of the labors of this great company of translators, whether English or foreign, the English translation shows extraordinary resource in dealing with the idioms of the original literature, especially of the Hebrew. The best example of this swift instinct for finding an English idiom which would come nearest to some wholly foreign one is shown in their rendering of a characteristic Hebrew construction. One mode of expressing emphasis in Hebrew is to repeat the infinitive of the verb with some finite form, as if we should say in English "to see I saw." This construction, which may be used with any verb, is rendered in the Authorised Version in the greatest variety of ways: *We saw certainly that the Lord was with thee; I have surely seen; Ye shall not surely die; O that my grief were throughly weighed; If thou altogether holdest thy peace; The earth shall reel to and fro; He shall mightily roar; I do earnestly remember.* In *Isaiah xxiv. 19* the translators find three different English idioms for this construction: *The earth is utterly broken down, the earth is clean dissolved, the earth is moved exceedingly.* In each of these cases, it will be remembered, the Hebrew is merely a repetition of the *break* or *dissolve* or *move* in the infinitive with the finite form of the verb. Another Hebrew idiom is the repetition of a noun or a numeral. Here again they find excellent English renderings. *Two-two* in the story of Noah is rendered by *two and two*; in the description of the cherubim *six wings six wings* is rendered *each had six wings.* *A heart and a heart* is rendered *a double heart*; *peace peace* is rendered *perfect peace.* In the story of the solemn anointing of Saul by Samuel, where the people shouted according to the Hebrew, *Let the king live,* our Bible boldly substituted the English cry, *God save the king.* In *Ezekiel xxx. 2,* where the literal translation would be, *Howl ye, woe to the day,* it translates *Howl ye, woe worth the day.* The phrase *God forbid,* which is so familiar in St. Paul's epistles, especially in *Romans,* is a rendering of a Greek construction which means literally *may it not be.* In the Old Testament *God forbid* is used for a word which means originally *unconsecrated* or *profane* or *abhorrent*; the Septuagint uses for it the same Greek

phrase which is translated in the New Testament
God forbid. The rendering of this Hebrew word in
the English appears in various forms; in the story of
Joseph's brethren, it is *God forbid that thy servants
should do according to this thing.* Where Abraham expostulates with the Lord against the destruction of Sodom, it is *That be far from thee to do
after this manner.* Where David spares Saul, it is
*The Lord forbid that I should do this thing unto
my master.* This comparative freedom from scruples
about a literal and uniform rendering of the words
of the original unquestionably made it possible for
the translation to have a spirit and vigor impossible
to scholars who are oppressed by a greater burden
of learning. The chief principle of all translators
of the sixteenth and seventeenth centuries seems to
have been to produce in lively and vigorous English the spirit of the original language. In some
cases the literalness of their rendering suffered; but
they produced translations which are independent
contributions to literature, where modern translators
give us works which are at best an imperfect means
of getting at the meanings of the originals.

An even deeper source of power than this aptness
in fitting the English idiom to that of the Hebrew or
the Greek and giving a new and richer life to the
rendering is the strong rhythm and the rich music

of the style, of which I have already spoken so often. In the case of the Old Testament the rhythm may be largely ascribed to the character of the Hebrew language. We have seen that in poetry the principle of parallelism established a strongly marked balance: in the case of the prose the balance is nearly as pervasive from the fact that sentences in Hebrew varied little in length; except in *Deuteronomy* they rarely go beyond a single clause, and in the narrative they are constantly of about the same length. Indeed, if they were printed in broken lines, as is the poetry in the Revised Version, the effect would be not far from the same. As a result of this regularity of balance the rhythm of the narrative passages is almost as strong as that of the poetry. Thus especially in the case of the Old Testament and of the Synoptic Gospels almost any translation would be more rhythmical than ordinary English prose of to-day. Another cause, as we have seen, reinforced this probability of a strong rhythm and gave it vitality. In part at any rate it reflects and expresses the intensity of feeling which accompanied all questions of religion in sixteenth century England. All through the period which saw the formation of our English Bible feelings on the subject of the lawfulness and the necessity of a translation were at fever heat. Adherence to one side or the other might be a matter of life or death. Nowadays scholars work at their translations in quiet and peace, walled in by their great apparatus of scholarship from the concerns of the world about them: in those days men undertook to prove the lawfulness and righteousness of the government of England by the quotation of texts of Scripture. Thus especially to men of the Puritan way of thinking the turn of every phrase in the Bible was a matter not only of the larger doctrines of the faith but also of immediate concern in this world's affairs. To some degree at any rate this earnestness wrought itself into the texture of our English Bible, expressing itself, as such feelings must, largely in a quickened and richer sound.

III

Before coming to an end, let us consider very briefly the character and place of the Bible in the great body of English literature and its contribution to that literature. Here again we must assume the fact of inspiration without attempting to define it or to draw a line between what is called literary inspiration and the higher and deeper inspiration which creates a religion. There can be no question that the two run into each other, and also that both are active in a region of the nature of man where there is little probability that he will ever have any accurate knowledge. We are driven by the existence of literature no less than by the existence of religion to acknowledge that there are forces inscrutable to us in our present state of knowledge which are instructive, potent, and constant in their influence on human life and action. When we have said that there are certain forms of speech and of writing which move men's imaginations and stir their souls, we have expressed the fact of inspiration and have gone nearly as far as it is possible to go in analyzing it.

Now there can be no doubt that above all other books in English the Bible has this power of stirring the imagination and moving the soul. Moreover, it has this power almost apart from religious belief: men who belong to no church, and who profess no religious belief, go to it with the same certainty of being stimulated and uplifted as do members of Christian churches; and it is not the disagreement of the churches as to its meaning which has led them to less dependence on its teachings. The power of the book to stir the imagination to a sense of realities which are on a higher plane than the affairs of everyday life is not limited to its use as a source of religious belief.

Yet this most native of all books is by origin wholly foreign, and in the case of the Old Testament it is as foreign as anything can be. The stories of

Genesis, Exodus, and *Numbers* were first gathered at
the little local shrines of Palestine at a time when
the children of Israel were just shedding their wild
nomadic habits; and the stories of *Judges* with the
glimpses they give us of bloody raids and tribal
feuds,—Gideon "teaching" the men of Succoth
with thorns of the wilderness and briars and with his
own hand slaying Zebah and Zalmunna, the lawless
foray of Dan, the sacrifice of Jephthah,—show how
little the settling down tamed their wild and bloody
temper. Even the histories of *Kings,*—of David
hewing out his kingdom with the help of the bloody
Joab, of Solomon putting his brother Adonijah to
the sword, or of the remorseless extirpation of the
worshippers of Baal by Jehu under the direction of
the prophet Elisha,—all such stories reflect a state
of civilisation which we look on as wholly Asiatic.
Even in the case of the New Testament the surround-
ings were not much less foreign. The Synoptic
Gospels and *Revelation* sprang from a life which
had not much more than a veneer of Roman civilisation. The first disciples were Syrian peasants and
fishermen, of a people whose descendants to-day seem
almost unassimilable to us. St. Paul was a man of
education, but of an education which probably had
little tincture of the Greek and Latin.

After all, however, one can feel the foreignness of

the Bible best by putting it alongside other works of
English literature, and noting how in almost every
way, it seems to contrast with them. Milton has used
the story of Samson in his *Samson Agonistes*, treat-
ing it in the manner of a Greek tragedy. But *Samson Agonistes* beside the original story seems like a
stage-play: for all Milton's grim austerity and earnestness his poem is artificial. Samson becomes an
introspective, seventeenth century Puritan, instead of
the hearty, inconstant giant who in the ancient cycle
of stories played his rough jokes on the Philistines.
Here is the way Milton conceives him:

> Unwillingly this rest
> Their superstition yields me; hence with leave
> Retiring from the popular noise, I seek
> This unfrequented place to find some ease;
> Ease to the body some, none to the mind
> From restless thoughts, that, like a deadly swarm
> Of hornets arm'd, no sooner found alone
> But rush upon me thronging, and present
> Times past, what once I was, and what am now.
>
> .   .   .   .   .
>
> But what is strength without a double share
> Of wisdom? vast, unwieldly, burdensome,
> Proudly secure, yet liable to fall
> By weakest subtleties; not made to rule,
> But to subserve where wisdom bears command.
> God, when he gave me strength, to show withal
> How slight the gift was, hung it in my hair.

Even apart from the frank anachronism of the char-
acterising, and the substitution of Milton himself for
Samson, the whole conception seems almost sophisti-
cated beside the simple directness of the Old Testament. Milton, the man of our own race, must imagine motives and thoughts and feelings in an elaborate
structure between the events and the mind of the
reader: the Israelite story-teller left the facts to speak
for themselves, as they have for all the centuries
since. The quiet self-confidence of this method makes
modern story telling, even in the restrained mechanism of the Greek drama, seem to labor and strive for
justification.

I have already in the chapter on the narrative
used Browning's *Saul* for purposes of contrast.
It is so good an example of almost everything
that the Bible is not that I will venture to quote a
few more lines from it in order to put them beside a
passage from the climax of *Job*:

> See the king—I would help him but cannot, the
> wishes fall through,
> Could I wrestle to raise him from sorrow, grow
> poor to enrich,
> To fill up his life, starve my own out, I would—
> knowing which,
> I know that my service is perfect.—Oh, speak
> through me now!

Would I suffer for him that I love?   So wouldst
  thou—so wilt thou!
So shall crown thee the topmost, ineffablest,
  uttermost crown—
And thy love fill infinitude wholly, nor leave
  up nor down
One spot for the creature to stand in! It is
  by no breath,
Turn of eye, wave of hand, that salvation joins
  issue with death!
As thy Love is discovered almighty, almighty
  be proved
Thy power, that exists with and for it, of being
  Beloved!

After that read the following:

Canst thou bind the sweet influences of Pleiades,
or loose the bands of Orion?

Canst thou bring forth Mazzaroth in his season?
or canst thou guide Arcturus with his sons?

Knowest thou the ordinances of heaven? canst
thou set the dominion thereof in the earth?

Canst thou lift up thy voice to the clouds, that
abundance of waters may cover thee?

Canst thou send lightnings that they may go,
and say unto thee, Here we are?[1]

Beside Browning's straining for superlatives and his
dancing whirlwind of words the grave, austere restraint of the East soars quietly to its portrayal of

[1] Job xxxviii. 31–35.

omnipotence. There is no effort in the prophets or in *Job* or the *Psalms*. The expression of emotion is often violent and overwrought; yet it has always at the same time a certain repose which comes from the effect of reserve power, and from the sense that the poet is not struggling with forces which are too mighty for him. This combination of extreme and excited intensity of emotion with a general gravity and soberness of tone is peculiarly Oriental.

Again, if one tries to imagine a play by Shakspere on a Biblical subject one will understand how entirely he belonged to the Renaissance, and how entirely the Renaissance was absorbed with the life of man and of this world. The mere fact that in such a play David and Solomon, or Jacob and Laban, would have appeared in a doublet and hose emphasizes the great gulf between Shakspere and this ancient literature. His interest would have been in the characters of the play, in their humanity, in the tangled web of their fate, and in the tragedies wrought by their weaknesses and their conflicting desires. It is only in the most shadowy way that the great forces which dominate *Job* and the *Psalms* and St. Paul's epistles and *Revelation* come into his pages. And when one puts even his greatest plays beside these books of the Bible one finds the modern writing almost trivial and ephemeral beside the old. Much

reading in the Bible will soon bring one to an understanding of the mood in which all art seems a juggling
with trifles, and an attempt to catch the unessential
when the everlasting verities are slipping by.   The
silent, unhurrying rumination of the East makes our
modern flood of literature seem garrulous and chatter-
ing: even the great literature of the Greeks loses beside
the compression and massiveness of the Old Testament.   It is this cool solidity of poise, this grave and
weighty compression of speech, that makes the Old
Testament literature so foreign.   It has no pride of
art, no interest in the subjective impressions of the
writer, no care even for the preservation of his name.
It is austerely preoccupied with the lasting and the
real, and above all, unceasingly possessed with the
sense of the immediate presence of a God who is
omnipotent and inscrutable.   This constant preoccu-
pation with the eternal and the superhuman gives
to this literature a sense of proportion which again
separates it from other literature.   Beside the will
of the Almighty the joys and griefs and ambitions of
any single writer are a vanity of vanities, a vexation of spirit, or as the Hebrew is more closely translated in the Revised Version, " a striving after wind."
It is as if, in the words of the marginal reading of
Ecclesiastes iii, God had " set eternity in their
heart."   In our modern literature it is hardly pos-

sible to find an author who has not some touch of the
restless egotism that is the curse of the artistic temperament: in the Bible there is no author who was
not free from it.

In this art which is not art, then, in this absorption with the solid facts of reality and the neglect of
man's comment and interpretation, in the unswerving instinct for the lasting, and the sense of the constant and immediate presence of an omnipotent God,
the Bible stands apart in our literature.

Yet on the other hand, the Bible is of all books
the most thoroughly woven into the thought and
language of English-speaking people. There is no
other book of which it can be said that for many generations all classes of the people were equally familiar with it. Moreover, this familiarity was at its
greatest when the language was taking on its permanent forms: the seventeenth and eighteenth centuries
largely settled the character of the English tongue;
and it was in those centuries that the Bible was the
household book. To the simple and uneducated its
messages and stories are as intelligible and as uplifting as to the most highly educated; indeed it is
only when cultivation luxuriates into sophistication
and decadence that the Bible loses its hold on the imagination. Bunyan and Ruskin, at the two extremes
both in time and in position in life, show the univer-

sal power of the book. Bunyan, taking it in the ut-
most literalness, found in every exigency of his self-
torturings comfort or despair in the texts which
flashed in on him. In the *Grace Abounding* I open
at random, and find such passages as these:

> But when I had been long vexed with this fear,
> and was scarce able to take one step more, just
> about the place where I received my other en-
> couragement, these words broke in on my mind:
> "Compel them to come in, that my house may be
> filled; and yet there is room." (Luke xiv. 22, 23.)

> I should often also think on Nebuchadnezzar,
> of whom 'tis said, "He had given him all the king-
> doms of the earth." (Dan. v. 18, 19.) Yet,
> thought I, if this great man had all his portion in
> this world, one hour in hell-fire would make him
> forget all. Which consideration was a great help
> to me.

> How lovely now was every one in my eyes, that
> I thought to be converted men and women! They
> shone, they walked like a people that carried the
> broad seal of heaven about them. Oh! I saw
> the lot was fallen to them in pleasant places, and
> they had a goodly heritage. (Ps. xvi.) But that
> which made me sick was that of Christ, in Mark:
> "He went up into a mountain, and called unto
> him whom he would, and they came unto him."
> (Mark iii. 13.)

> This scripture made me faint and fear, yet it
> kindled fire in my soul.

Pilgrim's Progress likewise can almost be resolved into a collection of texts from all over the Bible, put together to form the allegory.

Ruskin was almost as thoroughly saturated with the Bible; he gives us in the *Preterita* a list of the passages he learned by heart; and the allusions throughout his writings show how familiar the book was to him. These two men may stand as examples of what was true of all makers of English literature since the beginning of the seventeenth century, and of almost all speakers of the English language down to our own generation. Even to-day where you find a touch of the grand style in a piece of writing, you are almost sure to detect reminiscences of the Bible. Lincoln not only among Americans but among all English-speaking people of the nineteenth century is the man who most surely attained the great style, and we all know how naturally in his most solemn moments his style became infused with the phrases and the virtues of the English Bible. Here is a short passage from the Second Inaugural Address:

> The Almighty has his own purposes. "Woe unto the world because of offenses! for it must needs be that offenses come; but woe to that man by whom the offense cometh." If we shall suppose that American slavery is one of those offenses which, in the providence of God, must needs come,

but which, having continued through his appointed time, he now wills to remove, and that he gives to both North and South this terrible war, as the woe due to those by whom the offense came, shall we discern therein any departure from those divine attributes which the believers in a living God always ascribe to him? Fondly do we hope—fervently do we pray—that this mighty scourge of war may speedily pass away. Yet, if God wills that it continue until all the wealth piled by the bondman's two hundred and fifty years of unrequited toil shall be sunk, and until every drop of blood drawn with the lash shall be paid by another drawn with the sword, as was said three thousand years ago, so still it must be said, "The judgments of the Lord are true and righteous altogether."

One can find no better example, and one needs none, of the certainty with which this Biblical style expresses the deepest and strongest feelings of men of our race. Much of the Bible, especially of the Old Testament, can be described as primitive in thought; but only if "primitive" be taken to mean that such writings go down to the common roots of all human nature, and are grounded in feelings and ideas which are the common heritage of all men, and which are therefore perennial and universal. Thus this Biblical literature and this Biblical style in spite of their foreign origin are in a still deeper sense native, since their appeal reaches down below feelings and instincts which are peculiar to one age or to one country to those which belong to all.

IV

One does not need to say that the English Bible has had an enormous influence on the English language and literature. Not the least of its contributions is the standard which it has set for all writing in English that has an ambition to belong to literature. One can say that if any writing departs very far in any way from the characteristics of the English Bible it is not good English writing. In style it has been an axiom long accepted without question that the ultimate standard of English prose is set by the style of the Bible. For examples of limpid, convincing narrative we go to *Genesis*, to the story of Ruth, to the quiet earnestness of the gospels; for the mingled argument and explanation and exhortation in which lies the highest power of the other side of literature, we go to the prophets, and even more to the epistles of the New Testament; and for the glow of vehemence and feeling which burn away the limits between poetry and prose, and make prose style at its highest pitch able to stand beside the stirring vibrations of verse, we go to the *Psalms* or to

Job, or to the prophecies of Isaiah, or the triumphant declaration of immortality in *1 Corinthians*. If the whole range of English prose style were figured in the form of an arch, the style of the Bible would be the keystone; and it would be there not only because it is the highest point and culmination of prose writing, but also because it binds the whole structure together. On the one side would be the writing that tends more and more to the colloquial, which, beginning with such finished and exquisite talk as Dryden crystallised in his writings, runs off into the slack and hasty style of journalism; on the other side, such more splendidly and artfully colored prose as Sir Thomas Browne's or the ponderous weight of Dr. Johnson, that degenerate in the hands of lesser men into preciosity or pedantry. To bring the two sides into bearing on each other, we have the common standard; and the further any writing on either side falls away from that standard, the less it will have of the typical excellence of the national style.

In general, I suppose that in thus setting the English Bible as the measure of English prose style, one would name as the general qualities of that style simplicity and earnestness. In defining French prose style, one would think first, perhaps, of lucidity, added to keenness and subtlety; in defining German prose style, rather of thoroughness and the capacity for carrying strangely complicated burdens of thought; but in the case of English prose, since we have had neither an academy nor a cloistered body of learned men for whom books have been chiefly written, if there is to be a standard which shall be a common measure for Dryden, Swift, Goldsmith, and Burke, or in our own period for Macaulay, Newman, Ruskin, Thackeray, and Lincoln, we must find for that common measure a style which will be read by all classes of men, and which will carry the weight of high and earnest ideas. In France there is a gulf between literature and the peasants whom Millet painted; in England, Bunyan's *Pilgrim's Progress*, one of the monuments of the literature, was the work of a tinker; and one might recall, too, Stevenson's story of the Welsh blacksmith who learned to read in order to add *Robinson Crusoe* to his possibilities of experience. It is a striking fact that, as the generations pass by, the books which are still regularly and constantly reprinted are those like *Robinson Crusoe* and *Gulliver's Travels* and *The Pilgrim's Progress*, which appeal not only to a highly educated upper class, but to the moderately educated middle and lower classes: in literature, as in everything else in England and America, the final appeal is to the broad democracy. In the second place, it is notable that the books which do survive, at any rate in the case of prose,—for in the case of poetry final causes are deeper and more complex,—are almost all written by men with a purpose, men who have a mission to make the world better. There is something in the genius of the people which brings the language to its noblest heights when it carries a message that is to lift the people above themselves; and something in the genius of the language which makes it inevitable that when the language reaches these high points it shall show most strongly these two qualities of simplicity and earnestness.

With these qualities the style of the Bible is also notable for directness of statement, which gives to the style an unsurpassed power of carrying its readers with it; the books of the Bible are set forth as statements of facts, never as an apology or justification of the facts; and the effect of this confidence is to give to the Bible a virility and robustness which in themselves make it a worthy model of a great national style. The constant use of figurative language to expound hard doctrines, too, as in the discussion of faith in *Hebrews*, or in the first verses of *St. John*, explains the power that the Bible has had to speak to all generations, and to set each generation puzzling out for itself an interpretation in abstractions which inevitably pass with the particular stage of knowledge and thought for which they were made.

The mere fact that the words are Anglo-Saxon, rather than French or Latin, means nothing; the significance lies in the fact that Anglo-Saxon words still stand for the concrete, tangible objects of life, and that our words of theorising and abstraction we have drawn from the Latin; it is the difference between such phrases as "this is my body which is given for you" of the gospel, and "not only in quality of external signs and sacramental representations, but in their essential properties and substantial reality" of the theologians. In the Bible, the way in which the words carry to all men, whether learned or ignorant, the same sense of reality, of the actual things of life, depends on the fact that they are words of the simplest kind, naming the things which are the stuff of everyday experience. Their simplicity not only makes them sure of being understood by all men, but also of meaning always the same things to all men. With this simplicity of language goes always the dignity of the style: whether it be in the domestic details of Jacob's family life, or in the love of David for his son Absalom, or in the world-sweeping imagery of *Job* or of Isaiah, there is the same unstudied, unforced heightening of the substance by the form. At times, as in the prophets or in St. Paul's epistles, the style has a fire and a vehemence which leave no line between prose and poetry; but even in the narrative the earnestness and glowing faith of the writers and translators, needing a stronger medium than the subdued rhythm of ordinary prose, have produced an intenser vibration which brings the style near to the stronger and more rapid movement of verse.

Such, then, we may consider the general characteristics of the style of the Bible. Obviously such a style can be, for ordinary writers with ordinary purposes, only a standard: it is not often that there arises a man like Lincoln who has the weight of character and the sustained enthusiasm or a subject of the grave and dominant interest that such a style demands. To go back to the figure, the style of the Bible is at the apex of the arch, the most necessary, yet, as the highest, a unique example of English prose. Nevertheless, though the days of the apostles, as of the giants, have passed by, yet the standard remains; and directness of statement, lasting power of convincing, simplicity of words, earnestness and dignity, and a moving rhythm have been the qualities of every prose style which has become classical in English literature.

Furthermore, since style, when it approaches any adequacy of expression, reflects the character of its substance, one can say that in substance also the Bible is in a sense the norm and standard of our

English literature. Leaving out of consideration Shakspere, whom it is so hard to bring into any generalisation, one may roughly say that the spirit of English literature at its best is prophetic, that the essential characteristics of the books which are the record of the thoughts and feelings of the English race are virility, directness, unconsciousness, prepossession with the higher sides of life, and a noble and uplifting purpose. Spenser's *Faerie Queene* is a glorification of purity and the virtues of chivalry; Addison aimed to reform the licentious manners of his day; the one constant motive of Swift's morbid genius was to castigate the vices and follies of men; and Dr. Johnson, the stoutest Englishman of them all, was a conscious force for righteousness. The nineteenth century opened with the aspiring dreams of Wordsworth, Coleridge and Shelley; and its great prose writers, Thackeray, Dickens, Carlyle, Emerson, and the rest, were all consciously preachers. The ideal of art merely for the sake of beauty has never taken a deep hold on the men of our race. Keats, who above all English poets revelled in sheer beauty and sensuousness of form, is commonly and naturally thought of as a poet's poet. It remains true, therefore, in a broad way with the substance of English literature as with the style, that the English Bible stands as the norm about which all the rest can be

arranged and as the standard by which it is not unreasonable to estimate it.

Certainly an intimate acquaintance with the English Bible is the best possible preparation for a study
of English literature, or for the matter of that, of any
literature. A chief difficulty in coming to any absolute and permanent judgment in such matters is the
variety and the instability of taste. Few of the persons who own sets of Shakspere read much in his
plays; for the character of his speech is far enough
away from us to make it for most people something of
an effort to acquire the taste for reading him. The
fashions of the eighteenth century, moulded by Dryden and ossified by the followers of Dr. Johnson, are
a weariness of the flesh to most readers to-day; and
the only thing certain about our current literature is
that much of its conscious simplicity and naturalness
of expression will seem slipshod to the people of two
or three generations from now, when the pendulum
shall have swung back to other tendencies. Yet in all
this incessant change of tastes and fashions the Bible
holds its own. Indeed men were more familiar with
it in the days of the Johnsonian supremacy, when all
standards of style were almost diametrically opposed
to it, than they are to-day. Men of all classes and all
degrees of education have found equal delight in its
stories and its teachings, from John Bunyan, the

tinker, and the peasant father of Robert Burns to Scott and Browning and even the supercilious genius of Matthew Arnold; and to-day, when it is so little read even by church-going people, one can be certain of one thing, and that is that its effect will be in no way limited by station or education. Here, then, is a work which it seems safe to say is of something like universal appeal to men of our race, a book which one may therefore look on as touching the soul of the race as a whole. For this reason, therefore, if for no other, one must hope to see the study of the Bible begin to take a place in the study of English literature.

APPENDIX

THE following books will prove useful to persons who desire further knowledge of the problems discussed and the results attained by the Higher Criticism through a historical study of both the Old and the New Testament, or of the history of the English Bible. The copious references which they contain will lead a student as far as he cares to go. I have selected for mention books which are moderate in tone, cautious in judgment, and copious in their statement of evidence.

For a general introduction to the Higher Criticism of the Old Testament: W. Robertson Smith, *The Old Testament in the Jewish Church*, 2d edition, 1900.

For the background of the New Testament: A. C. McGiffert, *A History of Christianity in the Apostolic Age*, Revised edition, 1900.

For the Old Testament: S. R. Driver, *An Introduction to the Literature of the Old Testament*, 8th edition, 1898.

For the New Testament: Part II of *A Biblical Introduction*, by Bennett and Adeney, 2d edition, 1904.

For the English Bible: B. F. Westcott, *A General View of the History of the English Bible*, 3d edition (W. A. Wright), 1905; and R. Lovett, *The Printed English Bible*, in Present Day Primers, n.d.

For general reference Hastings' *Dictionary of the Bible*.

INDEX

Abstract words in New Testament, 181.

Acts, rhetorical style in, 72.

Alphabetic poems, 99.

Amalgamation of the sources of the Bible, 9, 309.

Amos, 18, 219, 246.

Apocalypses, a development from the prophecy, 250; the visions of, 257; originated in persecutions, 264; their imagery immaterial, 270.

Authorised Version is the Bible in English literature, 283; the origin of, 344; the principles followed by the translators, 347; the simplicity of its vocabulary, 368; the skill showed by the translators, 352, 372; the rhythm of, 375.

Bible, the unity of the, 1; in English literature, 376; the foreignness of, 8, 377; woven into English language and literature, 384.

Bishops' Bible, the, 339.

Browning's *Saul*, 82, 380.

Bunyan's *Pilgrim's Progress*, 75; *Grace Abounding*, 385.

Canon, the growth of, 284.

Canticles of *St. Luke*, 106.

Colet, John, 312.

Coverdale, his version, 328.

Daniel, the declaration of immortality in, 30, 266; the visions of, 258, 267.

Deuteronomy, the reforms of, 21; the influence of on the literature, 23, 62; the teaching of, 27.

Diversity of the sources of the Bible, 6.

Ecclesiastes, the general character of, 143; the personal note in, 144; its failure to solve the problem of retribution, 153.

Emotion, the expression of, 115, 121.

English language in the sixteenth century, 357.

English literature, the spirit of, 394.